CW00566618

Contents

Figures

Preface

The two travel accounts presented in this volume capture a vivid historical moment and map a period of profound social and intellectual change. The letters of the Dissenting minister and scientist George Cadogan Morgan, written from France in the summer of 1789, are an eye-witness account of the uprising in Paris that saw the storming of the Bastille; they also describe the response of the French provinces in the turbulent fortnight that followed. The autobiography of his son, Richard Price Morgan, evokes the 1790s London of his childhood, and the family's subsequent emigration to America. Between them, the two narratives raise interesting questions about the nature of historical witness, and the ways in which events are perceived and described in and over time. They show, too, how complex are the processes by which 'history' is made within families, how it is coloured and shaped by loyalties and inherited opinions, and how even a single family may have evolved competing versions or interpretations of events by the second or third generation.

Our edition of these previously unpublished texts is the result of a research collaboration. While working on a biography of Dr Richard Price (1723–91), Paul Frame became aware that letters, long thought lost, from Price's nephew George Cadogan Morgan had been deposited by descendants of the family at the Newberry Library, Chicago. Their rediscovery coincided with the start of an AHRC-funded project on 'Wales and the French Revolution' at the University of Wales Centre for Advanced Welsh and Celtic Studies, and, with the Newberry Library's permission, the decision was made to publish them as part of the project series. Mary-Ann Constantine edited and introduced the 1789 letters and the *Address to the Jacobine Societies*, and Paul Frame edited and introduced the autobiography of Richard Price Morgan. We have both read, discussed and contributed extensively to each other's work.

We have been exceptionally fortunate in the support of many individuals and institutions. This work would not have happened without the funding for the wider project which came from the University of Wales and the Arts and Humanities Research Council. We are very grateful to the Board of the Newberry Library, Chicago for permission to publish the texts: Martha Briggs, Jill Gage and David Spadafora have been especially helpful in providing copies, checking specific readings and offering much useful information. Descendants of the Morgan family in America, Ginger Smith and Ben Coogle, kindly gave us access to an unpublished Memoir written by George Cadogan Morgan's grand-daughter, Sarah Morgan Ashburner, while genealogical work currently being undertaken by David Perry, John Morgan and Nicola Bennetts enabled us to correct and expand our family tree. Peggy Tuck Sinko also helped with research in America and our thanks go to her and the Chicago Cubs.

We are also very grateful to staff at the National Library of Wales, the London Metropolitan Archive and the Bodleian Library, Oxford; to Bethan Jenkins, who undertook the painstaking transcription of Edward Rigby's letters and travel journal; also to Nia Davies at the Centre for typing out *An Address to the Jacobine Societies and other Patriotic Societies of the French*. We have drawn frequently on the knowledge and expertise of friends and colleagues, and are grateful to them all, but specific thanks go to Jeremy Black, Martin Fitzpatrick, Mark Philp, Harriet Guest, and to David Jenkins and Ian Smith of the National Waterfront Museum in Swansea. Colleagues on the 'Wales and the French Revolution' project offered continual moral and intellectual support, as did the advisory panel: thanks to John Barrell, Gavin Edwards and Dafydd Johnston for comments on drafts of the introduction. A special thanks to David Parsons for taking on the job of first copy editor and for creating digital versions of the maps, and to Ralph Harrington for permission to use the wonderful volcano on the cover. Gwen Gruffudd has been a punctilious second copy editor, and, like everyone else on the team, we are much indebted both to her professionalism, and to that of Sarah Lewis, Siân Chapman and Dafydd Jones at the University of Wales Press.

October 2012   Mary-Ann Constantine and Paul Frame

Acknowledgements

The Newberry Library, Chicago: Fig. 1
David Parsons: Fig. 2
Paul Frame: Fig. 3
David Parsons and Paul Frame: Figs. 4, 5

Abbreviations

DAB	*Dictionary of American Biography* (20 vols., New York, 1928–36)
DWB	*The Dictionary of Welsh Biography down to 1940* (London, 1959)
ECCO	Eighteenth Century Collections Online
NLW	National Library of Wales
ODNB	*Oxford Dictionary of National Biography* at *http://www.oxforddnb.com*
OED	*Oxford English Dictionary* at *http://www.oed.com*
Rigby-Eastlake	Lady [Elizabeth] Eastlake (ed.), *Dr Rigby's Letters from France &c. in 1789* (London, 1880)
SMA, 'Memoir'	Sarah Morgan Ashburner, unpublished memoir

George Cadogan Morgan
Travels in Revolutionary France

met with artificial Caves and rocks — but their Residence ill became them, they appear'd in circumstances in which Nature never placed them, and in which it is impossible that anything but the Monstrous folly of man should ever bring them. — We saw attempts likewise to make gurgling streams, by increasing the declivity of the Water, and by placing pebbles in its Bed, But the neighbouring Meadow, and a quiet muddy stream which runs close to the Babbler silently proclaim its absurdity — In short in the Grounds I saw nothing but the Mangling hands of Art, Stone walls, cropp'd Hedges, Imitations of Nature without attending to Circumstances, and a profusion of wealth without doing the least Credit to the Intellects of Him who squanders it. The House is little different from all other great Mansion Houses, — It is divided into rooms immensely large, and dazzling with gold, and the Most glaring Colours. It Contains a Cabinet of Natural Curiosities most excellently Arrang'd by Bonau one of the first Naturalists in France, who happen'd to be at Chantilly at the same time and who was very communicative indeed — My Head, my Legs, my Eyes, and my very heart ach'd at length with fatigue. We saw a vast deal, and left unseen a vast deal more. We returned to the Inn and immediately sett off for Paris where we now are in health and safety — an account of what I have seen here and a long letter to my Uncle I will send by the earliest Opportunities

Paris July 13th 89. 4 oClock in the Morning,

The accounts You will hear of this last Nights tumults in Paris have induced me to be thus early in my assurances of our safety — the Distress, the Confusion; the Destroying madness of the Scene I have just witness'd have actually equall'd those of a Town taken

Introduction: 'A World of New Ideas'

Early in July 1789 four men set out from Dover on a nine-week European tour that would take them down through France to Marseilles, Nice and the Italian and Swiss Alps, and back through Alsace and the Low Countries. Like hundreds of British tourists before and since, they went with the expectation of enjoying new landscapes, encountering new cultures, trying different kinds of food, and visiting notable monuments. More open-minded than many, they also took a keen interest in how these Continental societies organized matters such as agriculture, education and care of the sick. They had planned ahead, bringing letters of introduction to local mayors and merchants, as well as to various British and American expatriates. Their connections at home made them well aware of the rapidly evolving political situation in France, of the convocation of the Estates-General in May that year, and of the birth of the National Assembly a mere week or two before they set out. Yet, like the Calais innkeeper who confidently assured them that they would find Paris 'perfectly free from disturbance',[1] they could never have predicted that their arrival in the French capital in the second week of July would coincide with the eruption of popular unrest, the storming of the Bastille, and other extraordinary events of the French Revolution.

All four travellers must have recorded their experiences in letters home to their families, and, by huge good fortune, the accounts of three of them have survived. The letters of the Norwich doctor Edward Rigby were published in 1880 by his daughter, Lady Eastlake, and her edition has often been cited by historians of the French Revolution. The unedited manuscripts of these, discussed below, are in fact a more reliable source, since Eastlake did not hesitate to rewrite as she thought fit.[2] The letters of Samuel Boddington, the son of a prominent London merchant, have already been used to good effect by Jeremy Black in his studies of the Grand Tour.[3] Those of Ollyett Woodhouse either do not survive or have yet to be tracked down. The letters of the Glamorgan-born Dissenting minister and scientist George

Cadogan Morgan have until now only been known partially, from quotations cited in other works.[4] They are here published for the first time in their entirety,[5] together with a political pamphlet written by Morgan three years later at a critical moment in the Revolution. A lively autobiographical account by his son, Richard Price Morgan, reveals what happened to the next generation of this radical Dissenting family as, after their father's early death, they tried to make their lives in America.

Both men's accounts are striking testimonies of places and events that shaped the modern world: they are the responses of individuals caught up in the flow of history. The force of that flow is exhilarating and frightening, and like all travellers and adventurers, however well prepared, they cannot always control the pace and direction of the journey. Both narratives involve vivid descriptions of river journeys, and if George Cadogan Morgan is doing no more than other tourists have done before him when he takes a ferry down the Rhône, he is still awed by the strength of the forces at work: 'indeed, the velocity when the river is flooded is so great as to take away from the boatman all the power of his helm.' His son, precariously navigating timber rafts down the Mississippi, notes in his more matter-of-fact way that it 'required much care . . . to avoid being carried precipitously by a four mile an hour current against various dangerous obstacles, that are continually presenting themselves'.

Revolutionary France and early nineteenth-century America are, for these British travellers, *terra incognita*, and both are in their way dangerous. But the father and the son share a fundamental resilience, and an optimism about human nature that makes them ideal travellers, willing to negotiate obstacles and risk the loss of 'power at the helm'. Their gain is that of all those who travel with open minds. As George Cadogan puts it at the end of his account, still dizzy with delight at his experiences in the Swiss Alps: 'It has cost me a deal of trouble, but it has rewarded me with a world of new ideas.'

George Cadogan Morgan: a life

George Cadogan Morgan was born in Bridgend in 1754, the son of a doctor, William Morgan, and of Sarah Price, sister of the political philosopher Richard Price.[6] He was educated at Cowbridge School, where he became Head Boy and showed a talent for the classics. He then spent a year in Oxford, at Jesus College, before moving, after his father's death, to complete his education at the Dissenting academy in Hoxton, where he was taught by his uncle Richard Price as well as by Andrew Kippis, Samuel Morton Savage and Abraham Rees. Financial reasons seem to have played a part in this decision, but there is no doubt that his religious convictions shifted decisively at this period: he is said to have once declared Oxford and Cambridge to be 'full of debaucheries and luxuries'.[7] In 1776, aged only twenty-two, he was invited to preach at the Unitarian Octagon Chapel in Norwich. In 1783 he married Anne (Nancy) Hurry, from a prominent Dissenting family in Great Yarmouth: they would, in fifteen years together, have nine children, a daughter and eight sons, and she would prove an extraordinarily resilient mother after her husband's early death.[8] In Norwich, Morgan pursued scientific studies, writing a paper on electricity and combustion which was published by the Royal Society.[9] He seems at this point in his life to have been liberally inclined (he supported, for example, the work of the Society for Constitutional Information), but not yet radical: a speech made in 1784 shows him to be an advocate of parliamentary reform for wider representation, but has none of the fire of his writing and opinions in the 1790s. A certain taste for conflict is nevertheless revealed in a long, ill-tempered pamphlet of 1782 attacking the Revd F. J. Brand, who, he claims, has insulted his 'literary and moral character' and, unforgivably, criticized the writings of Richard Price.[10] It seems likely, too, that his time in Norwich brought him into contact with Edward Rigby, a doctor of gynaecology and future mayor of the city, also with radical sympathies.

In 1785 Morgan moved to Great Yarmouth, where he began to take paying pupils at home in addition to his preaching duties. Two years later he was invited to take up a ministry in Hackney. Here, besides preaching alongside his increasingly frail uncle at the Gravel Pit Meeting House, he taught courses in the classics, mathematics and science at the recently established New College at Hackney – where William Godwin was among his students – and continued to tutor several of his own pupils at home.[11] Some of the scientific lectures from this period would appear as *Lectures on Electricity* in 1794. For reasons apparently connected with the somewhat volatile nature of the college at this time (it was riven with factionalism and financially unstable) he did not take up Price's ministry upon the latter's retirement,[12] and in 1791 – the year Price died – he moved his family and pupils to Southgate in Middlesex, where he lived close to his brother William Morgan, the actuary, and to the Boddington family, with whom he had close ties. Throughout the 1790s his home was a busy hub of progressive education and increasingly radical Dissent. Gatherings of like-minded friends met, according to his son, 'every Saturday afternoon, to discuss the political condition of the world, and the interesting events daily occurring on the continent'. A flavour of these meetings is captured in an entry from William Godwin's diary for September 1794, which reads: 'Dine at Morgan's, w. Battie, Boddington & Amelia; adv. Ives Hurry & Walters; talk of God &

Burke. Sleep at Southgate.'[13] If Richard Price Morgan's memories of early childhood are to be trusted, they did more than talk:

> some of my first recollections were the patriotic songs of the period. For while trotted on the knee, I was frequently entertained with the 'Marseilles Hymn', 'Ca ira' and a variety of lively French national tunes.[14]

Morgan's social circles were, as far as we can tell, primarily defined by the overlapping spheres of religious Dissent and radical politics. The sources are frustratingly sparse, but one gets little sense here of 'Welshness' as a cohesive factor. His mother spoke Welsh, and his brother William could apparently 'turn a Welsh song into elegant English on the spur of the moment',[15] but we know nothing about George Cadogan's knowledge or use of the Welsh language, though it seems entirely likely that he spoke it as a child. His name does not appear in the lists of the Gwyneddigion or the Cymmrodorion, the two main London-Welsh societies of the period, and nothing in his surviving works shows any particular antiquarian or linguistic interest in matters to do with Wales. Yet, scattered as they were across London and East Anglia, the different branches of the Morgan family remained very much in touch with their South Walian roots. As George Cadogan's son Richard would later remember, a network of cousins, aunts and uncles preserved Glamorgan as a place of renewal and of family sociability for many generations. Caroline Williams records nice vignettes of George swimming energetically in the sea ('the person of Mr Morgan,' noted his obituary, 'was about the middle size, tending to corpulency but athletic and powerful in an uncommon degree'); or, with his brother William and their respective elder daughters – 'the two Sarahs' – visiting an aged aunt.[16] Glamorgan ties apart, however, there is little evidence for a consciously Welsh identity, and almost none at all in the letters from France. Just once, travelling near Marseilles, he seems implicitly to acknowledge his Welshness when he teases Rigby for being 'loud and boisterous' over 'two stupendous mountains': 'I affected great indifference at the sight, and intreated Rigby to be less trouble-some when he next saw what was astonishing only to the Marshland Eyes of a Norfolk Man'. Elsewhere, however, he is happy enough to describe himself as 'one of John Bull's calves'.

The 'interesting events' abroad moved Morgan, in the critical summer of 1792, to pen an anonymous *Address to the Jacobine Societies*, urging the French to seize their opportunity to obliterate the institution of monarchy – 'the most destroying Pestilence that ever desolated the Universe'. The powerful language of this essay, discussed further below, doubtless echoes what his son calls the 'bold political eloquence with which he electrified his hearers'. That his sympathies were not muted by events in the difficult years that followed is suggested by the comments of Amelia Alderson (later Opie) in 1794, on the publication of the names of the jury for the upcoming trial of Horne Tooke:

> My usual spirits have been lowered this morning by hearing Mr Boddington and Mr Morgan mark the printed list of the jury. Every one almost is marked by them as unfit to be trusted; for almost every man is a rascal, and a contractor, and in the pay of government some way or another. What hope is there then for these objects of ministerial rancour?[17]

Like many radicals in the 1790s, however, Morgan learned to curb both his tongue and his pen: 'I hoped,' he wrote to his mother, 'to have published my uncle's life . . . but I am sadly frightened by poor Johnstone's conviction.'[18] The bookseller and radical sympathizer Joseph Johnson, founder and publisher of the liberal *Analytical Review*, was convicted in July 1798 for his part in the publication of Tom Paine's *Rights of Man* (1791/2). George Cadogan Morgan's biography of Richard Price did not, therefore, see the light of day in the 1790s – it is possible that the reception history of Price's work would have been quite different if it had – but was completed by his brother William after his death, and published as *Memoirs of the Life of the Rev. Richard Price* in 1815.

During the summer of 1798, which would be his last, he kept a close eye on events in Ireland, and lamented to his mother that 'the state of things in that country can admit of no change for the worse', adding many graphic details of 'roads covered in putrid bodies. In every direction burnt or burning houses. The villages changed into barracks and in many places daily executions. Some flogged, some half hanged and the horrid spear spikes elevated with the bleeding heads of the rebels fixed on them.'[19] The level of detail here is intriguing, and one would give a great deal to know more about the 'good authority' that supplied such disturbing information – and, indeed, about the general awareness of the conflict amongst the British public as a whole. And there is not, it must be said, quite enough context in the extracts of letters quoted by Caroline Williams to be certain exactly what, beyond horror at the carnage and deep concern for the ordinary people involved, Morgan's political response to the Irish rebellion may have been.

The Southgate house was full of children, the Morgans' own and five more from two other families, without counting the young men who came as pupils, and house guests like Amelia Alderson who came for lengthy visits.[20] Richard Price Morgan, writing in old age, is not always correct in his dates and his facts, but his evocation of those early years filled with companions and shaped by the progressive educational ideals of his father is engaging. His description of his father's study – 'strikingly characteristic of the great mind that furnished it' – has the glamorous awe of childhood about it, and is testimony to the centrality of education in the Morgan household:

> His schoolroom was his study, an immence apartment, not less than sixty feet in length, and twenty-five feet wide, and proportionably high, with book shelves requiring a step ladder to get access to all the valuable works in his extensive library. Considerable space was appropriated to his philosophical apparatus, speci-mens for the study of natural history, anatomy and mineralogy, occupied the shelves of large glass cases, while a broad table supported electrical machines, jars and other experimental models, as well as globes and a grand telescope, manu-factured by Dolland, which had been a legacy from Dr. Price.[21]

Morgan's scientific curiosity may have led to his unexpected death on 17 November 1798, aged only forty-four; his published obituary described an 'affection of the chest' leading to 'pulmonary fever', but the family account claims that he 'inhaled some poison, which carried him off after a short fever'.[22] He left Anne with eight children, and pregnant with another. Her story and those of her children are recalled in the memoir that forms the last part of this volume.

George Cadogan Morgan lies buried in Southgate. One of many people from this period whose lives were busy with the pursuit of knowledge and the progress of humankind, he has left relatively little mark on the historical record. A poem (under the pen name 'Ignotus', but possibly by his wife or daughter) in *The Monthly Magazine* the following spring lamented that he was 'cropt like a May-day flower in all its bloom',[23] and it is frustrating to think what he might have accomplished had he lived longer. His letters from France reveal him to have been an affectionate husband and father and an observant traveller, possessed of a robust faith in human nature that allowed him, like many others at this critical moment, to believe that the whole of European society was on the verge of changing for the better.

Letters from France, summer 1789

In 1789 George Cadogan Morgan was thirty-five. In late June of that year he and his family moved from Clapton into a house in Hackney owned by the merchant Benjamin Boddington and leased by him for £90 per annum.

A mere fortnight later Morgan, Boddington's twenty-three-year-old son
Samuel and another young man, Ollyett Woodhouse, set off for Dover on
their own version of the Grand Tour; they were joined from Norwich by
Edward Rigby, then in his early forties, who proved a popular addition to
the group: 'Mr Rigby,' wrote Samuel to his stepmother on the first evening
of their journey, 'fully answers the description Mr Morgan gave of him he
is indeed a very pleasant man.'[24]

The connections between the four men are worth exploring as they give
some idea of the motivation for the journey and the dynamics of the group.
Samuel Boddington (1766–1843), though already working in the family
business at Mark Lane, seems to have been tutored by Morgan in 1787; his
younger brother Thomas was certainly receiving 'preparatory education for
New College Hackney' from him between 1787 and 1789, and doubtless
his schooling was one of the many commitments that made Morgan reluctant
to allow the tour, tightly scheduled for July and August, to extend much
into September, revolutionary delays notwithstanding. The Boddingtons
were a prominent Dissenting family, actively involved in parliamentary and
religious reform, and close to the Morgans over two generations.[25] It is likely
that Ollyett Woodhouse, from another Norwich Dissenting family, was also
a pupil of Morgan's. A cousin of Amelia Alderson Opie, who was distantly
related to George Cadogan through his wife's family,[26] Woodhouse could
have been one of several 'young men of liberal families', who came via
family contacts in Norfolk.[27] Given Morgan's semi-defined role as mentor,
it is not impossible that the Boddingtons and/or the Woodhouses at least
subsidized the costs of the tour.[28]

The journey was thus, as these journeys so often were, primarily educational
in intent, and, in line with Morgan's progressive theories which encouraged
pupil and teacher to learn, experiment and observe together, all made the
most of the opportunity it afforded. Cultural differences – food, dress, religion
– are of course frequently commented upon, and Morgan, the classicist,
turns more than once to Caesar or Homer to make his point. But much is
scientific. Agricultural observations form a key-note in all three surviving
accounts, especially in the scribbled notebooks of Rigby and Boddington,
which are often simply lists of crops they see from the road. Rigby's interest
is practical as well as theoretical; a friend and neighbour of Coke of Holkham,
he translated an agricultural treatise from Italian and, as his daughter informs
us, applied the new methods to the land he owned at Framingham in Norfolk
('well do I remember,' she wrote, 'the gigantic size of certain Swedish turnips
and mangel-wurzel laid on the lawn for the inspection of friends, and particularly a certain monster cabbage').[29] Morgan likewise is keen to tell his wife
how the land is used in the different areas of France, 'tho' each inch of

ground was cultivated, yet there was scarcely any pasturage. Corn, beans and flax covered the whole ground.' All three writers comment surprisingly often on the apparent fertility and abundance of produce all around them (and make frequent reference to children and pregnant women). They all assure their families that the 'scarcity, magnified into a Famine' is by no means as evident as they had been led to believe at home. In this respect at least their tourist status appears to have insulated them from the harsh economic realities of that summer, occasioned by the disastrous harvest of the previous year: the prices of grain and bread had been escalating rapidly since the spring, and reached their highest point in Paris on 14 July 1789.[30]

Rigby, as a doctor, assiduously visits hospitals and is at times horrified, but also quite frequently (at Dijon, for example) impressed; Morgan the natural scientist discourses on sea levels at Dover, has his thermometer ready to record the heat of a Provence afternoon, and attempts to calculate the height of mountains. They all, experimentally, boil water on a summit in the Alps. A nice episode recorded by Boddington (though not, modestly, by Morgan himself) reveals the international dimension to their pursuit of knowledge. At the Prince of Condé's palace in Chantilly, almost the only thing that meets with the approval of our group (unanimous in their dislike of its ostentation and the sterility of formal French garden design) is the famous Cabinet of Natural Curiosities assembled by the naturalist Bomare, who happened to be

> writing descriptions on the different fossils when we entered the room. We had a striking trait of the Polite manners of the French in the attentions he showed us. Mr Rigby having made some remark which discover'd his knowledge of Fossils Reaumur [sic] immediately enter'd into conversation with him & Mr Morgans name being mentioned he very politely thank'd him for the pleasure he had received in perusing his papers in the Phylosophical Transaction. He attended us for near an hour pointing out the most curious articles in the collection.[31]

This incident raises the question of language. It is not always evident how the British travellers communicate with the people they encounter, many of whom go out of their way to offer help and advice: did the helpful merchant in Toulon, or the likeable M. Pastor in Geneva, speak English, one wonders. Morgan's first letter reveals some trouble with decoding spoken French 'which, owing to the rapid manner in which they express themselves, is to me as yet unintelligible'. Of the three writers, Boddington appears to have the most fluent grasp of the language and enjoys peppering his letters home with throw-away phrases. Once they reach Paris, and for the remainder of the journey thereafter (although he is entirely invisible in the accounts of Rigby and Morgan) the party also has the benefit of a valet called Scheilds, 'a most useful clever fellow', who doubtless acted where needed as an interpreter.[32]

There is much that could be said about how the three narratives relate to each other – the triple 'voice' is a remarkable gift to the historian and the student of travel literature – and to other travel narratives of the period. A great deal of what they see and experience is on the beaten track of the Grand Tour, and these accounts add to the wealth of detail we already have on topics such as costume (particularly female), food, religion, hygiene and landscape (particularly vividly documented by Rigby and Boddington, both of whom share a decidedly romantic aesthetic). A closer analysis of the content and the interplay of the three accounts must be deferred for another study, and, although one can never wholly separate the political from the merely mundane (even the fleas, those 'legions of blood and fury', seem subliminally significant given the context) this introduction will now focus more narrowly on the political implications of George Cadogan Morgan's tour, paying particular attention to the nature of the letters' testimony to the events in Paris.

Political drama in Paris

The primary importance of these letters, of course, is their eye-witness account of many of the key events in those first days of the Revolution. Morgan's close connection with Richard Price is also significant, as the two lost letters he wrote to his uncle from Paris directly informed Price's understanding of the situation, and would shape his famous *Discourse on the Love of Our Country* delivered later that year, which in turn would spark the pamphlet debate taken up, amongst others, by Burke, Paine and Wollstonecraft. The letters to Price were published in the *Gazetteer* on 13 August and 14 September 1789. Somewhat astonishingly, given the survival of earlier and later issues of this newspaper, not a single copy of these particular issues is known to still exist, an absence which it is tempting to ascribe to political intervention, although there is no proof of this. All that remains of Morgan's detailed descriptions of the scenes and events that took place around 14 July are a few citations in other works – Burke's *Reflections* among them – where they are aired merely in order to be attacked by critics thoroughly hostile to their pro-French, and pro-Revolutionary, sentiment. The rediscovery of the letters to his wife is thus doubly precious. Their value increases further when we realize that the often-cited testimony of Edward Rigby to the events in Paris, an account of some sixty pages in Eastlake's volume, is a heavily revised version of a now *missing* source: no manuscript letter in the collection corresponds to the published material, though in several places Eastlake has used Rigby's journal to enrich her text.[33]

A determination to welcome the events in Paris, however personally inconvenient or indeed threatening, is – at times to the point of comedy – a key-note of Morgan's letters to his wife. Writing at four in the morning on 13 July from their hotel room next to the seething Palais Royal, Morgan recounts how earlier in the night a crowd hunting for weapons had, after much hammering, forced its way into the gunsmiths on the floor below them, 'but found no arms as another company had previously seiz'd upon the whole of the gunsmith's stock'. Instead of venting their frustration on the frightened tourists, however, 'they soon relieved us by retiring in great tranquility'. Such moments of unexpected politesse occur more than once. Attempting to leave Paris, they are repeatedly turned back from the gates 'amidst taunts, hissings, abuse and insults', behaviour which Morgan cordially interprets as a result of the Parisians' perception of betrayal of their Revolutionary cause, adding that 'the politeness of some individuals amply made up for the severity of the multitude'.

One notable feature of the travellers' time in Paris is their regular attendance at the theatre. On the day of their arrival they saw Sedaine and Grétry's *Richard Coeur de Lion* and *Le petit souper de famille* at the Théâtre Italien; the following evening, in the same place, they saw the famous mezzo-soprano Mme Dugazon, 'who is the Mrs Siddons of Paris', in *Raoul Barbe Bleue* ('nothing more or less,' says Morgan, 'than the old story of Blue Beard and Sister Ann'). On the 10th they were at the Opera, where they saw the dancer Auguste Vestris.[34] Morgan's attitude to all this entertainment is decidedly negative, and he is unwilling to admit to enjoying any of it: 'At the Opera, the pride of the French, all was noise and nonsense, improbability and distortion. I wish'd it over before it was half finished.' Versailles, on the other hand, where they spent the day and night of the 11th, proved a more uplifting kind of theatre:

> There indeed I was delighted – such a spectacle as gratified my fondest feelings appeared in the Grand Body of the Representatives assembled to establish Liberty in one of the first nations upon Earth.

They could scarcely have arrived at a more dramatic moment. The new National Assembly had reached a particularly tense point in its relations with the Court. Having watched Lafayette present the bill for the Declaration of the Rights of Man and Citizen (which would be passed in August), the group went in search of Mirabeau and Target, to whom, through Richard Price, they had letters of introduction.[35] The former was unavailable but (according to the account in *Rigby-Eastlake*) Target was willing to discuss the impending crisis forced by the relentless build-up of troops around the city of Paris. He said that many members of the Assembly suspected that the king intended to move against them at any moment; that many of them by now indeed feared for their lives, but that he was 'not without a reasonable hope that the army would declare for us'.[36]

Outwardly, though, things were still quiet. Having attended and enjoyed the 'spectacle' of the king and queen at Versailles even less than his trips to the theatre – 'The splendid minions of a Court in all their gaudy tinsel gave me but little pleasure, whilst yet warm with the grandeur of what I saw on the preceding day' – Morgan and his companions travelled back to Paris on the morning of Sunday 12th with no difficulty. A few hours later they were dining in the Rue St Michel, 'and while we sat at table one of the company ask'd us whether we had heard of Necker's flight'. This second dismissal and flight of the Genevan-born director-general of finance, Jacques Necker (1732–1804), was a significant contributory factor in sparking the revolt in Paris.[37] To discover more, the group decided to attend the theatre, because 'it would certainly give signs of the multitude's disposition': and from this point on, for the next few days, the drama is entirely political.

René Farge's painstaking account of the events of 12 July, much of which hangs on the exact opening hours of the Paris theatres, allows us to time the unfolding action of the next few hours very precisely, and to place Morgan's group in relation to such legendary episodes as Camille Desmoulins's speech at the Palais Royal, and the disastrous attempt to restore order by the Prince de Lambesc at the nearby Jardin des Tuileries.[38] The theatres played an important role in the popular expression of the revolt, and their forced closure, as if in 'mourning', by the crowds marked a significant moment in the Revolutionary narrative. At about half past three the crowd headed off to shut down the various central theatres, with one group stopping at the home of the wax-work museum owner Paul Curtius to collect busts of Necker and the Duc d'Orléans. From inside the Théâtre Français,[39] Morgan and his friends experienced it thus:

At this moment the curtain was rais'd and the manager came forward. "Sirs," said he, "You are to have no play this evening." "The reason why?" was immediately resounded from every quarter of the house. – The manager answer'd, that the <u>People</u> then at his door had commanded it. A burst of the most impetuous applause discover'd to us the disposition of the assembly.

Leaving the theatre, they then proceeded with a huge crowd back to the Palais Royal, the venue for some of the Revolution's more theatrical moments. In the eyes of many, indeed, it was the crucible of the uprising. Owned by the king's troublesome cousin Louis-Philippe, Duc d'Orléans (who would become known as 'Philippe Égalité' for his espousal of republicanism under the Revolutionary régime),[40] the Palais Royal had been recently reinvented as a place for shopping, eating and entertainment, a place that licentiously, and subversively, mixed classes and genres. It rapidly became a focal point for tourists, and a hub for news and gossip:

> Imagine a large rectangle surrounded by a very fine building, intersected by cut walks, refresh'd by several pieces of water with *jet d'eaus* in the middle, crowded by men with powdered heads and with their hats under their arms, and thickly beset with ladies of all kinds, adorn'd likewise by very rich shops form'd like the best in London, and here and there presenting to the eye companies of men and women sitting in the open air.

Orléans's rivalry with the court at Versailles meant that the presses based at the Palais escaped the normal laws of copyright and censorship, and they turned out a deluge of mostly radical pamphlets: 'thirteen today, sixteen yesterday and ninety-two last week' according to Arthur Young, who was 'all amazement at the ministry permitting such nests and hotbeds of sedition and revolt'.[41]

Rigby's journal records that our group reached the Palais Royal 'about six', thus missing (Eastlake's version notwithstanding) Camille Desmoulins's speech at the Café Foy, but in time to hear many others, equally agitated.[42] About an hour later (Boddington says 'about 7 o'clock')[43] they saw 'a Man in a green Coat came running with Marks of Alarm' who 'called to Arms – for the French Dragons had attacked the People at the Champs Elizees – & that he himself was wounded.'[44]

This man was very probably François Pépin, identified as the bearer of the wax bust of the Duc d'Orléans during the afternoon demonstrations, who was wounded in the leg during a clash between the Royal Dragoons and several thousand people in the Place Louis XV at around six o'clock. This encounter, as Paul Spagnoli has shown, has been played down by many historians, but seems to have been just as significant in changing the mood of the crowd that evening as the notorious incursion of the Royal Allemand into the Tuileries gardens some two hours later. This latter event, known as Lambesc's Charge, rapidly assumed an iconic significance in the revolutionary narrative of the events of the *journée* which was taken on unquestioned for the next two hundred years.[45] Yet while the story of the 'massacre' in the Tuileries proves to have very little foundation in fact (no deaths can be directly attributed to what seems to have been an attempt at retreat, not attack), the earlier confrontation between the angry crowd who had just come from closing down the theatres, and the Royal Dragoons who believed the people were preparing to march on Versailles, represents a serious moment of conflict and resulted in at least one death.

Spagnoli has plenty of other evidence to support his argument, but he does draw on Eastlake's version of Edward Rigby, which, as we have seen, is not wholly reliable. It is interesting to find, then, that Rigby's and Morgan's manuscript versions of events actually support his case rather better than the published version: *Rigby-Eastlake* has the wounded man call out 'To arms citizens, the Dragoons have fired on the people in the *Tuileries gardens*',[46] where the notebook clearly has 'Champs Elizes', that is, the space immediately adjacent to the Place Louis XV on the other side. The notebook version is thus entirely consistent with Spagnoli's conclusion that Pépin was referring to the earlier incident, and suggests that either Rigby or Eastlake retrospect-ively altered the location to fit the 'revised' version, which developed very rapidly, collapsing the various flashpoints of that evening into the fiasco with Lambesc. Indeed, in the published Rigby version the importance of the Tuileries episode is actually prefigured: 'These gardens were soon to acquire a new celebrity, as the spot where the revolutionary explosion first took place.'[47]

Morgan's letter is equally clear on the matter, with plenty of time elapsing between the arrival of the wounded man (Pépin) and news of the action by the Swiss Guards (already, at this point, turned by rumour into a massacre of 'fifty of the populace'). Arriving at the Palais Royal with the crowd from the theatre, Morgan says that they listened for a while to various orators haranguing the public:

In this boiling and unsettled state of commotion we had continued some time when we saw a man enter in all the most distorted attitudes of imprecation and rage. "To arms," says he. "I have been wounded by the Dragoons, and they are this moment firing upon your fellow citizens." Hundreds immediately echo'd back "to Arms", and a vast portion of the multitude immediately follow'd their guides. There were now very few individuals remaining in the quadrangle of the Palace and my companions stood prophecying the horrors of the approaching night, when we saw the mob return led by a most desperate fellow, sweating & raving and swearing and holding up an empty helmet as a standard. None of the company chose to be near the scene of action, we therefore returned to our hotel and from the windows survey'd the increasing distraction and rage of the populace – within the space of half an hour tranquility was restor'd in our street, but we heard distant shouts and saw new multitudes rushing down thro' every alley and street. As the scene of danger seem'd to be removed we ventured once more into the Palais Royal, and there learnt that the barriers of the town were all on fire – that the Swiss Guards had fired and [that] fifty of the populace had fallen, but that the crowd could not be dispersed.

The travellers, fortuitously, had chosen to stay at the expensive Grand Hôtel du Palais Royal in the Rue de Valois: 'However we have not grudg'd the money,' noted Morgan with his usual positive attitude, 'as our situation at the awful moment of the revolt enabled us to see, what others who lodged in a different part of the town heard from us with astonishment.' They were thus, caught up in the ebb and flow of an excited crowd, able to retreat more than once in the course of the night to the comparative safety of their room, where they listened to the confusion outside: 'Every now and then the report of a cannon then a volley of musket. Carriages going past into the country. Men hallowing and women screaming. In short it was one continued scene of alarm and confusion.'[48] Besides contributing to a more precise mapping of the day's events, the three men's accounts vividly evoke the turbulence of the night of the 12th–13th.

The travellers seem to have spent the next day trying and failing to leave Paris; they would not, in fact, manage to get out of the city for another full week, although they made several attempts. They were thus captive but not at all unwilling witnesses to many further extraordinary developments, most of which are glanced at only elliptically (and, for posterity, frustratingly) in Morgan's letters to his wife as 'those great events which I have described very minutely in a letter to my Uncle'. They were also extremely fortunate in their Paris-based contacts, including the helpful Mr Dallas (married to a Norwich friend of the Rigbys), who went out of his way to guide them around the sights and assist them in their dealings with French bureaucracy; and Richard Price's friend and correspondent Thomas Jefferson, then American ambassador, who informed them of the progress of events in other parts of the city and 'assured Mr Morgan that our situation and Character as Englishmen secured us from any Danger'.[49]

The inevitably patchy nature of finding oneself in the middle of a great historical event is nicely exemplified by their activities on Tuesday, 14 July. Having experienced the very moment of the Revolutionary 'explosion' in the Palais Royal, all three writers express admiration at the rapidity with which order had been restored by the 'citizen guards'.[50] Feeling that things had settled down, they decided to spend the afternoon visiting the gardens of the Duc d'Orléans at Monceaux. Returning at about five o'clock they heard news of a disturbance at the Bastille, and made to head in that direction, calling in first at the hotel. From there, hearing a commotion, they went out to find a large crowd heading down the Rue St Honoré for the Palais Royal, 'bringing a Paper on which was written La Bastille est prise & les Portes sont ouvertes'.[51] This was followed shortly afterwards by a more grisly sight. 'There,' wrote Boddington, 'I first beheld the horrid effects of war. The heads of the Governor and the Commandant of the Bastile just cut off from their bodies carrying in triumph.'[52] This episode is altogether lacking from Morgan's account, and must have been described in the lost letters to Price. It is interesting to see the efforts made by both Boddington and Rigby to ascertain the facts of the storming of the Bastille in the hours and days that followed: thus Rigby's journal for Wednesday, 15 July revises what he heard the previous day with a 'true account', while Boddington on the 19th acknowledges that 'there are various accounts of this memorable action'.[53]

The night of the 14th seems to have been another anxious one, with rumours of reprisals by the king's forces: Boddington notes that the flagstones of the pavement in front of their hotel were all 'taken up and carried to the house opposite' as a potential weapon. But by Wednesday the mood was again much calmer. Rigby's journal for Wednesday, 15 July shows that he rose early, and, although the timing is rather unclear, he appears to have gone down from the hotel into the Rue St Honoré and seen two of the Bastille's 'eight' prisoners being brought by a crowd to the Palais Royal. One of them is especially interesting:

> Count D'Auche a Prisoner in from the Bastille was found this Morning in one of the deepest Dungeons, the Road to which was the most private intricate possible – he had been confined 42 years. He was a Major in the Cavalry – he was draped in a greasy reddish Cloak – his beard was very long & his Hair which had not been combed during this long Period was grown very long – closely matted together – was divided into two Parts & reached lower than his Knees – exhibiting a most extraordinary Phenomenon.[54]

In a letter written on Sunday, 19th, Samuel Boddington likewise tells his family that:

> one of them a Count D'Auche had been confined two and forty years in one of the dark dungeons. I never beheld so affecting a spectacle. His beard was of a great length and his hair which appeared never to have been combed was entangled in large nets as if it had been wove. It was parted into two long parts and coming over his shoulders reached below his knees. His face was [illegible] but quite pale, and he looked about him as one should conceive a man to do who for the first time had the use of his eyes.[55]

While Rigby's journal entry does not make it wholly clear that he actually *saw* the man in question, it seems, given Boddington's testimony, perfectly probable – although, since Boddington's letter implies that the procession was on the evening of the 14th, there is uncertainty about when this happened. The Eastlake version claims that he did see him, and goes into three pages of considerable detail describing his reaction to this man, again focusing on his poor eyesight and his extraordinary hair and beard ('matted together and divided into two long tails, very much like the tail of a monkey').[56] Indeed, he confesses to finding the man's plight so distressing that he was 'no longer able to bear the sight. I turned from the crowd. I burst into tears'; he then went and found his companions who 'had all a sight of the released prisoners'.[57]

The episode is profoundly intriguing. The bearded man would appear to be (or to have been explained to them shortly afterwards as) the Comte de Lorges, whose tragic history would be elaborated at length by the journalist J. L. Carra, and published in September; an engraving showing the moment of his discovery in the dungeon was also published.[58] This pitiful character would be absorbed into the developing story of the Revolution, and his incarceration of thirty-two (not forty-two) years would come to symbolize the tyranny of the old regime. But who in fact was he? Recent criticism has described him as a 'myth', and indeed a 'narratological necessity': the Comte de Lorges, apparently, 'never existed', and historians agree that only seven prisoners were liberated from the Bastille.[59] But our travellers clearly saw someone. If we had this description from *Rigby-Eastlake* alone, we would be inclined to read it as another example of Lady Eastlake making sure that her father's letter included the 'complete' Revolutionary experience (although, to be fair, in this instance she adds a baffled footnote trying to identify this man), but both the manuscript accounts are vivid and precise in their descriptions of the man and his hair, and both give him a name which at least approximates to the mythical 'Lorges'. Without proving the existence of the elusive Count, we can say that on the evening of the 14th or the morning after, a half-blind long-bearded old man was paraded through the streets as a released prisoner, and that his 'story' and his 'name' were generally known very shortly thereafter – much sooner than recent commentators have claimed.[60]

On the Wednesday, too, came news that the king had agreed to comply with the requests of the National Assembly, and planned to come to Paris to greet the people. Thinking once again that things would now settle down, the party headed for the Hôtel de Ville in search of passports. The *Rigby-Eastlake* material contains a dramatic and highly circumstantial account of the group's attempt to leave Paris on the Wednesday, which involved them being turned back from check-points several times, at first merely as a matter of course, but, after someone discovered pistols in the carriage, with increasing hostility. They returned three times that day to the Hôtel de Ville (where at one point their carriage was surrounded by an angry crowd), before giving up and spending the night with Mr Dallas at the Hôtel Saint Michel.

On Friday, 17 July, they had an excellent view of the procession accompanying the king's entrance from the balcony of a Mr Sykes in the Place Palais Royal. Once again, frustratingly, the highly circumstantial account in the published *Rigby-Eastlake* letter cannot be corroborated in every detail. This episode is crucial in resolving a long-running debate on the source of Richard Price's controversial phrase 'a King led in triumph' in his *Discourse on the Love of Our Country* – a phrase which Edmund Burke mistakenly, or wilfully, took to refer to the more brutal subsequent events of the October Days, and which he cites as proof of Price's support for violent revolution. We know that Morgan definitely gave an account of the event in the lost letters to Price, and seems to have used the much stronger phrase 'dragged in submissive triumph' in the extracts quoted by his detractors.[61] On Saturday, 18 July the party revisited the Bastille, which they had seen shortly after their arrival, and watched it being dismantled, stone by stone. It seems that they regretfully but prudently turned down an invitation to go inside and inspect the dungeons. Having finally procured passports, they left Paris at half past five in the morning 'without Interception' on Sunday, 19th, and headed for Dijon via Fontainebleau.

All of them seem to have been deeply moved by what they saw. Morgan reflected that 'the King's entrance without his guards into Paris, the demolition of the Bastile, and the restoration of Peace and Liberty to the noble Parisians amply repaid our loss of time and the fatigue of our spirits.' Rigby, more expansively, told his family:

> I have been Witness to the most extraordinary Revolution which perhaps ever took Place in human Society – a great & wise People struggled for Freedom & the Rights of Humanity – their Courage, Prudence & Perseverance have been rewarded by Success; & an Event which will contribute to the Happiness of Millions who are living & to Millions & Millions of their Posterity has taken Place, with very little Loss of Blood, & with but a few Days Interruption to the common Business of the Place.[62]

Travels through France

The four travellers and Scheilds, the servant who would remain with them for the tour, rode the crest of the breaking news down through France. Indeed, in some places they were the first to bring word:

In every village as we passed along we were stop'd by the crowd agitated by inquiries about news from Paris. We wav'd our cockades;[63] we briefly announced that "the Bastile was demolish'd – that the Governor's head was off; that the Army was disbanded, and that the King without Guards had thrown himself on the mercy of the free peoples." – We are generally dismissed with loud applause and with the cry of "Vive la Nation. Toujours le tiers État!"

A few days after Morgan and his party had calmed a particularly pressing crowd by this means, Arthur Young, just outside Lisle, had a similar encounter:

I was questioned for not having a cockade of the *tiers état*. They said it was ordained by the tiers, and, if I was not a Seigneur, I ought to obey. *But suppose I am a Seigneur, what then, my friends?* – What then? They replied sternly, why be hanged; for that is most likely what you deserve. It was plain this was no moment for joking, the boys and girls began to gather, whose assembling has everywhere been the preliminaries of mischief; and if I had not declared myself an Englishman, and ignorant of the ordinance, I had not escaped very well. I immediately bought a cockade, but the hussey pinned it into my hat so loosely, that before I got to Lisle it blew into the river, and I was again in the same danger.[64]

Young's response to such 'assemblings' is, as one would expect from his more sceptical attitude to politics in general, noticeably different from Morgan's, emphasizing the sinister aspects of the crowd and the compulsion to conform to the new ordinance – to wear the cockade or risk being 'hanged'. France, in the fortnight after the fall of the Bastille, was, after all, an extremely jittery place, and it is hard not to feel that in Morgan's case sheer enthusiasm for the cause acted as a kind of prophylactic during incidents that could easily have turned unpleasant. Just outside Dijon it happened again:

A crowd with cockades and muskets stop'd up the road. Our postilions crack'd their whips and made an effort as in former times to force their way thro' the multitude with the accustom'd defiance of all those who serv'd the Grand Monarch. But the spirit of Liberty was now in its full pride and in a moment our traces were cut and our carriage immoveable & altogether at the mercy of the crowd. However, the Commander rode up to us, expressed his concern for our embarrassment with great politeness, and beg'd that we would pardon the little excesses of a people who had just thrown off their fetters. We found that the armed force which had stop'd us belonged to a small town which had followed the example of hundreds more; and with swords and bayonets were determined to teach the Priests, the Noblesse and the King that they were human beings as well as themselves.

Once again, Morgan appears extremely sanguine in the face of real potential danger. 'Little excesses' such as this were a characteristic feature of the French countryside in the weeks that followed the uprising in Paris. Georges Lefebvre's classic study, *La Grande Peur de 1789*, has tracked the nervous state of huge swathes of the French population during precisely this period. He concludes that although the causes of the various panics that swept regions of France were often minor if not chimerical, the very real result – to which Morgan here bears ample witness – is that small villages and communes organized themselves into armed, self-governing units of citizens, which would soon be drawn into the implementation of national Revolutionary ideology.[65]

Beyond the militarization of local populations (particularly noted in Lyons, which, as Morgan recognized, had started its own revolution independently of Paris),[66] the travellers also record in the course of their journey an increasing hostility to the aristocracy. Dijon, for reasons to do with the elections to the Estates General in 1788, was particularly swift to move against its own nobility, as Morgan's account of a conversation with the Guards who accompanied them to the hotel bears out:

> They shook their heads and said, that they would take care to keep the Noblesse quiet; for whom, they assured us, they meant to erect a Bastile at Dijon. At present it is a sad calamity in France to be a nobleman – or one of his relations. They are fairly driven out of the towns, and should any new disturbance arise, I am apt to think, they would lose something more than their titles.[67]

By the end of the month they are in Aix-en-Provence, in time to witness another dramatic moment:

> We entered this town just as 4,000 Marsilians departed, who had marched hither commanded by a priest in full force to require the liberation of 60 prisoners whom the Noblesse had confined. The prison doors were thrown open and these Sons of Liberty marched with the captives in triumph to Marseilles. The intendant of Aix narrowly escap'd destruction. He is fled to Italy and is amongst the proscribed.

Among the prisoners, notes Rigby, were 'several Women, & two Babies which had been born since the Imprisonment of their Mothers; there were also other Prisoners who had been confined several years; I saw one unhappy Woman who had been confined nine Years, for striking her Fellow servant, & was held there mainly by the Cruelty of her Master.'[68] At Marseilles shortly afterwards the triumphal processions of crowds parading these released prisoners made it difficult for them to get about the streets: 'We found them here as martial as at Paris,' noted Morgan. 'The[y] had proscribed 30 of the Noblesse and the number of 14,000 Citizens had enrolled themselves for arms.'[69]

Armed citizens, cockades, check-points, processions, demonstrations and occasional tangles with bureaucracy (at Antibes the Governor objects to their passports 'solely that he might hear the news from Paris'): these are the outward and evident signs of political upheaval, all duly noted in letters home. But politics permeates their writing in other ways too, and all three travellers punctuate their accounts with remarkably similar comments of enthusiasm or disapproval at what they find. Perhaps the most frequently expressed sentiment of this kind is amazement at the productivity of the land, and what this promises in a more equal future:

> If such has been the situation of a country under the iron hand of despotism what may not be expected from it now the shackles of industry are broken and a free government is about to be established . . . They who could best afford it have paid no taxes but have rioted in abundance obtained from the industry of the honest peasant. Their day is now over.[70]

Of the three, Morgan's attitude is the most stridently anti-royal. His perception of the hunting forests at Chantilly and Fontainebleau as unproductive wastelands prevents him from acknowledging any beauty in the scene, 'while my companions were in raptures with the shade, the beauty, and the variety of the woods thro' which they passed, I was employed in drawing the picture which the same ground would have afforded, if like the surrounding country it were cover'd with cornfields and villages.' (The theme, taken up more than once, would be expanded even more acerbically in his 1792 pamphlet.) He is, more than once, a reluctant visitor to grand edifices, churches and palaces, all symbols in their way of oppression. And though all the travellers disapprove heartily of monasteries and nunneries and are scathing about the apparent superficiality of the religious services they attend, Morgan's narrative is also the most tinged with an anti-Catholicism which at times borders on bigotry. 'Avignon,' he writes, 'is part of the Pope's dominions, and we had no sooner entered the territories of his holiness than we saw a scene of drunkenness and irregularity, the remote semblance of which we had not discovered in the whole Kingdom of France. Our inn was nasty, our beds full of buggs.' And Chalon, which Boddington claims is 'a pleasant town on the banks of the Saône', is for Morgan 'the residence of vermin', and 'a dirty town replete with buggs and fleas and priests'.

At Protestant Geneva, on the other hand, 'We stroll'd about from one street to another, admiring the varieties of Industry and like the true Sons of Liberty ascribing all to the absence of Kings and Priests and their whole train of oppressors.'[71] Even the dreadful disappointment of not finding letters from their families waiting for them poste restante cannot take the shine off this city, where 'people know no distinctions but those which arise from superior virtues or abilities'[72] (and where, as it happens, royalty is not entirely absent, Prince Edward the duke of Kent being currently resident, and displaying, in Morgan's words, 'a brilliancy of character worthy the fountain from which he sprang. – His mistress, his houses, his contempt of his tutors, and his royal extravagance afford the town no small diversion').

One of the most compelling parts of Morgan's narrative is the final long letter dated 17 August, from Vevey, which contains a magnificent account of their adventures in the Alps. The subject deserves more detailed attention elsewhere, as 1789 is relatively early for tourists doing the 'Mont Blanc experience', and there are many practical details (accommodation, routes taken, methods of transport, guides) of great interest to the historian. Just over a decade later the young J. M. W. Turner covered much of the same ground, leaving a stunning visual record of the landscapes – the crags, the billows of ice, the twisted trees – that Morgan and Rigby are at some pains to describe to their families.[73] Morgan's accounts of the Glacier des Bossons and of the famous Mer de Glace are also potentially interesting for the study of glaciology. And there are, amidst episodes of high comedy deriving from the unsuitability of their clothing and their typically British disregard for planning ahead, some moments that touch on the sublime. The most dramatic of these, I suggest, can best be understood as political.

Exactly a year after Morgan and his companions, Wordsworth, on a walking tour with his college friend Robert Jones, would find himself confronting the same landscape. As has been frequently noted, his whole experience of the Alps, recollected in *The Prelude*, is curiously anticlimactic – particularly when the friends discover that they have actually 'crossed the Alps' without realizing it. Wordsworth's initial response to Mont Blanc itself is one of disappointment:

> That day we first
> Beheld the summit of Mont Blanc, and griev'd
> To have a soulless image on the eye
> Which had usurp'd upon a living thought
> That nevermore could be.[74]

Not so George Cadogan, whose description of Mont Blanc by sunrise is not only a text-book example of a writer trying to capture the sublime, but, by an unexpected twist, itself an act of sublimation. On the day of their trek from Chamonix to Martigny via the Col de Balme, the group rise at two in the morning in order to capture the full interaction of moonlight and encroaching day being played out like a drama on the 'gleamy summit' of the mountain. Morgan dwells at some length on the effects of the light, and then something extraordinary happens:

> I was attentively watching this change of delightful appearances when I saw a bright cloud bursting from one of the snowy precipices. It descended with vast fragments of ice and rock. Our Guides shouted, and desir'd us to mark what followed. In a few moments our ears were assail'd by a roar to which that of thunder is trifling. This was one of those falls from the sides of the mountains which form the Glaciers. We have but one thing now, said I, to wish for and this scene of sublimity would be compleated.

The wish is, to say the least, an unexpected one:

> Let Mont Blanc open wide his jaws and disclose the horrors of his entrails. Let him belch forth a torrent of fire and whirl into the air his concealed stores of combustible matter. Let a destroying lava dissipate the snow and combined torrents of liquid fire & ice pour into the valley. Let the surrounding rocks shake and totter and the ground below us undulate. Add a Volcano to our views, and we shall then see what the world's greatest sublimities cannot surpass.

Where, in a text not noted for its flights of fancy, does this vividly imagined volcano come from? Morgan is, perhaps even with a touch of humour, rolling out all the elements of the sublime to convey the sheer thrill of the moment. But it is hard not to read this eruption – destructive, energetic, frightening, beautiful, world-changing – as a sublimated metaphor for what he has seen over the past few weeks. Even today historians reach for volcano metaphors to describe the seismic cultural shifts of this period; and there were many who made the connection explicit at the time.[75] It is significant, too, that the written-up text as we have it stops here with the words 'The End'. Although the travellers would be another fortnight on the road, visiting Germany and the Low Countries, those experiences were not subsequently included in Morgan's tour.

The Revolutionary tense: travel writing, time and narrative control

If the Revolution thus grandly reveals itself in the text as metaphor, it also registers its disruptive presence at the more structural level of narrative.

Recent work by Gavin Edwards offers a useful way of understanding how George Cadogan Morgan tried to maintain a sequential narrative flow to his letters that would reflect the course of his journey – and how the events in Paris interfered with it. Edwards's *Narrative Order 1789–1819* explores the various pressures exerted on the telling of stories during this period of social and semantic upheaval: whatever their ideological positioning, he suggests, the work of many British writers of the 1790s reveals the impact of 'radical, repeated and unpredictable change'.[76] This uncertainty about the power of narrative to convey lived experience truthfully is manifested at many levels, from the plotting and outcome(s) of a novel such as Godwin's *Caleb Williams,* to the nuances of a single word in a poem by Wordsworth. Particularly relevant to our material is the problem of hindsight, discussed by Edwards in relation to Watkin Tench's *Narrative of the Expedition to Botany Bay* (1789) and its sequel, *An Account of the Settlement at Port Jackson* (1793). These are factual histories based on personal journals, and record Tench's experiences as an officer of the First Fleet sent to establish a British colony in Australia; a third volume, *Letters Written in France to a Friend in London* (1796) describes the six months Tench spent as a prisoner of war in France in 1794. Edwards patiently unpicks the process by which the raw material of the journals was converted into published narrative, homing in on the disturbances wrought by the process of writing-up on the standpoint in time of the authorial voice, whose retrospective knowledge of the significance of, say, 1789, inevitably 'bleeds back' into the record. At one especially telling point Tench abandons his historical account and reverts to the journal in an attempt to recapture a particularly troubling moment as it was lived:

> Let me for a moment quit the cold track of narrative: – let me not fritter away by servile adaptation, those reflections, and the feelings they gave birth to: – let me transcribe them fresh as they arose, ardent and generous, though hopeless and romantic.[77]

The 'adapted' or processed narrative is 'cold', sequential and considered, but a true account of history, Tench implies ('questioning his whole narrativizing enterprise', as Edwards puts it)[78] must also sometimes give way to the 'ardent' and 'romantic' impressions of the moment, however cynical the voice of hindsight.

Though not included in Edwards's discussion, another writer from this period acutely aware of the distinction between immediate and reflective (Tench's 'hot' and 'cold') writing is the agriculturalist Arthur Young, who, as we have seen, was travelling through France at the same time as George

Cadogan Morgan. At the very beginning of his *Travels* (1792), Young announces:

> There are two methods of writing travels; to register the journey itself, or the result of it. In the former case, it is a diary, under which head are to be classed all those books of travels written in the form of letters. The latter usually falls into the shape of essays on distinct subjects.[79]

Weighing up the pros and cons of both, he applauds the greater authenticity of the journal or letter form, which 'hath the advantage of carrying with it a greater degree of credibility; and, of course, more weight. A traveller who thus registers his observations is detected the moment he writes of things he has not seen.'[80] But he notes too its pitfalls: 'prolixity' and 'repetition', and the fact that 'subjects of importance . . . are given by scraps as received, without order, and without connection'.[81] To solve this problem, Young effectively writes his book twice. His three 'immediate' travel accounts for the years 1787, 1788 and 1789 are followed by five weighty 'Essays on Agriculture' intended to distil and organize the material he has gathered. The book, however, was not published until 1792. Thus, even for its first audience, it was a text filtered through time and through unthinkable levels of social reorganization – the suppression of religious orders, the abolition of nobility, deep uncertainty about the future of the monarchy – all of which must inevitably have coloured their reading. Young himself, though for the most part letting his narrative stand, cannot help but footnote his own confident entry for 27 June 1789: 'The whole business now seems over, and the revolution complete' with the wry acknowledgment: 'The events that follow'd were as little to be thought of as of myself being made King of France.'[82]

In their different ways, then, both Watkin Tench and Arthur Young acknowledge and attempt to deal with the complex layering of 'Revolutionary' time in their writings. Their thoughts can, to some extent, be applied to the texts written by George Cadogan Morgan in 1789. The precise nature of those texts does however, first require further consideration. Whereas the letters of both Rigby and Boddington are the actual items written and sent from France, complete with sealing wax, date stamps, crossings-out and scribbled additions, the Morgan manuscript is a fair copy, written out in a neat eighteenth-century hand (which we assume but cannot prove to be the author's).[83] Dates and places are preserved, but the opening and closing salutations are absent. Thus where Rigby typically starts 'My dear Loves' and finishes with 'God bless you; your affectionate Edw. Rigby', Morgan's letters refer immediately to the progress of the journey: 'I finished the letter

I wrote to you from Lisle just as we were summon'd to take our peregrination through the town', and tend to finish abruptly. A limited amount of editorial pruning has taken place, then, to produce this fair copy, and we may speculate, from the other two writers, that some details have been lost from the beginnings and ends of some letters – information or queries about matters at home, the names of friends, expressions of affection. Internal evidence shows that at least one letter, written at Dover, has been omitted from the beginning of the sequence, and common sense suggests that Morgan did not cease writing home after 17 August, the date of the last letter here, in spite of the volcanic flourish and an emphatic 'The End'. An additional page of manuscript summarizes the contents of each letter as though giving chapter headings, which suggests that the author/copyist deliberately chose to restrict the narrative of the tour to France and the Alps. That the editorial pruning was, nevertheless, limited, can be surmised from the naturalness of the tone, the fact that various intimate references to his wife and children are preserved, and, above all, the absence of the kind of hindsight evidenced by Watkin Tench. Morgan was not, as far as we know, writing with publication in mind, though we cannot be completely certain in this respect: the two letters to Price were published, the first while Morgan was still abroad, and this fair copy of the tour may well have been intended as a record for other eyes, perhaps to be passed around informally amongst friends. While I would argue that the copying-out of the letters has not, despite some shaping, altered them fundamentally, all of the above factors need to be borne in mind when determining the 'temperature' of the text, that is, the nature of its historical witness.

I shall focus here on the three letters that describe his time in Paris. The first (Letter II) was written on 9 July, when the group had been in the city for a day and a half. From Rigby and Boddington we learn that they have already been to the Théâtre Italien twice, walked the *grands boulevards*, eaten in the Palais Royal, visited Notre Dame, the King's Library and the Gobelins tapestry works. Morgan's letter at this point, however, is still catching up with the journey, and devotes some two and a half thousand words to describing his impressions of Lisle and Chantilly. Of Paris itself we get the briefest glimpse in the closing line:

> We returned to the inn and immediately sett off for Paris where we now are in health and safety. An account of what I have seen here and a long letter to my Uncle I will send by the earliest opportunities.

The immediate present, which we know to have been busy, is not allowed to intrude on his resolutely sequential narrative of the journey thus far. He

may be sitting at a desk on the third floor of the Grand Hôtel, or sipping
Bordeaux in a busy cafe at the Palais Royal itself, but he does not chose to
evoke these immediate surroundings before 'catching up'. This is his general
pattern for the whole tour, his way of controlling the narrative of the journey.
It creates an odd little *décallage*: a space, a slippage, where the place and time
of writing noted at the top of the letter almost never correspond to the
material in the letter itself. That space or gap in time is, of course, extended
by a few days for Morgan's primary 'audience', his wife; when she receives
the letter from Lyons in which he describes being in Dijon, he is in fact
already in Marseilles. This process of writing up with a two- or three-day
time-lag allows for a mostly past-tense, reflective narrative. Occasional
moments when the present intrudes are often at the end of letters brought
to a sudden halt – 'My companions are eager to be on their walk – and the
post is to set off soon –'.

The major exception to this past-tense narrative, however, is Letter III.
It opens with urgency:

> Paris, July 13th, 89, 4 o'clock in the morning

> The accounts you will hear of this last night's tumults in Paris have induced me
> to be thus early in my assurances of our safety. – The distress, the confusion, the
> destroying madness of the scene I have just witness'd have actually equall'd those
> of a town taken by storm. – They have far exceeded any ideas I could have form'd
> of insurrection in its violence and of popular rage in its extravagance. – Yesterday
> noon our party returned from Versailles to Paris.

The tenses here are interesting on several counts. Firstly, at four in the
morning of the 13th, in the heart of the Revolutionary moment, Morgan
is worried about the *future* impact of the news on his wife – 'the accounts
you will hear'. Second is the brief intrusion of the moment itself – 'the scene
I have just witness'd'. And third is the instinctive return to his normal controlled
past-tense narrative which, however, is much closer in time than usual,
and which takes us from 'yesterday noon' (12 July) step by step, from mid-
afternoon dinner in the Rue St Michel, through the ebb and surge of the
crowds around the Palais Royal, until the reader has almost caught up with
the time and place at the head of the paper:

> *About 10 o'clock* the uniformity of the noise was interrupted by the violence of a
> party who assail'd the doors of a gunsmith living in a room just under ours. The
> crash of the stones and stakes which the populace drove against the doors set our
> whole hotel into an uproar. The women shriek'd – some of the lodgers were

immediately for flying, but they were strangers and could not tell us how they would direct their steps. At length the populace forc'd their way in, but found no arms as another company had previously seiz'd upon the whole of the gunsmith's stock. They soon relieved us by retiring in great tranquility.

That peaceful denouement notwithstanding, this is now urgent, immediate, gripping reportage – the Revolution is literally knocking at their door. By now, and in a manner completely unlike his other letters home, Morgan is writing in a form of present tense:

The whole night *has been employed* in surveying the mob as they pass and repass. Their multitudes *is* immense, amongst them *I have number'd* some hundreds of the soldiery. *All are arm'd – and the whole city is still in confusion and riot.* The mischief of the night I have not yet heard. The return of day *has smooth'd* a little the formidable aspect of the scene – *I observe* a vast number of families leave the town and we shall as soon as possible follow their example – *our danger is all over.*

This letter, which disturbs the travel narrative by crashing in ahead of itself – hammering on the door as it were, enacting the moment – nicely exemplifies Gavin Edwards's theory of Revolution-induced narrative disruption. Letter IV, written from Dijon on 21 July, two days after they finally left Paris, shows how clearly Morgan himself was aware of that intrusive Revolutionary moment breaking up his account: 'The commencement of the revolt at Paris interrupted that part of my correspondence which successively referr'd to the several scenes and places thro' which I passed.'

The opening sentence of this letter once again reveals that complex collision of the future and the past that all travel entails. Morgan has yet to get to Lyons, where he will find out whether his wife has heard from him in Paris:

I shall hope to find letters at Lyons with information that *you have frequently heard from me* while at Paris. In that scene of tumult and danger, I seiz'd every possible opportunity for telling you that I was well and safe – I have written twice to my Uncle, and I shall be very anxious till I am assur'd that the packets have reach'd his hands.

Those opening lines raise further possibilities: the written-up text does not contain any more 'present-tense' letters of reassurance from Paris after the one written on the 13th. Did they fail to get through, or did Morgan consciously omit them from his neat copy, feeling that they added nothing more to the sequential narrative? Or, alternatively, did the two long and detailed letters to Richard Price stand in for further letters home? Either way, Morgan is quite determined not to have his journey-narrative interrupted any more. He rewinds to Chantilly, and makes himself arrive in Paris almost as if the Revolution hadn't happened:

> The commencement of the revolt at Paris interrupted that part of my corres-pondence which successively referr'd to the several scenes and places thro' which I passed. I stop'd at Chantilly, from whence I travelled to the capital with eyes widely open to observe the difference of its approach compared with that of London . . .

Almost, but not quite. One single line (quoted earlier in this introduction) about finding a hotel near the Palais Royal contains a brief flash of hindsight: 'our situation at the awful moment of the revolt enabled us to see, what others . . . heard from us with astonishment.' In other words, the events of 12, 13 and 14 July 1789 have already 'spilled back' into his account of the 9th and 10th.

For the historian of 1789, such moments in the text are worth noting, but should ultimately make little difference. Morgan's narrative is by any reasonable standard a reliable historical witness to the events of that extra-ordinary summer, and it is to be hoped that his letters will be of use to those researchers aiming for ever more precise calibrations of time and place in their accounts of the Revolution itself. The additional material in the letters and journals of Edward Rigby and Samuel Boddington, to be explored in a future publication, promise to reveal in even more detail how the events of 1789 were received, understood, and, indeed, manipulated, by people at the time.

For the reader interested in *how* writers manage those events from a narratological point of view, these moments of disruption are of great value; Morgan's later letters, as he travels down through France, would certainly repay further investigation along these lines. Travel writing, because of its odd relation to both space and time, is an especially rewarding subject for the analysis of narrative strategies that deal with notions of time and how it is perceived, not just by the writer, but by his or her readers, days, years or centuries after the act of writing. Because, of course, the 'spillage' of hindsight affects us, as modern readers, more than anyone. As these letters show, times of revolution and war often feel both oddly speeded up (because so much happens so quickly) and slowed down (because the flow of events is so dense). The result resembles a geologically busy period. Two or three years of this kind of activity produce strata of knowledge that cannot help but weigh down on our own readings of a particular place in a particular year. There are many instances of this in Morgan's letters, but one striking example occurs during their visit to Lyons, which they reached on 24 July. On a guided tour of the local antiquities, Morgan expresses his usual scepticism when faced with 'the bones of 1800 martyrs who had been killed on the spot' – a shrine which presumably commemorated the Christian Martyrs of Lyons, whose mass execution by Romans in AD 177 is recorded in contemporary accounts.[84] It is difficult to read this passage now, knowing something of Revolutionary France, without also thinking 'forward' to the massacres of October 1793: the number of dead is an uncanny premonition of those who would be killed in the infamous *mitraillades* that formed the aftermath of the siege of Lyons, when the Committee of Public Safety issued its 'famous, ferocious decree' against the rebellious town.[85] Some 1,700 people were executed in public squares: 'killed', to borrow Morgan's words, 'on the spot'. For the modern reader, past and future atrocities flicker ominously across the text. George Cadogan Morgan's letters are indeed a vivid slice through one historical moment, but they resonate well beyond the summer of 1789.

History is full of such echoes and premonitions. In 1794, shortly before Tooke and Hardy were tried for treason at the Old Bailey, the young author Amelia Alderson wrote from the Morgan household in Southgate to a close friend in Norwich. In her letter she sounds out of sorts, apprehensive – 'for the state of the times and other things press upon my mind continually'. Both she and her father, she says, are deeply 'interested and agitated by the probable event of the approaching trials' since their outcome will have repercussions on many lives beyond those of the accused:

> On this, at least, I hope we are at all events resolved; to emigrate, if the event of the trial be fatal; that is, provided the Morgans do not give up their present resolution, and that we can carry a little society along with us, in which we can be happy, should Philadelphia disappoint our expectations. I write to you on this subject in confidence; as we do not wish our intention to be much known at present.[86]

Had things been different, George Cadogan Morgan might have left us his account of the arduous Atlantic crossing, his impressions of Philadelphia, and of the family's attempt to start afresh in a society that beckoned so many of Britain's liberal minds in the 1790s. As it was, his wife and children made the journey some fourteen years later, without him.

Editorial note

This edition of George Cadogan Morgan's letters is based on an eighteenth-century manuscript copy of the lost originals. I have removed most of the capitalization, presented underline as italic, replaced some of the many dashes with commas and full stops, standardized the representation of direct and reported speech, and occasionally broken long passages with a paragraph. Original spellings and misspellings ('currious', 'dissapointed', 'cheif') are retained throughout, and have not been signalled further with *sic*. Morgan's erratic French spellings have also been retained but are noted and corrected in the endnotes (e.g. 'Maçon' for 'Mâcon', 'Le Mer du Glace' for 'La Mer de Glace').

For those concerned with issues of punctuation and textual presentation in this period, we are hoping to produce a digital 'raw' text of the letters, along with those of Edward Rigby and Samuel Boddington, in due course.

Notes

1   Lady [Elizabeth] Eastlake (ed.), *Dr Rigby's Letters from France &c. in 1789* (London, 1880), p. 34 (hereafter cited as *Rigby-Eastlake*). See pp. 11–12, for a discussion of the reliability of this source.

2   Oxford, Bodleian Library, Special Collections, Dep. c. 115, 'Dr Rigby's Letters from France' (hereafter 'Rigby Letters') and Dep. e. 43 (hereafter 'Rigby Journal').

3   Jeremy Black, 'On the Grand Tour in a Year of Revolution', *Francia*, 13 (1985), 333–53, and *idem*, *The British Abroad: The Grand Tour in the Eighteenth Century* (Stroud, 2003). Boddington's journal and letters of the tour are held at the London Metropolitan Archive, MS 10823/5A (hereafter 'Boddington Journal') and MS 10823/5B (hereafter 'Boddington Letters').

4   See Caroline E. Williams, *A Welsh Family from the Beginning of the 18th Century* (2nd edn., London, 1893), which draws a vivid picture of the Morgan family through several generations, and cites these letters and others at various points. Lengthy extracts from the first few letters were also published by George Bransby-Williams as 'Letters from Revolutionary France', *The New English Review Magazine*, II, no. 2 (February 1949), 114–21. They are also included in the typescript family history entitled 'A Family Budget', compiled by George Bransby-Williams in 1952 (facsimile held at the National Library of Wales, NLW facs. 665).

5   Morgan-Gardner Family Papers, Newberry Library, Chicago. This text of George Cadogan Morgan's letters is a neat copy, probably made shortly after the event, and described more fully on pp. 26–7. Attempts to locate the original letters have not been successful.

6   The most detailed biography is D. O. Thomas, 'George Cadogan Morgan', *The Price-Priestley Newsletter*, 3 (1979), 53–70; see also the *ODNB* entry by the same

author, and the anonymous but lengthy obituary, 'Account of the Late Mr George Cadogan Morgan', *The Monthly Magazine*, VI (1798), 475–80. Although this latter piece claims categorically that 'he never sat for his picture' (p. 480), a portrait by John Opie is supposed to have existed, although it was no longer in the possession of the family by the mid-nineteenth century (Williams, *A Welsh Family*, p. 81). George Cadogan Morgan's close relationship with his uncle, Richard Price, is discussed on pp. 124–5 and 140–1.

[7] D. A. Rees, 'George Cadogan Morgan at Oxford', *Enlightenment and Dissent*, 1 (1982), 89.

[8] The eldest child and only daughter, Sarah Price Morgan, was born in 1783 or 1784; her brothers were George Cadogan, William Ashburner, Richard Price, Luke Ashburner, Edmund Cobb, John Sextus, Septimus and Henry, who was born after his father's death. See the Fig. 3, p. 122, and Richard Price Morgan's account below. For details of Nancy's family, see Thomas Hurry-Houghton, *Memorials of the Family of Hurry of Great Yarmouth, Norfolk, and of America, Australia, and South Africa* (Liverpool, 1926).

[9] George Cadogan Morgan, 'Observations on the Light of Bodies in a State of Combustion', *Philosophical Transactions*, 75 (1785), 190–212. This is the paper referred to in the incident at Chantilly, p. 10. For Morgan's involvement in contemporary debate on the nature and uses of electricity, see Simon Schaffer, 'Charged Atmospheres: Promethean Science and the Royal Society', in Bill Bryson (ed.), *Seeing Further: The Story of Science and the Royal Society* (London, 2010), pp. 131–56.

[10] *Idem, An Appeal to the Public, in Answer to a Letter from the Rev. Mr. Brand to ★★★★★ ★★★★★★★* (Norwich, 1782).

[11] For this period see also D. O. Thomas (ed.), 'Richard Price's Journal for the Period 25 March 1787 to 6 February 1791', *National Library of Wales Journal*, 21 (1979–80), 366–413; W. Bernard Peach and D. O. Thomas (eds.), *The Correspondence of Richard Price* (3 vols., Durham, 1983–94), III, p. 106.

[12] On the history of the New College, Hackney, 'the ultimate endeavour among liberal dissenters', see Stephen Burley, 'Hazlitt the Dissenter: Religion, Philosophy and Politics 1766–1816' (unpublished University of Oxford DPhil thesis, 2011), pp. 78–141, and the online article, *idem, New College, Hackney (1786–96): A Selection of Printed and Archival Sources* (2nd edn., 2011, at *http://www.english.qmul. ac.uk/drwilliams/pubs/nc%20hackney.html*). Richard Price was one of the founding members. Although financial mismanagement played a large part in undermining the institution's optimistic beginnings in the 1780s, Burley shows that 'professional jealousies' also played their part. For Morgan's part in the arguments over the succession to Price (the post was filled in the end by Joseph Priestley), see Burley, 'Hazlitt the Dissenter', pp. 94–110.

[13] Godwin's diary shows that he met Morgan six times between 1789 and 1798; see Victoria Myers, David O'Shaughnessy and Mark Philp (eds.), *The Diary of William Godwin* (Oxford, 2010) at *http://godwindiary.bodleian.ox.ac.uk*. He also appears, in a less than flattering light, in a letter from Godwin to Amelia Alderson,

who stayed with the Morgans in Southgate for several months in 1794: 'you are wretchedly deceived,' says Godwin, 'if you take Mr Morgan for a great genius.' As John Barrell points out, the criticism was somewhat less than disinterested (review of Pamela Clemit (ed.), *The Letters of William Godwin, Vol I: 1778–97* (Oxford, 2011), *London Review of Books*, 33, no. 17 (8 September 2011), 21–3). See also Harriet Guest, 'Amelia Alderson Opie: Sociability and Politics', *Bodleian Library Record*, 24, no. 1 (2011), 44–50.

[14] See the account by Richard Price Morgan on p. 141.

[15] Williams, *A Welsh Family*, p. 137. For William Morgan see p. 199 n. 10.

[16] Williams, *A Welsh Family*, p. 129; the obituary appeared in *The Monthly Magazine*, VI (1798), 475–80.

[17] C. L. Brightwell, *Memorials of the Life of Amelia Opie* (Norwich, 1854), p. 46. This could be yet another Boddington: John, a close friend of Alderson's at this time.

[18] Williams, *A Welsh Family*, p. 122. On the silenced generation of the 1790s, see Kenneth R. Johnston, 'Whose History? My Place or Yours? Republican Assumptions and Romantic Traditions', in Damian Walford Davies (ed.), *Romanticism, History, Historicism: Essays on an Orthodoxy* (London, 2009), pp. 79–102.

[19] Williams, *A Welsh Family*, pp. 122–4.

[20] Information from a recently discovered memoir by George Cadogan's granddaughter, Sarah Ashburner Morgan, suggests that the Morgans received an income for taking on the care and education of the Ashburner and Boddington children. See p. 207 n. 87.

[21] The Dollonds were makers of optical instruments; see p. 200 n. 19.

[22] See Anon., 'Account of the Late Mr George Cadogan Morgan', 475–80; Williams, *A Welsh Family*, p. 129.

[23] *The Monthly Magazine*, VIII (1799), 985.

[24] 'Boddington Letters', Letter 1, 3 July 1789. For Edward Rigby (1747–1821), see the *ODNB* entry, and the memoir by his daughter in *Rigby-Eastlake*.

[25] The Boddington family held estates in the West Indies and Samuel inherited a large fortune from his father who was a director of the South Sea Company and of the Million Bank, which Samuel had also joined by 1793. A fair amount of information about the family and their outlook on life can be gleaned from Benjamin Boddington, senior's journal (London Metropolitan Archives, MS 1083/4), which intersperses the dates of births, deaths and marriages with occasional interjections, mostly of a religious nature. For the unsuccessful marriage of Samuel Boddington and Grace Ashburner, see p. 143.

[26] Anne Hurry's first cousin Elizabeth (1751–91; a daughter of Samuel Hurry) married Robert Alderson (1753–1833), the younger brother of Dr James Alderson (father of Amelia Opie), in Norwich in 1784. Note that Caroline Williams, *A Welsh Family*, p. 86, is doubly mistaken in having Anne's *sister*, 'one of the daughters [of William Hurry]', married to *James* Alderson (which would have made Amelia Opie George Cadogan Morgan's niece). For the Hurry family, see pp. 139–40; and *The Monthly Repository of Theology and General Literature*, V (1810), 402.

[27] Ollyett Woodhouse (1769–1822) was the brother of Robert Woodhouse the mathematician; both were part of the Godwin circle. He later became advocate

general of Bombay. For Amelia Opie's affection for her cousin, see 'On the Anniversary of the Birth-day of my Dear Relation Ollyett Woodhouse, Advocate General of Bombay, which recurred soon after I had heard of his Death, 1822', and 'Stanzas on the Death of the Same' in *eadem*, *Lays for the Dead* (London, 1834), pp. 16–21. See also Brightwell, *Memorials of the Life of Amelia Opie*.

[28] Only Boddington discusses financial arrangements in any detail (the sending and cashing of bills); this may be because he received a personal allowance from his father.

[29] *Rigby-Eastlake*, pp. ix–x.

[30] William Doyle, *The Oxford History of the French Revolution* (2nd edn., Oxford, 2002), p. 86; Jacques Godechot, *The Taking of the Bastille, July 14th, 1789*, trans. Jean Stewart (London, 1970), p. 122.

[31] 'Boddington Letters', Letter 3, 8 July 1789.

[32] 'Boddington Letters', Letter 11, 2 August 1789.

[33] A detailed study of Rigby's papers and their relation to the published account is currently being undertaken by Mary-Ann Constantine and Bethan Jenkins. For a history of the *Gazetteer*, then under the editorship of the Scot James Perry, see Robert L. Haig, *The Gazetteer 1735–1797: A Study in the Eighteenth-Century English Newspaper* (Carbondale, 1960). The significance of the lost letters to Price is discussed by D. O. Thomas, 'Edmund Burke and the Reverend Dissenting Gentlemen', *Notes & Queries*, 29 (1982), 202–4, and by Paul Frame in chapters seventeen and eighteen of his biography, *Liberty's Apostle: The Life and Times of Richard Price 1723–91* (Cardiff, forthcoming).

[34] Auguste Vestris (1760–1842) was one of the most renowned dancers of the age; in 1781 he and his father, the equally famous Gaëtan Vestris, had taken London by storm. Both father and son were painted by Gainsborough. See Martin Postle, 'Thomas Gainsborough's "Lost" Portrait of Auguste Vestris', *The British Art Journal*, IV, no. 1 (Spring 2003), 64–8.

[35] Guy-Jean-Baptiste Target, who would be elected president of the National Assembly the following January, was a celebrated Parisian lawyer sympathetic to the Protestant cause. See Sarah Maza, *Private Lives and Public Affairs: the Causes Célèbres of Pre-revolutionary France* (Berkeley, 1993); Paul Boulloche, *Un avocat du XVIIIè siècle* (Paris, 1893). For the colourful Honoré-Gabriel Riqueti, Comte de Mirabeau, see Antonina Vallentin, *Mirabeau: A Man of the French Revolution* (Clifton, 1948); Simon Schama, *Citizens: A Chronicle of the French Revolution* (paperback edn., London, 1989), *passim*.

[36] *Rigby-Eastlake*, p. 40. For the extraordinary few months which saw the development of the Estates General into the National Assembly, see Timothy Tackett, *Becoming a Revolutionary: The Deputies of the French National Assembly and the Emergence of a Revolutionary Culture (1789–1790)* (1996; paperback edn., Pennsylvania, 2006).

[37] See Robert D. Harris, *Necker and the Revolution of 1789* (New York, 1986).

[38] René Farge, *Un épisode de la journée du 12 juillet 1789: Camille Desmoulins au jardin du Palais-Royal* (Paris, 1914).

[39] 'Rigby Journal', p. 23[r]. This was presumably the Théâtre Français du Fauborg St Germain (now the Odéon).

[40] Orléans was suspected at the time of orchestrating the events of the uprising, though most historians are sceptical of any organized plot (see, e.g., Godechot, *The Taking of the Bastille*, pp. 143–5). For his life and character, see Tom Ambrose, *Godfather of the Revolution: The Life of Philippe Egalité Duc d'Orléans* (London, 2007).

[41] Arthur Young, *Travels, during the Years 1787, 1788 and 1789, undertaken more particularly with a View of ascertaining the Cultivation, Wealth, Resources, and National Prosperity of the Kingdom of France* (Bury St Edmunds, 1792), p. 104. The life of the Palais is vividly evoked in Louis-Sébastien Mercier, *Tableau de Paris* (12 vols., Paris, 1781–8), I, pp. 257–60, and described in detail in Robert M. Isherwood, *Farce and Fantasy: Popular Entertainment in Eighteenth-Century Paris* (New York, 1986), pp. 217–50; see also Schama, *Citizens*, pp. 114–16.

[42] For the growth of the 'myth' of Desmoulins's speech in the Palais Royal, see Farge, *Un épisode de la journée du 12 juillet*. The account in *Rigby-Eastlake* (p. 46) names Desmoulins as one of the speakers, but if Farge is right this cannot be the case.

[43] 'Boddington Letters', Letter 4, 13 July 1789.

[44] 'Rigby Journal', p. 33.

[45] Paul G. Spagnoli, 'The Revolution Begins: Lambesc's Charge 12 July 1789', *French Historical Studies*, 17, no. 2 (Autumn 1991), 466–97.

[46] *Rigby-Eastlake*, p. 46 [my emphasis].

[47] Ibid., p. 44.

[48] 'Boddington Letters', Letter 4, 13 July 1789; cited in Black, 'On the Grand Tour', p. 336.

[49] 'Boddington Letters', Letter 5, 14 July 1789. For Jefferson, see William Howard Adams, *The Paris Years of Thomas Jefferson* (New Haven, 1997). For positive responses to English visitors during the Revolution, see Victoria Thompson, 'Foreign Bodies: British Travel to Paris and the Troubled National Self, 1789–1830', *Studies in Travel Writing*, 15, no. 3 (September 2011), 250. I am grateful to Liz Edwards for this reference.

[50] For the [re]organization of the forces of law and order in Paris just prior to and during the uprising, see Godechot, *The Taking of the Bastille*; Dale Lothrop Clifford, 'The National Guard and the Parisian Community 1789–1790', *French Historical Studies*, 16, no. 4 (1990), 849–78; and Jean Chagniot, *Paris et l'armée au XVIIIè siècle: Étude politique et sociale* (Paris, 1985).

[51] 'Rigby Journal', p. 35^v.

[52] 'Boddington Letters', Letter 6, 19 July 1789; cited in Black 'On the Grand Tour', p. 337. For the events of the day and movement of the crowds, see Doyle, *Oxford History*, pp. 108–11; Godechot, *The Taking of the Bastille*, pp. 204–46.

[53] 'Rigby Journal' p. 38^v; 'Boddington Letters', Letter 6, 19 July 1789.

[54] 'Rigby Journal', pp. 37–8.

[55] 'Boddington Letters', Letter 6, 19 July 1789; cited in Black, 'On the Grand Tour', p. 338.

[56] *Rigby-Eastlake*, p. 68.

[57] Ibid., p. 70.

58   J. L. Carra, *Le Comte de Lorges, prisonnier à la Bastille pendant trente-deux ans, enfermé en 1757, du temps de Damiens, et mis en liberté le 14 Juillet 1789* (Paris, [September] 1789). A dramatic contemporary picture of the moment of his release can be seen at the website of the Bibliothèque nationale: 'Délivrance de M. le Comte de Lorges, prisonnier à la Bastille depuis 32 ans' at *http://gallica.bnf.fr/ark:/12148/btv1b8410741p/*.

59   For the seven prisoners released on the 14th see Godechot, *The Taking of the Bastille*, pp. 91–2. For the growth of the legend of the mysterious Comte, see Hans-Jürgen Lüsebrink and Rolf Reichardt, *The Bastille: A History of a Symbol of Despotism and Freedom*, trans. Norbert Schürer (Durham, 1997), pp. 67–8; David Bindman, *The Shadow of the Guillotine: Britain and the French Revolution* (London, 1989), pp. 38–42 and 220. Robert Druce states: 'in spite of the fact that he never existed, it was almost a dramatic (and, I would suggest, narratological) necessity to invent the Comte de Lorges'. *Idem*, 'From *A Tale of Two Cities* to *Mam'zelle Guillotine*: The French Revolution seen through Popular Fiction', in C. C. Barfoot and Theo D'haen (eds.), *Tropes of Revolution: Writers' Reactions to Real and Imagined Revolutions 1789–1989* (Amsterdam, 1991), p. 331.

60   'By the end of August, this old man had a fixed name – Count de Lorges – and his time in prison had lengthened to forty years'. Lüsebrink and Reichardt, *The Bastille*, p. 68.

61   Rigby's published account speaks of 'witnessing the spectacle of the monarch thus, I might almost say, led captive' (*Rigby-Eastlake*, p. 88), but the phrase is not in the journal.

62   'Rigby Letters', Letter 9, 18 July 1789.

63   For the significance and development of the Revolutionary cockades see p. 48 n. 82.

64   Young, *Travels*, p. 145.

65   G. Lefebvre, *La Grande Peur de 1789* (Paris, 1932); see also David Andress, *The French Revolution and the People* (London, 2004), pp. 113–14.

66   See p. 84 n. 61.

67   'In July 1789,' according to Lee Baker, 'the new city council (which appointed itself as the Bastille fell) confined all nobles to their homes because "they oppose the public good", and, by "plotting against the people" were the "enemies of liberty"'. *Idem*, 'The French Revolution as Local Experience: The Terror in Dijon', *The Historian*, 67 (2005), 700.

68   'Rigby Letters', Letter 14, 29 July 1789.

69   The events of 29 July were described by Mathieu Blanc-Gilli (deputy to the Legislative Assembly for La Bouche du Rhône) in *Le triomphe de l'humanité: récit de l'expédition du peuple de Marseille à Aix pour délivrer les prisonniers de différens pays de Provence, accusés de séditieux* [copy in Marseilles not seen, but recorded as number 89:7357 in Pierre Conlon, *Le siècle des lumières: bibliographie chronologique, Tome XXVI: 1789, Auteurs* (Geneva, 2008), p. 49].

70   'Boddington Letters', Letter 8, 24 July 1789.

71   Geneva was a self-governing republic from 1541.

72 'Boddington Letters', Letter 14, 17 August 1789.

73 These are beautifully documented in David Hill, *Turner in the Alps* (London, 1992).

74 William Wordsworth, *The Prelude* (1805), Book 6, lines 452–6.

75 See, for example, the volcano which engulfs the 'tyrants' of Europe and the Pope at the end of Sylvain Maréchal's play, *Le Jugement dernier des Rois, Prophétie en un Acte, en prose . . . jouée sur le Théâtre de la République, au mois Vendemiaire et jours suivant l'an second de la République Francaise* (Paris, 1793). Or Charles-François Dumouriez's scathing assessment of the 'young men' who fought in America: 'They brought home ill-digested ideas, and wishing to adapt them to the national genius, they set on fire, and lighted up a volcano which has covered with rubbish and with ruins this land of happiness'. *Idem, The Life of General Dumouriez* (3 vols., London, 1796), II, p. 10. For further examples and an interesting analysis of the figure, see David McCallum, 'The Volcano: From Enlightenment to Revolution', *Nottingham French Studies*, 45, no. 1 (Spring 2006), 52–68. I am grateful to Heather Williams for this reference.

76 Gavin Edwards, *Narrative Order 1789–1819: Life and Story in an Age of Revolution* (Basingstoke, 2006), p. 14.

77 Edwards, *Narrative Order*, p. 77.

78 Ibid.

79 Young, *Travels*, p. 1.

80 Ibid.

81 Ibid., p. 2.

82 Ibid., p. 124.

83 I am grateful to David Spadafora of Newberry Library for the information that the paper carries the 'Britannia' watermark known to have been in use around 1788.

84 See Jean Rougé and Robert Turcan (eds.), *Les Martyrs de Lyon, 177: Colloque, Lyon, 20–23 septembre 1977* (Paris, 1978).

85 This began, 'La ville de Lyon sera détruite' (The town of Lyons shall be destroyed), renamed the place 'Ville-Affranchie' (Liberated Town), and ordered that a column be raised on the ruins of the town inscribed: 'Lyon fit la guerre à la Liberté; Lyon n'est plus' (Lyons made war on Liberty; Lyons is no longer). See W. D. Edmonds, *Jacobinism and the Revolt of Lyon 1789–1793* (Oxford, 1990), p. 280. For a helpful review of the conflicted historical readings of this episode, see Paul Mansfield, 'The Repression of Lyon, 1793–4: Origins, Responsibility and Significance', *French History*, 2, no. 1 (1988), 74–101.

86 Brightwell, *Memorials of the Life of Amelia Opie*, p. 45. For the experiences of some of George Cadogan's contemporaries, and the radical impulse to head west, see W. M. Verhoeven, 'Land-jobbing in the Western Territories: Radicalism, Transatlantic Emigration and the 1790s American Travel Narrative', in Amanda Gilroy (ed.), *Romantic Geographies: Discourses of Travel 1775–1844* (Manchester, 2000), pp. 185–203.

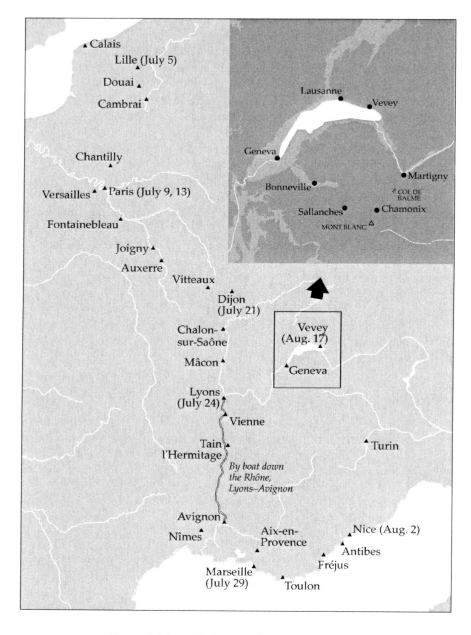

Figure 2. Map: The journey through France 1789

Letters From France, Summer 1789

Letter I

Lisle, July 5, 1789

We reached this place just as the gates were shutting last night. The scene displayed by the city as we entered was altogether novel and striking. Every street was crowded with men, women and children. Multitudes of soldiers were rushing from every quarter to the guard house which is placed in the very middle of the market place.[1] At the same moment about 40 drummers were roaring the tattoo, and the largest bell I ever heard began to sound the ninth hour. The activity and bustle of the multitudes who paraded before our window did not cease till 11 o'clock, when we finished our dinner, the only meal of the day, and retired to our beds, which we found in several cells belonging to the very room in which we fed. Tho' the fasting and the heat and the fatigue of the journey had prepared me for sleep, yet such was the annoyance of the buggs that I have rested very little and have willingly resigned my bed to the conquering legions before 5 o'clock in the morning. I again see the market place, tho' so early, cramm'd with people. Several stalls are loaded with provisions, and I hear a tinkling of bells from all the churches, so that this singularity of appearance, altogether different from anything that I have ever yet seen in England, must be ascribed to the united powers of the stomach and of superstition.

When I last wrote to you[2] I was at Calais where my attention was distracted by a thousand novelties of sound and appearance.[3] The town you well know is fortified and the walls of course form a circumference of two miles nearly – they furnish a walk of 30 feet in width and enable a spectator to take a bird's eye view of every street in the town. In every direction of my sight I could see nothing but the promiscuous motion of soldiers upon their arms, or amusing themselves with different games, or carrying & cleaning their provisions or mending their cloaths – with these were blended boys at play, women clattering with their high wooden heels against the pavement, and a most numerous body of fishermen and tradesmen busy in their various occupations. I see nothing of that meagerness or poverty which my prejudices as one of John Bull's calves taught me to expect in the soldiers. Their cloaths are clean and whole; their persons are as tall and robust as those of Englishmen and I am sure that they look much too healthy for the victims either of famine or of want. There is a delightful simplicity in the attire and the gait of the women. They walk without hats and the generality wear long cloakes which reach down to their heels. The matrons have hoods to their cloakes. These are thrown over their heads and are generally made of a most gaudy printed linnen. The height of their heels gives all the women a most remarkable singularity in their walk. There is the same vivacity in their movements as there is in their conversation which, owing to the rapid manner in which they express themselves, is to me as yet unintelligible.

The population of Calais is wonderfully great. You scarcely see a house without a pregnant woman or a child on the lap, who cannot fail to do well if there be aught cherishing in warmth and cloathing, for the head and body of the child is wound round with a load of flannell.[4] However, I observe they set the children on their legs very soon and the limbs of all the boys appeared so strong and straight as to correspond with this care in nursing. Amongst hundreds I saw not one that was either ricketty or deformed. The houses in Calais are well built, but tho' every family seems to have enough, I saw none of those gardens and stables and other luxuries which display the opulence of the middling people in England.

In this place I saw little either of the parade or impertinence of the popish religion.[5] A crucifix is gibbeted over the gate and to the side of a wooden Jesus is fastened a little doll about the size of Sarah's, which they told me was the Virgin Mary.[6] Hundreds of women and soldiers are continually passing by this crucifix, and every now and then you may see a devotee separating from her companions and resting a few minutes on her knees – I saw but one man and he was old who was thus devout. The homage received by the wood was cheifly given by the women and children. Like all other travellers I strolled into the church – where I saw nothing but crucifixes and Virgins and very bad pictures and very long candles. I could not help admiring the boxes made for auricular confession. There was a place made for the priest in the middle, and on each side a cell for the supplicant so that he might have a separate person whispering at each ear during the same moment.

The inns were superb at Calais; we might have fed, had we chosen, like princes, but we never sit for a long time, we make a point of being constantly on the foot, and after supper we found hundreds walking upon the ramparts and in the streets. But amongst the whole we never saw one person who appeared to be either drunk or dissolute, what a different scene is display'd by the gin-drinkers and whoremongers of Yarmouth and Norwich, where you cannot walk a hundred yards together without being insulted by the obscenity of the women or the drunkenness of the men.

We left Calais before 5 o'clock yesterday morning – and as we departed from the town were met by numbers of your sex laden with heavy burthens for the market. Not one horse or pudding cart[7] could I see. Nor one appearance of that ease and indolence which distinguish the farmer and their ladies in England. I could not help reflecting on the multitudes of human beings which are added to the strength of this country by assuming this labour and feeding on that subsistence which is given to the horses in Great Britain. You will have an idea of the French low countries when I assure you that for 80 miles together I never was without 8 or 9 villages in my view, interspersed with numberless cottages. Not a spot of ground appeared otherwise than cultivated to the highest degree.[8] We never travell'd 100 yards together without having several inhabitants in our view. I saw not one house in ruins or even empty. Every church was surrounded with a populous village – and every cottage appeared to be the residence of children. Be it added that tho' each inch of ground was cultivated, yet there was scarcely any pasturage. Corn, beans and flax covered the whole ground. In short, while I travell'd on the road, I wondered how the productions I saw could be devour'd, but when I enter'd the villages and towns I wondered where provisions could be had for the inhabitants. At present there is a great scarcity which in England is magnified into a famine;[9] what we sell for a penny costs every individual here 3d. Government has ordered that no bran be separated from the flour. This renders the bread rather dissagreeable but taking it altogether, the food of the country is formed for the most Epicurean appetite.

Letter II

Paris, July 9th, 1789

I finished the letter I wrote to you from Lisle just as we were summoned to take our peregrination thro' the town.[10] Our guide carried us to the citadel, to the cathedral, to several of the large churches, to a convent, and to a monastery. The several objects I saw were so many varieties of slavery, mummery, and folly – soldiers sweating upon their arms – priests smothered with the weight of their garments, and the weight of their fat. Nuns visible only thro' iron grates – & amongst the rest hundreds of boys and girls, barr'd and bolted up between the dark walls of convents to receive what they call in this country their education. How can a spirit of Independence or Freedom ever warm a heart so early and so long accustom'd to uninterrupted confinement and to the most unrelenting severity. To an Englishman nothing can be more singular and novel than the scene presented by the Sunday as well in Lisle as in other popish countries. Every shop is open, every business carried on as usual – a perpetual jingle of bells rings in the ears. The doors of the churches are crowded with successive multitudes who go to, or return from mass, and the priests sit in perpetual employment at the altars, where they play their parts in a manner which I dare say must be the object of frequent laughter even to themselves. Their backs are always to the audience, who stand so as to have a continual sight of a large white cross painted on a richly embroidered robe which covers the shoulders of the priest. All his devotion is paid to a small silver crucifix plac'd on the altar – every now and then he turns half round, makes a bow to one part of the table, and soon after to another. In the meantime the organ roars from all its pipes, a large company of singers open their throats, attended by the sounds of all the most noisy instruments which can be collected. The church is all around hung with paintings not less execrably bad than the music, which is really like the braying of two asses in concert. Under the influence of these curious incitements to devotion, you see the congregation running over the service of the mass book as quickly as possible. Some old women sigh'd and lifted up their eyes, but all the rest read and talked just as the fit seiz'd them. Olyett and Mr. Boddington interrupted the devotion of many amongst the ladies, whose eyes quitted the crucifix and the Virgin for the smart appearance of our English beaux.[11] Not one minute passes without the entrance or the exit of new devotees. I saw one whole regiment perform mass. They march'd into and fill'd the whole body of the church. Not one hat was taken off, but every individual stood wiping the wet off his arms and talking to his next neighbour. – I staid some time in expectation of seeing the mass begin. The band of the regiment had play'd for some time, and the priest had perform'd some gestures to the crucifix, when I heard the drums strike up, and perceiv'd the soldiers in motion. "Sir," said I, to a gentleman who stood by, "we are a long time before we begin." He smiled: "Sir," said he, "it is all over." "Over! Why," replied I, "the soldiers had scarcely wiped their arms." "That's nothing," answered he, "they are supposed to say mass to themselves. The priest presented the crucifix, and they ought to have pray'd." I was mute with astonishment when the gentleman endeavor'd to relax my features by saying that the religion of the French was a very easy thing indeed. "Yes, sir," said I, "it is easy because it is nothing at all." "True," answered the gentleman, "I wish the same observation could not be applied to their morality."[12]

Tired with churches and the scenes they presented, we returned to our lodging where we stayed just long enough to dine. But as we departed from Lisle we took a new view of the streets and every object had now changed its appearance. The religious ceremonies of the day were over – all were dressed in their best habits. You might trace the direction of every individual's steps either to the Play House or some other place of amusement – in short, the whole was dissipation and gaiety. As we pass'd thro' the villages we observed the influence of the same cheerful spirit. The peasants either danc'd or sung or paraded the roads in large bodies. If to enjoy is to be grateful, the devotion of the French is very great indeed. I must confess for my own part that I regarded their innocent mirth with feelings far more pleasant than those call'd forth by a troop of Methodists returning from an interview with the best of beings, with a gloom on their brows, and the rancour of bigotry in their hearts. I had rather break the Sabbath with the former than keep it with the latter.

After passing over about 20 miles of a country crowded with inhabitants and rich with the most luxuriant fertility, we reach'd Douay which is one of the French Universities and contains more students than even Oxford itself.[13] Their colleges are an exact resemblance of our own. I visited one of them to whose president Mr. Rigby had brought some letters of recommendation.[14] – This, like every other place of education in Flanders, is a perfect prison. We were admitted after a dozen locks were open'd. The Governors have endeavor'd to make the confinement palatable by furnishing the students with various opportunities for amusement. In their gardens I observ'd two tennis grounds, several walks and contrivances for some games which I did not understand. The president seem'd to be very proud of his College, and more than once repeated the superiority of his numbers to those of Oxford. But from the size of his students and from some other circumstances, I found that they took them at all ages and that they united with the character of a university that of a large school.[15]

We reach'd Cambray late in the evening, and were guided by candle light to see the Cathedral and Palace of the renowned Fenelon.[16] Our observation in these edifices was call'd to nothing but a vast profusion of marble and of gold and silver. The Arch Bishop's monument was shewn us with great parade, but it is a miserable thing.[17] We were carried from one sight to another, but we looked only to be disappointed, and to regret that every new curiosity serv'd only to delay the better gratification which we expected from our supper.

The next day's journey was a long one indeed. We travell'd 91 miles thro' populous villages, crowded towns, and a country in which as yet we have not discover'd one barren spot or cottage in ruins – or one testimony either of indolence or dissipation in the inhabitants. Within ten miles of our journey's termination, we stopped for a change of horses in a little town, the most beautiful I ever saw.[18] It is situated on the banks of a river as large as the Thames at Richmond. Every house is neat and seems to be the residence of health and comfort. Even the ditches are all cultivated by the industry of the inhabitants who seem to employ every spot of the rich soil on which they live. Above this town hangs a hill of some height cover'd with woods and windmills – and at the brow of it commences the Prince of Condé's Forest.[19]

We turned out of the great road and travell'd thro' this immense tract which is near 40 miles in circumference, and is wholly devoted to the insipid pleasures of one poor creature whose power enables him to keep out the prolific industry of the surrounding inhabitants, which appears by the culture and population that intrudes upon the very edge of the forest. Thro' a continued vista of 12 miles and a half we hasten'd to Chantilly. We saw a few wild stags and a quantity of game in the vast solitude; all animal life seem to fly before the wasteful hand of tyranny – and while my companions were in raptures with the shade, the beauty, and the variety of the woods thro' which they passed, I was employed in drawing the picture which the same ground would have afforded, if like the surrounding country it were cover'd with cornfields and villages.[20] From the forest we entered into the Prince of Condé's Park. We soon learnt from the shorn appearance of the walks and trees that the Mansion House was not far distant. We suddenly burst from the woods into a valley whose first appearance astonished and filled us with agreeable sensations. The sky was perfectly serene and clear. The sun was just setting. A large stream of water gushed from the side of the forest and by the hands of art was made to fall in a spreading cascade. The stream was skirted with woods and temples. At some distance from us we saw a dozen *jet d'eaus*[21] spouting to a considerable height in the air.

Behind these *jet d'eaus* the houses appear'd like one vast mass of fire, owing to the reflection of the sun's beams from the countless windows. The banks of the stream were cover'd with different companies of the Prince's domestics, all superbly dress'd. Numberless parties from the neighbouring town of Chantilly were basking themselves in the same situation. The feeling and expressions of my companions were those of enchantment and rapture. It was with eagerness that we waited the approach of the next morning, six hours of which were employ'd in seeing the various parts of this costly place. As we walked through the park we were saluted by the most dauntless approach of the game which came up to the very path on which we trod, and by being made so common and so tame lose in my opinion the only distinction by which they can give pleasure. We were first led to a building far more splendid and capacious than the palace itself. It was built for a stable or ecurie and contains 400 English hunters. It is the residence likewise of the Prince's hounds, and the whole of it employs more expense than would people the whole surrounding forest with happy peasants. The endless variety and wretched taste of the grounds and gardens very soon fatigued our spirits.[22] We were carried to the Tent of Silvia, and we saw nothing but shorn banks shaded by a few hanging trees. The devastation and deformities of the shears appeared in all quarters, and which soever way we look'd, the eye peep'd thro' a boundless walk protected on each side by a wall of shrubs. Our guide leads us thro' the Labyrinth, an object which to an inform'd mind must ever be associated with pain and horror. But this was not the labyrinth of Dedalus. Its sides were made only of a thin hedge, and if I could not find, I should soon be able to cut my way thro. In the islands which a very peaceful stream surrounded, we met with artificial caves and rocks, but their residence ill became them, they appear'd in circumstances in which Nature never placed them, and in which it is impossible that anything but the monstrous folly of man should ever bring them. We saw attempts likewise to make gurgling streams, by increasing the declivity of the water, and by placing pebbles in its bed. But the neighbouring meadow, and a quiet muddy stream which runs close to the babbler silently proclaim its absurdity. In short, in the grounds I saw nothing but the mangling hands of Art, stone walls, cropp'd hedges, imitations of Nature without attending to circumstances, and a profusion of wealth without doing the least credit to the intellects of him who squanders it.

The house is little different from all other great mansion houses. It is divided into rooms immensely large, and dazzling with gold, and the most glaring colours. It contains a Cabinet of Natural Curiosities, most excellently arrang'd by Bomare one of the first naturalists in France, who happen'd to be at Chantilly at the same time and who was very communicative indeed.[23] My head, my legs, my eyes and my very heart ach'd at length with fatigue. We saw a vast deal, and left unseen a vast deal more. We returned to the inn and immediately sett off for Paris where we now are in health and safety. An account of what I have seen here and a long letter to my Uncle I will send by the earliest opportunities.[24]

Letter III

Paris, July 13th, 89, 4 o'clock in the morning[25]

The accounts you will hear of this last night's tumults in Paris have induced me to be thus early in my assurances of our safety. – The distress, the confusion, the destroying madness of the scene I have just witness'd have actually equall'd those of a town taken by storm. – They have far exceeded any ideas I could have form'd of insurrection in its violence and of popular rage in its extravagance. – Yesterday noon our party returned from Versailles to Paris. We had left the court in all apparent tranquility. Nor was the event which has caused all the tumults even whisper'd in the neighbourhood of the Palace. We dined at our arrival in the Rue de St. Michel, and while we sat at table one of the company ask'd us whether we had heard of Necker's flight.[26] – As we had just arrived from Versailles our possitive assurances satisfy'd those who were present that the rumour was false. We agreed however to go to the theatre which was open and which would certainly give signs of the multitude's disposition.[27] We had scarcely sat down in one of the boxes when a gentleman with the greatest distraction in his looks assur'd us that no play was to be perform'd, that Necker was by that time 160 miles from Paris, and that a most terrifying uproar prevail'd in the city. At this moment the curtain was rais'd and the manager came forward. "Sirs," said he, "You are to have no play this evening." "The reason why?" was immediately resounded from every quarter of the house. – The manager answer'd, that the People then at his door had commanded it. A burst of the most impetuous applause discover'd to us the disposition of the assembly.[28] We hasten to the doors and every countenance expressed rage or the most anxious apprehensions. – Our company hurried immediately towards the Palais Royal.[29] – But every street was almost blocked up with inhabitants, and neither the voice nor the walk of one individual was otherwise than rapid and impetuous. From several companies of the mob we heard the cry "Aux Armes". – When we reached the Palais we heard thousands of voices all uttering the denunciations of vengeance at the same instant. – No settled design seem'd to guide the populace. They collected themselves into innumerable parties and not two of the orators who harrangued them seem'd to speak in the same language.

In this boiling and unsettled state of commotion we had continued some time when we saw a man enter in all the most distorted attitudes of imprecation and rage. "To arms," says he. "I have been wounded by the Dragoons, and they are this moment firing upon your fellow citizens."[30] Hundreds immediately echo'd back "to Arms", and a vast portion of the multitude immediately follow'd their guides. There were now very few individuals remaining in the quadrangle of the Palace and my companions stood prophecying the horrors of the approaching night, when we saw the mob return led by a most desperate fellow, sweating & raving and swearing and holding up an empty helmet as a standard. None of the company chose to be near the scene of action, we therefore returned to our hotel[31] and from the windows survey'd the increasing distraction and rage of the populace – within the space of half an hour tranquility was restor'd in our street, but we heard distant shouts and saw new multitudes rushing down thro' every alley and street. As the scene of danger seem'd to be removed we ventured once more into the Palais Royal, and there learnt that the barriers of the town were all on fire[32] – that the Swiss Guards had fired and that fifty of the populace had fallen, but that the crowd could not be dispersed.[33] We were now alarm'd by a number of ladies and gentlemen mixed with several of the lower people who rushed towards us with shrieks and with all the terror of persons who saw danger immediately approaching. – Our company partook of the hurry and terrors of the crowd – and once more we lodged ourselves safely in our citadel.

It was now night and we could only hear the steps and shouts of those who pass'd to and fro. The sky was red with the several fires. We could hear the reports of the guns from a variety of quarters and we witness'd the cries of mothers and wives who stuck to their husbands and their sons pressing them not to unite with the general rage. About 10 o'clock the uniformity of the noise was interrupted by the violence of a party who assail'd the doors of a gunsmith living in a room just under ours.[34] The crash of the stones and stakes which the populace drove against the doors set our whole hotel into an uproar. The women shriek'd – some of the lodgers were immediately for flying, but they were strangers and could not tell us how they would direct their steps. At length the populace forc'd their way in, but found no arms as another company had previously seiz'd upon the whole of the gunsmith's stock. They soon relieved us by retiring in great tranquility.

The whole night has been employed in surveying the mob as they pass and repass. Their multitudes is immense, amongst them I have number'd some hundreds of the soldiery.[35] All are arm'd – and the whole city is still in confusion and riot. The mischief of the night I have not yet heard. The return of day has smooth'd a little the formidable aspect of the scene – I observe a vast number of families leave the town and we shall as soon as possible follow their example – our danger is all over. The scene of action is removed to a part of the town far remote from us. Those of the mob who stray thus far are generally intoxicated.

Letter IV

Dijon, July 21st

I shall hope to find letters at Lyons with information that you have frequently heard from me while at Paris. In that scene of tumult and danger, I seiz'd every possible opportunity for telling you that I was well and safe – I have written twice to my Uncle, and I shall be very anxious till I am assur'd that the packets have reach'd his hands.[36] The commencement of the revolt at Paris interrupted that part of my correspondence which successively referr'd to the several scenes and places thro' which I passed. I stop'd at Chantilly, from whence I travelled to the capital with eyes widely open to observe the difference of its approach compared with that of London – but instead of meeting with 100's of stage coaches – buggys – phaetons – carriages, carts and gentlemen on horseback, with a large crowded foot path, you see the gates of Paris before you are sensible of its vicinity.[37] A fine well cultivated country abounding with corn of all kinds extends to the very walls. Corn waggons loaded with the peasants returning from market were the only vehicles I saw till I got within the barrier or the place where all the tolls and customs are paid.[38] Here a scene of confusion begins. Hackney coaches,[39] carts, and thousands of men, women and children are all blended together. It was in the afternoon of a dry day and the dust buried all in a cloud. At this hour every family seem to be sitting at the door of each house and the street consequently appear'd to be pav'd with inhabitants. We moved in heavy procession to the Palais Royal, where we agreed for a most extravagant lodging, each paid for his bed two guineas a week.[40] The unnecessary expense of a coach amounts to as much, and every other article was proportionably dear. However, we have not grudg'd the money as our situation at the awful moment of the revolt enabled us to see what others who lodged in a different part of the town heard from us with astonishment.

The first night of our arrival we had scarcely finished our tea when we hastened to the inner part of the Palais, where crowds of the Parisians meet every evening to talk politics, to drink coffee or to sup. Imagine a large rectangle surrounded by a very fine building, intersected by cut walks, refresh'd by several pieces of water with *jet d'eaus* in the middle, crowded by men with powdered heads and with their hats under their arms, and thickly beset with ladies of all kinds, adorn'd likewise by very rich shops form'd like the best in London, and here and there presenting to the eye companies of men and women sitting in the open air. Draw a picture from all these particulars and you will have an idea of the Palais Royal.[41] – We frequently walk on this lively spot and on every occasion found new reason to admire the spirit, the politeness, and the information of the company. I followed the inclination of my fellow travellers, and for three days successively tired in looking at public buildings and curiosities and in fatiguing myself each night at some public place. Rich palaces and churches abound in this City, but they are testimonies of power, of affluence, and of the superstition which has reign'd in this City; the productions of good taste are rarely met with in Paris. But the people are improving, and their new buildings shew that they are far beyond the English in architecture. Their Players' Operas are more apposite to the appearance of Nature than at Drury Lane etc. I went to see Madam Du Gazon[42] who is the Mrs Siddons of Paris, and I think she rants with equal success and popularity. But poor woman, she was forc'd to sing her dying groans, and consequently all the softer sounds of her pantings and sobbings were lost amidst the uproar of bassoons, haut-boys, &c. The people notwithstanding were in rapture, tho' the play and its events were nothing more or less than the old story of Blue Beard and Sister Ann.[43] At the Opera, the pride of the French, all was noise and nonsense, improbability and distortion. I wish'd it over before it was half finished – Mr. Boddington slept and poor Rigby felt wants from the very beginning which made him curse over and over the tediousness of the Opera.

On Saturday we set off for Versailles. There, indeed, such a spectacle as gratified my fondest feelings appeared in the Grand Body of the Representatives assembled to establish Liberty in one of the first nations upon Earth.[44] But this subject I have dwelt upon in one of my letters to my Uncle. The Sunday morning I attended the crowd to the Gallery at Versailles. The splendid minions of a Court in all their gaudy tinsel gave me but little pleasure, whilst yet warm with the grandeur of what I saw on the preceding day. However, like the rest of the company, I stared at the King and thought him a little superior to our own. I stared at the Queen, and saw the true image of pride and lasciviousness. The Palace, the gardens, the pictures, all these we gaz'd at and paid dearly for our sight. The particulars of my rout to Versailles I shall hereafter talk over with you. On our return from this place we found Paris all in confusion, and we saw the beginning of those great events which I have described very minutely in a letter to my Uncle. By the civil commotions of the capital we were detained four days longer than we expected.

We made one attempt to quit the town, and we had well nigh paid dearly for our attempt. The mob thought we wished to turn our backs upon them in danger, and when we had reach'd the gates they sent us back from centinel to centinel, amidst taunts, hissings, abuse and insults to our own lodging where they search'd every rag of our baggage and treated us in every respect as if we had been spies.[45] However, the politeness of some individuals amply made up for the severity of the multitude. – On Sunday morning we procured a passport. Our baggage was again searched partially. But the King's entrance without his guards into Paris, the demolition of the Bastile, and the restoration of Peace and Liberty to the noble Parisians amply repaid our loss of time and the fatigue of our spirits. My journey from Paris to Dijon which was delightful, and an account of what is currious and interesting in this place, I shall hereafter describe – My companions are eager to be on their walk – and the post is to set off soon –.

Letter V

Lyons, 24th July

My last letter was dated from Dijon whither we were conveyed from Paris after a journey of two days th[r]o' a country crowded with inhabitants, and diversified by singularities I had never seen before – the uninterrupted extent of cornfields which reached from French Flanders to Paris we did not pass over till we found by its thick forest and shorn vistas that we approached the King's Palace at Fontainbleau.[46] This is situated in the centre of an amphitheatre whose boundary is form'd by a bulwark of rocks intercepted by numberless lofty trees which seem to grow from the very fissures of the stone. The King has not visited this palace for several years, both the neighbouring town therefore and the Royal Building appear as if they would soon totter. We travell'd over several miles of forest in which we saw no life but that of bushes and trees. But the returning appearance of villages and of cheerful inhabitants soon assured us that we had escap'd the desolated regions of the King's splendor and pleasures. We now entered into the land of vine yards. An extent as far as the eye could reach open'd before us, the whole of which resembled an undulation of high hills crowding upon the backs and peeping over the shoulders of each other. But not one summit was bare, not one side shaggy. No barren rocks stared upon us, but every hill was mantled with a vine yard. Declivities on which I should stand with some difficulty were perfectly covered, nay the tendrils droop'd over the very edge of the road. What the prodigality of our countrymen would consign to the growth of willows and bulrushes was here a perfect garden. You know that a vineyard is much more valuable than a piece of corn-ground of equal extent. Hence as the riches of the French soil increase, so does the population. The distance which separated their large towns & villages seem'd to diminish.

A few posts from Fontainbleau conveyed us to the banks of the Seyne, a river nearly as large as the Thames, at Windsor. For thirty miles together we traversed either upon its edge or upon a ridge of high grounds which hung just over it. The river was quite full. It ran at the rate of a mile and a half every hour, add moreover that it was as clear as crystal. Every 100 yards it presented us with a new view. Once [in a] while it stole along amongst vineyards, another time it was bordered by a successive chain of villages. We sometimes thought we should lose it in a deep valley, but by following its course, we soon found the valley open and discover to us the same fertility diversified by unexpected circumstances of what is picturesque & beautiful. Thro' a country thus form'd to fix and gratify the eyes we passed to a little town called Joigny. This is an excellent termination of the views belonging to the Seyne. It is well built; it descends along the slope of an eminence, and to the ornaments of a church, and of several chateaux, are added those of a large bridge and of a river cover'd with boats and barges.[47]

In every village as we passed along we were stop'd by the crowd agitated by inquiries about news from Paris. We wav'd our cockades;[48] we briefly announced that "the Bastile was demolish'd — that the Governor's head was off; that the Army was disbanded, and that the King without Guards had thrown himself on the mercy of the free peoples." — We are generally dismissed with loud applause and with the cry of "Vive la Nation. Toujours le tiers État!" But when we reached Joigny the carriage was fairly stop'd by the inquisitive multitude, and their eagerness for sometime alarm'd me. At last to a polite venerable old gentleman we delivered our intelligence who received it with joy and dispersed it amongst the surrounding crowd. It was in the sight of Joigny that I first thought of the superior pleasures which might be enjoyed with an affectionate family in the South of France. Should retirement be my future destiny, it certainly would not be in England — but enough — I almost envy the addition of Liberty to the other numerous advantages to this great and delightful country. From Joigny we passed [into] the Auxerre.[49] But after the diversified prospects we had seen, we felt no taste for the luxuriancy of a wide flat country, more rich and populous but equally insipid with that of the country of Norfolk. The town of Auxerre itself is pleasantly situated on the banks of the Seyne,[50] and the appearance of an immense palace, of a Gothic cathedral and of several churches singularly constructed fixed my attention and have impress'd it on my memory.[51]

Our next day's journey to Dijon presented us with no great difference in the aspect of the country. We lost the Seyne but we were still amongst vineyards and towns and villages. We were stop'd by similar inquiries, and as we travers'd along we found that we did not outrun the footsteps of Liberty and Revolt. At Villeaux a very difficult ascent delay'd our progress a whole hour. At length we reach'd the lofty summit of a mountain with full expectations of some vast prospect to reward our toil. But alas we saw nothing excepting the summits of other high grounds whose full cultivation gave us new testimonies of the general industry that reigns in France. For ten miles we crawled over the uninteresting inequalities of this soil; at length we reach'd its boundary. This is a sudden declivity having on its brow a massey castle and a large town. It commanded a view of the Romantic valley at whose extremity stands the town of Dijon. The road on each side was compressed by precipices covered with shrubs, but within 5 miles of Dijon the night overtook us and while we were gazing at the brilliancy of the glow worms which studded the rocks we all fell asleep. Our slumbers, however, were soon interrupted by the appearance of lights, by the shouts of a crowd, and by the clatter of bayonets and guns. We were now at the gates of Dijon, and the Citizens were in arms. They had followed the example of Paris, and they stop'd every carriage which entered the town. A Guard attended us to our hotel who seem'd inquisitive about news from the capital. We told them that all was tranquil. They shook their heads and said, that they would take care to keep the Noblesse quiet; for whom, they assured us, they meant to erect a Bastile at Dijon. At present it is a sad calamity in France to be a nobleman – or one of his relations. They are fairly driven out of the towns, and should any new disturbance arise, I am apt to think, they would lose something more than their titles.[52] At Dijon, Rigby found a hospital to admire, and he was the only person of the company who left Dijon with any impressions which he wished to retain.[53] Our journey to Lyons and all its circumstances I shall describe to you in my next letter. We have not yet seen all that is to be seen on this Romantic spot. I shall write to you again from Avignon which lies 150 miles to the south of this town.

I was enchanted when I learnt by your letters that I could write anything amusing to my dear Sarah and George.[54] Tell them that if they liv'd in this country they would be dress'd like the finest gentleman and ladies they ever saw. Miss Sarah would strut along with a large roll on her head, with her locks frizzled and powdered, with a stay that would make her sides as stiff and erect as a brick wall, with a fan as big as herself in her hand, and with a petticoat that would sweep up all the dust from her own to her cousin's house. Tell her likewise, that she would have high heels, and if there were room for it, a cork rump as big as Mary's real one. I have seen ladies but little older than herself thus dress'd in France. Tell Mr. George that his hair would be powdered. That a long queue would hang down his back. That he would have [a] coat with flaps and sleeves big enough to set his wind-mill agoing. His waistcoat could likewise be laced, his breeches would change his little thighs into the shape of a rolling pin, and that every time he met Papa or Mama he would be obliged to bow till his nose touch'd the ground. One of the most ludicrous sights I have yet seen in France was a procession of these little men in miniature led by a School Master who was an overgrown boy dress'd in the same ludicrous manner. The better sort of ladies are in all the large towns dress'd like the English ladies. The gentlemen are more formal. Few of them walk along the streets without his hat in his hand and without having a bagwig[55] and silk coat. The citizens & middling people resemble in their dress the same rank in England. But they are much more polite and obliging.

Our diet is much liked by our companions. We seldom sit down to less than 8 dishes of meat, but they are all too complex for my taste.[56] I slept last night in a bed for the first time since I left Lisle. All but Rigby have been victims to the bugs in their turns. To avoid these legions of fury and blood I have generally lain upon the floor or a couch, wrap'd up in a blanket. We are now in the region of fleas. In our bed room last night Olyett had scarcely stood 5 Minutes before they form'd a perfect half boot by their swarms that fixed on his legs. It appears this morning that in the course of the night they have given singular magnitude and expression to the features of Mr. Boddington's face. We expect to be still more annoy'd as we go down the Rhone.[57]

Letter VI

July 29th, Marseilles, 1789

We are all safe and well at the remotest boundary of our journey. Our time and money are half spent, and we pride ourselves in having managed our concerns with much accuracy. Henceforth our faces will be obliquely directed toward England, but before our full fronts are fixed homewards we have a great space yet to traverse over, and a great many places to behold. Tomorrow we pass on to Toulon and thence we shall slowly advance along the Mediterranean coast till we reach Nice. Our next route will be to Geneva where I hope to find letters from you.

When I last finished or rather interrupted the thread of my story I halted at Dijon. Our road from this place had not continued a mile thro' vineyards and cornfields before a wide plain open'd and displayed at its extremity a view of the Alps towering into the clouds and forming a vast amphitheatre of near 200 miles in diameter. They appeared black as night and rose into the heaven in all the possible varieties of points and craggs and precipices. We gazed upon them with increasing wonder for several leagues, and were at length rous'd from the silence of our admiration by the sound of the drum & the familiar shout of *Toujours le tiers État*. A crowd with cockades and muskets stop'd up the road. Our postilions crack'd their whips and made an effort as in former times to force their way thro' the multitude with the accustom'd defiance of all those who serv'd the Grand Monarch. But the spirit of Liberty was now in its full pride and in a moment our traces were cut and our carriage immoveable & altogether at the mercy of the crowd. However, the Commander rode up to us, expressed his concern for our embarrassment with great politeness, and beg'd that we would pardon the little excesses of a people who had just thrown off their fetters. We found that the armed force which had stop'd us belonged to a small town which had followed the example of hundreds more; and with swords and bayonets were determined to teach the Priests, the Noblesse and the King that they were human beings as well as themselves.[58]

The following night we lodged at Chalon, a dirty town replete with buggs and fleas and priests. However, this residence of vermin is on the banks of the Soane, and a growing trade co-operating with the spirit of Liberty will soon assimilate them to the advantages and beauties of the spot on which it is built. A finer stream than the Soane I never yet beheld. It is as full, pellucid and large as the Thames at Richmond. It flows with greater velocity and directs its passage thro' scenes of fertility and affluence which are to be seldom met with in Europe. With the dawn of the following morning we set off for Lyons. The heavens were without a cloud. The inequalities of the country were perpetually furnishing us with some new varieties of the Soane and of its banks, when all at once our wheels began to shriek and one of them to smoak, the postilions could not stop as they were hastening down a hill. When we reached the valley our carriage was immoveable. The wood of the wheel was on fire and every speed was used to extinguish it; nor could we succeed till we buried the axle in one of the postilion's jack boots which we had previously fill'd with water. But the combustion was such as to require that we should all walk 5 miles while the carriage followed us to a little town where we were delayed 4 hours.[59]

This incident obliged us to rest the following night at Mâcon,[60] a most charming town which forms a quay of near a mile in length along the banks of the Soane. Our inn fronted the river and the Alps bounded our prospect which was altogether picturesque and noble. Hundreds of people walked below us enjoying the mildness of the evening and the mutual cheerfulness which marks all the society of France. Two grand bridges strided over the stream. A weighty bulk of clouds hung over the Alps, and the dusky extent which was spread at their feet was perpetually illuminated by flashes of lightening. I gaz'd at this scenery till the hum of the crowds below us had ceased. I slept on the floor as usual in terror of the buggs, but with my windows open and my eyes fix'd on the clouds and the Alps. From Mâcon we travelled thro' a continued series of villages and towns. They really seem'd to touch each other, and the high grounds which rose above them display'd little besides the same testimonies of population and industry. Within 12 miles of Lyons we began to discover the influence of its commercial powers.[61] We entered an amphitheatre of about 20 miles in diameter bounded by very lofty mountains and fertilized by the Soane and its ramifications, but instead of cottages we behold rich Chatteaux, plantations intruded in the vineyards, and fantastic ornaments of different kinds diversified the sides of the mountains.

We were an hour and a half ascending one of the descents. We reach'd the top expecting the view on the other side with great eagerness. At the same instant all of us panted for breath and struggled to exclaim, *How wonderful!* The highest front of the Alps seemed, while we had been admiring in the valley below, boldly to have advanced within a few steps of us. One black bulk appeared to be crowded upon another and over all Mont Blanc shot into clouds shining with the same yellow colour as itself. The grandeur of this mountainous scene did not allow us for some minutes to look at the declivity along which our road winded to the environs of Lyons. The similarity however, of this singular region is not to be found in the world. Conceive each row of houses in a large city to [be] separated from each other by a valley having its sides cover'd with vineyards, and its lower regions wash'd by a running stream of the clearest water; paint this valley as diversified with rocks & cascades, with woods untouched by the shears or pruning hook and with meadows in all the verdure of spring. But to have a compleat idea of the neighbourhood of Lyons, you must further suppose every house in the rows I have alluded to as seperate from the next to it, by a garden, by summer houses, and by all the ornaments of a rich country retirement. We descended thro' these enchanting suburbs to the banks of the Soane, which flow'd thro' a passage separated on each side by a space of about 50 yards from two lofty precipices. On that opposite to us we beheld the staring fronts of an old castle of the Arsenal, and of many public buildings. Over our heads we saw a multitude of houses perched with all the wantonness of singularity on jutting rock and precipices. Between the river and this for-midable bulwark runs a long street formed of houses 7 stories high. These seem to touch each other on high and from each window in them the noise of an English coach call'd a most curious collection of visages. At the doors below crowds of the ugly, the ragged, and the dirty individuals of your sex greeted us with a stare, with a nod, with a smile, or with a shout in favor of *le tiers État*.[62] However, in the whole course of my life I never passed thro' such a concentration of stinks. Garlick, rotten cabbages, fryes, roastings, inlets & outlets [from] a thousand sooty kitchens and ten thousand rank individuals pour'd forth at once all their poisons into our nostrils. But putrefaction is the source of New Life.[63] This was the case here, thousands of children crawl'd around us, and not a door opened without displaying the majesty of a pregnant woman.

When we cross'd the Soane we entered the city itself and passed over a grand quay to our inn. Our eagerness for new scenes was whetted by the variety of our late gratifications. We dined and hurry'd to have a sight of the Rhone. My mind had been prepared by the discussion of ancient poetry and of modern travellers so as not to be surprised by the rapidity of its torrent.[64] I notwithstanding gaz'd at it with wonder. It has the perpetual flow of a very precipitate floodgate, the whole body of it moves with the same uniform velocity. We changed our situation, supposing we had first observed the place most favorable to its speed, but the whole length of a quay which stretches for two miles gave us a fine specimen of what we found to be alike wonderful for 200 miles successively. We regretted the hours of this evening which we spent at a play. We found it to be perfectly modeled after the childish foppery we had previously seen at Paris.

Next morning a very polite merchant attended us & we agreed for 9 *louis* to take our passage down the Rhone. We then clamber'd up the precipices to take a view of the antiquities of Lyons. These consisted of 7 or 8 Arches about 40 feet high, the remains of an Acqueduct thro' which the luxurious

Romans conveyed their water over 21 miles length of the inequalities which diversifies this country. Our guide carried us to an underground chapel & shewed us the bones of 1800 martyrs who had been killed on the spot.[65] An inscription over the door advised us to look with compassion on the walls ting'd with their blood, but gave us no dates or particulars relative to this extraordinary tale. A Roman bath, very perfect, finished the sights of the morning. Our obliging friend, the merchant, carried us to his country seat in the afternoon.[66] We were enchanted with the beauty of his prospect, with the displays of affluence and hospitality which mark'd every appurtenance of his country house and some of the company tore themselves with regret from the beautiful females who allur'd us by every expression of politeness and affability to continue some little time longer at their Villa. The merchant assured us that nearly half the inhabitants of Lyons slept at some country house during the summer season, and that his own house was the inferior of hundreds more splendid. With £200 per annum we might live creditably amongst the princes of the neighbourhood – Rigby seizes me with saying we shall lose the post. I am therefore interrupted very suddenly.

Letter VII

Nice, August 2nd, 1789

I am near 150 Miles distant from the place whence I directed my last letter. I now breath the pure air, I gaze upon the delightful views, but I at the same time feel the scorching sun of Italy. We are all, however, perfectly well and are annoyed by no inconveniences save those of the fleas, buggs and musquitoes. Never lived a poor creature to whom their prion[67] or partiality has been more troublesome than myself. I am marked as if I had but lately recovered from the chicken pox, and I rival the cleanliest Scotchman in the eagerness of scratching. My sufferings will abate as I travel Northward, and I hope to return with scars only as the testimonies of my warfare. When I wrote last I was suddenly interrupted by the post. My detail of adventures reached only to Lyons where we spent two days and enjoyed very great pleasure.

New and romantic views perpetually fixed our attention, and every step we took was embarrassed by the multitudes who crowd the streets. This town is said to contain 180,000 inhabitants, and such is its climate that ⅔ of this vast body are always employed in the open air. The narrowness of the streets adds to the multitudinous appearance of Lyons. The horrid combination of smells which at first infected our nostrils inspir'd us with the wish that the attainment of a little more elbow room would be amongst the earliest acquisitions of their free government – but we had not walked two hours in the heat of their sun before we fled to the gratifying shadow of a narrow street in defiance of all its odours. The height of the houses is here immense; in one of them which did not strike me as very large, a merchant assured us that 600 persons lived; of the number he was one. The rent of this house amounted to 2000 guineas per annum – but during 9 months of the year, said he, all our families are in the country, so is the family of the meanest tradesman. You see, the Lyonese have always been remarkable for their independent and republican spirit, and we found that the citizens had taken up arms some time before the Revolution at Paris.[68] We saw the ruins of a barrier which the populace had burnt, and we saw many other testimonies of that Liberty which is now the fondest object of every Frenchman's wishes.

We entered the boat we had hired to carry us down the Rhone early in the morning.[69] We glided along the Soane with our eyes fixed on Lyons, and its delightful suburbs. New hills, new buildings, new varieties in the position of rocks, cascades, and mountains diverted our thoughts till we reach'd the junction of the two rivers. The rapid stream of the Rhone was perceptible at some distance, but we moved near a mile after the rivers had flowed in one bed before the rapidity we saw close to us was sensible. As soon as the boat enter'd the Rhone, it shot almost like an arrow from a bow. The men immediately laid down their oars, and all in the profoundest silence stood looking at the rapid succession of trees, bushes, and rocks which seem'd to fly along the shore. For twenty miles together we wing'd, as it were, our course amidst fertile hills covered with vineyards and chatteaux and with a village or town at their base before we reach'd Vienne. Here we were stopp'd to be searched by the Custom House Officer – and to be pestered with fruit sellers and beggars. We hasten'd to see the Roman Antiquities of this spot and plac'd ourselves under the guidance of a female, who exposed us to the sun and buryed us in the dirt for an hour together; when I was almost melted away I asked her where she was leading us. She stared and grinned and said she did not know. I stared likewise and was going to relieve the burthen of my limbs by sitting in the middle of a dirty street, when I heard the voice of a salutation from a rock near us. Here we found a Gentleman busily employed in cutting out a grave for the remains of a friend who was an Englishman.[70] His sorrow bad him to treat us with very great kindness indeed. He eas'd his mind by telling us the history of his friend's calamities and then offered his services to us. He led us to the several antiquities of the place. He showed us the extensive boundaries of the town in the time of the Romans. He specified the height of the vast amphitheatre of mountains which surrounded us, and concluded his civilities by carrying us to his own house, where he gratified our parch'd lips with some of the best wine which the country affords.

When we returned to our boat every part of it was like an oven. In the shade furnish'd by the boards which were rais'd for our defence, Farenheit's Therm. rose to 84°. We continued our rapid course thro' mountains covered to the very summit with the labours of the spade and plough – and hitherto found more reason to admire the fertility than the grandeur of our successive views. For leagues and leagues likewise we found no great variety in the scene, and tho' we travelled with amazing velocity yet such was the effect of fatigue on Rigby's tongue and such the silence of our unemployed boatman that we fell asleep just as the sun was setting. After an hour's forgetfulness, the sound of drums and the cry of *toujours le tiers Etat* opened our eyes upon the sable greatness of a craggy amphitheatre which inclosed the Rhone whose wide extent gave at this instant the appearance of a vast lake. From the dark masses which seem'd to fill the air we soon directed our attention to a very cleanly damsel who shewed us the way of her dwelling. The Spirit of Liberty had lined the streets thro' which we passed with armed Citizens. We found everything very nice and clean in our lodging – and the damsel's strong assurances that no buggs infested her beds, gave me courage to enjoy a night's rest which I did not expect.[71]

At 4 in the morning the drums of the Citizens gave us the signal and as the sun arose we entered the boat. The mountains thro' which we pass'd this day were rather more wild than those we saw on the preceding day. But the whole variety of the scene was formed by the numberless towns and villages which appeared on the rocks and in the valleys. The industry of the inhabitants had entirely exterminated the woods which in general contribute very much to the grandeur of mountainous prospects. We saw a vast abundance of old castles plac'd in the most fanciful situations. We had now hasten'd over 70 miles. The appearance of Pont St. Esprit refreshed our eyes and awoke our apprehensions. This bridge is nearly as wide again as that of Blackfryars. Its arches are as large, but it strides over the Rhone with such lightness and ease as to seem wholly suspended in the air.[72] The stream rushes thro' its arches with amazing velocity; indeed, the velocity when the river is flooded is so great as to take away from the boatman all the power of his helm. The Rhone was now rather low and we flew under the bridge without danger. The country diversified its countenance but very seldom, and with no striking marks of expression during the remainder of our journey. The water likewise became less rapid, and we landed for these reasons with some degree of relief just as the darkness thicken'd under the walls of Avignon. In the space of two days the Rhone had carried us 200 miles. This circumstance will give you some idea of what I regard as the most striking peculiarity of this journey. I mean the rapidity of a stream near half a mile wide in some places, and in most places near 30 feet.

Avignon is part of the Pope's dominions, and we had no sooner entered the territories of his holiness than we saw a scene of drunkenness and irregularity, the remote semblance of which we had not discovered in the whole Kingdom of France.[73] Our inn was nasty, our beds full of buggs. The streets were all night annoy'd by riots and shouts, the clatter of wooden shoes and by thundering strokes at our own and the doors of the other inhabitants. Add to all these disturbers of my sleep a most violent pain in my bowels, and you will conceive how disagreeably I spent the night. The next morning the tinkling of bells from twenty churches announced that superstition of the day which so well coincided with the irregularities of the dark. We found, however, no small gratification in viewing the Romantic craggs on which part of this town is built. The Rhone whirls along under its walls, and on the cliff overhanging the opposite shore is erected a huge castle. The walls of those buildings give protection to a large French town just under it. But in every view the most prominent object is most commonly a rich monastery or a convent. From Avignon we crossed the country and passed thro' olive orchards and mulberry grounds to Pont du Garde. We now began to perceive more sensibly the effects of a warm climate on the vegetation of the country. The air was rendered perfectly fragrant by the rosemary, the lavender, the thyme and the numberless aromatic plants which sprung spontaneously from the soil. Indeed, such herbs as in our country are altogether inodourous, we found here to emit the most delicious scents. For the first time we now heard the harsh sound of a fly, millions of whose species crowd the olive trees, and rend the air with their dissonance through- out the whole of the south of France.[74] The novelty of this day's prospect was in some degree rendered less gratifying by the devastations of the last frost, who[se] cold had withered the olive trees of leagues and leagues of the surrounding country. Indeed, we were haunted by the comfortless appearance of blasted orchards till we reached Marseilles.[75]

The singularities of the Pont du Garde are described by every French traveller.[76] It rises 120 yards into the air, consisting of 3 rows of arches resting one upon the other. It is part of an aqueduct which conveyed the water from a distance of 29 miles to Nismes. The expence of erecting it must have been enormous, and must impress every mind with a great idea of the luxury and power of the Romans. The fountain which springs at Nismes affords excellent water, but to enjoy the flowing mountain spring the wonderful fabric I have been describing was constructed. The valley below the Pont du Garde is very picturesque, it is the bed of a boiling stream which holds constant war against the sides of vast rocks, which interrupt its course. An immense bed of pebbles below the bridge inform'd us of the fury of this stream when it pours down the waters deposited by a storm on the neighbour- ing mountains.

We reach'd Nismes early in the afternoon and spent three hours in the survey of its distinguished antiquities. The town is now considerable as 2000 of its citizens are in arms to establish the liberties of their country. But the size of the amphitheatre and the magnificence of its ancient baths reduce its present magnitude to that of meaness compared with its Roman grandeur. We spent a short night at Nismes and past an uninteresting but long journey the next day to Aix, the capital of Provence. We entered this town just as 4000 Marsilians departed, who had marched hither commanded by a priest in full force to require the liberation of 60 prisoners whom the Noblesse had confined.[77] The prison doors were thrown open and these Sons of Liberty marched with the captives in triumph to Marseilles. The intendant of Aix narrowly escap'd destruction. He is fled to Italy and is amongst the proscribed. At Aix we saw nothing but well built streets and a most pleasant walk cool'd by three antient fountains. Our view of the surrounding country was bounded on all sides by the most romantick mountains, whose rough sides and staring prominences rose into a sky which is scarcely ever disturbed by clouds or foggs.

The continuation of our journey from Aix to Marseilles was a succession of beauties and sublimities but we look'd to the opening of every mountain with eyes eagerly on the watch for a view of the Mediterranean. At length our horses clambered up the summit of rocks which overhangs the town and such was the view it commanded that I am sure it would have kill'd the lady whom Mrs. Montague patronized because it was her genius to faint whenever she saw a fine prospect.[78] The wide expanse of the sea appeared as green as grass – on each side of one protruding bay stood Marseilles, consisting of houses and streets and churches and public edifices, well built. At the mouth of the bay two rocky islands seem to float amidst the waves. These islands were guarded by castles and serve as an excellent protection to the harbour. A chain of cliffs tower aloft in the rear of the town and bend in in a crescent form till their horns are cut short by the sea. The Lazaretto is placed at one of these horns, at the extremity of the other is a fort which commands the town. A plain of about one mile in diameter between the mountains and the towns is filled with the rich country houses of the Citizens.

We could hardly pass thro' the streets of Marseilles owing to the armed multitudes who were carrying the prisoners they had taken at Aix from one place to another in triumph. We found them here as martial as at Paris. The[y] had proscribed 30 of the Noblesse and the number of 14,000 Citizens had enrolled themselves for arms. This place seems to be the seat of affluence. Its harbour contained 600 ships and new buildings were rising in every quarter of the town. Our stay here did not exceed one day.

The following morning we set off for Toulon and as we penetrated the Alps we discovered that the grandeur we had beheld was trifling compared with what we had to see. The mountains raised higher. The vegetation became more luxuriant. Every declivity seemed like the side of an English green-house, for it was covered with groves of myrtle [&] tamarisk. The buggs had deprived me of sleep during several nights. In defiance, therefore, at the enchanting scenes of the road we pursued, the God Morpheus spread his wings before my eyes. I was dreaming of what is dear to me in England when I heard Rigby loud and boisterous in the exclamation of sudden ecstacy. I forc'd my head out of the coach window and found that we moved along in the depths of a valley shaded by two stupendous mountains covered with pines and myrtles. Not a piece of naked rock or unfruitful earth appeared, but on the edge of one mountain the sun seemed to have rested himself amongst the branches of lofty pines and cedars. However, I affected great indifference at the sight, and intreated Rigby to be less troublesome when he next saw what was astonishing only to the Marshland Eyes of a Norfolk Man. I endeavor'd to sleep again, but the declivities forc'd us out of our carriage and the fatigue of a walk made all the sublimities of

Nature insipid. The influence of hunger co-operated; and the finest of countries would soon have resembled a desert if a dish of fresh anchovies had not given us new spirits and with them new relish for the food of our eyes. We passed from one mountain to another till a vast bulwark of precipices appeared to block up all further progress. But the road turned round a sharp angle and led us into a compleat inclosure of craggs whence the sky appeared only to those who gave themselves the head-ache in looking up. The road was just wide enough for our wheels, and we passed close to the bed of a most furious torrent. In this imprisonment of precipices we passed along for some time before we recovered our views of a more verdant scene. Just as we broke loose from our caverns a vast olive orchard displayed itself and at its extremity a pretty country house surrounded with almond and orange trees.

We reached Toulon early in the afternoon, and spent the remainder of the day in surveying the town and harbour –[79] the latter is very commodious, and the former, when viewed from the sea, appeared with great advantage at the base of some very high precipices. It was now the 30th day of July, and we had ripe grapes for supper. We bought melons of great weight and most highly flavour'd for 4d each. The gentleness and heat of the climate appeared from many other circumstances. We were obliged to keep our windows open all night, and we beheld numbers of the common people lying without any covering in the open air. As the evening approached every inhabitant hasten'd to the public walk. The women protected only by a single jacket and petticoat – and the men cloath'd in the slightest and lightest habiliments. Our journey to Frejus was only a repetition of what we had seen before, but the roads were execrable, and in the most terrible fatigue we met with terrible accommodations at our hotel. The buggs soon forced me from a couch on which I lay, and the stone floor on which I lay'd myself awoke me before 4 the next morning with every [sic] stiff and painful limbs.

An ascent of 5 miles was the commencement of the next day's journey. Our legs dragg'd us up with difficulty. The horses followed slowly, but tho' we had often feasted our sight with prospects, yet the frequent displays of the Mediterranean was cause of so many novelties that our legs were much relieved by our eyes. When we reached Antibes the Governor objected to our passport, but we found that he did this solely that he might learn the news of Paris. Along the sea coast a pleasant ride brought us over the vale into Italy.[80] We reside in a house cleanly and comfortable. We have already spent a day and a half here, and tomorrow morning we are to turn our faces directly homeward over the high Alps. The curiosity of the English Consul brought him to our lodging this morning. He wished to hear news from France, and he returned our civilities by an invitation which we did not accept of.[81] I shall count the hours which seperate me from Geneva, where I shall hope to hear something from Yourself, &c.

Letter VIII

Vevey, August 17th, 1789

In less than two hours after I finished [my] last letter,[82] I was summon'd to join my companions who with eyes half open were taking their farewell view of Geneva. In this town we saw all the joyful effects of Liberty and Equality amongst the human species. Every street was crowded with busy individuals. No lazy priests were interspersed with the multitude, no lounging officers saluted us with the stare of impertinence and astonishment. We entered the gates without the delay of a single question, and we pass'd amongst the inhabitants as if they had something more interesting to regard than the peculiarities of idle travellers; the first day the dissapointment of receiving no letters from you render'd me insensible to the animation of that scene which surrounded me. Such is the impotence of Reason when the heart is sick, that I fancy'd everything foolish and suffered that folly to torment me.[83]

We stroll'd about from one street to another, admiring the varieties of Industry and like the true Sons of Liberty ascribing all to the absence of Kings and Priests and their whole train of oppressors.[84] We lodged at a mile's distance from the town on the edge of the lake. We therefore convey'd ourselves home in a boat and enjoyed a full view of Geneva. It rises very boldly at the extremity of the lake where that beautifull expanse of water covering a space of 60 miles in length and in some places 24 miles wide divides into two rapid streams which flow as clear as crystal and by their union some distance below form an island which included the whole of ancient Geneva at that renown'd moment when it was taken by Julius Caesar.[85] At present an extensive suburbs is included within the walls, and the whole appears like a well built citadel rais'd to guard the entrance of the water.

A Mr. Pastor,[86] with all the expressions of republican pride, shew'd us their Town Hall, the place where their Council meet, and with singular emphasis directed our eyes to a wooden bench in one of the streets. There, says he, our Judges sit to try criminals – that all their fellow Citizens may testify the justice of their sentence. In the afternoon we took a voyage upon the lake, and for three hours our eyes pass'd successively from one rich chatteau to another, and when our view was finished we learnt from our Guides that we had only seen a league of that rich edge which extended with a similar variety of beauties for 20 leagues together. On the second day we visited the watch manufactories, and I learnt that I could not gratify my dear Sarah as I fully intended by purchasing a real watch without laying out more money than I could afford. I found trinkets as dear as in England, and was asham'd & mortified at the necessity of coming away without buying a single article. Mr. Pastor was very pressing in his importunities for two or three days more of our Company. You have yet seen, says he, but few of our *Ladies.* – I have seen, says I, a great number of the wives and daughters of your Citizens, and it is impossible that you should shew us what will do you greater credit. Nature has done everything to force them upon our attention, and they do nothing to discredit Nature. They wear no stays, they daub themselves with no paint. The dancing master has not distorted their limbs, and every part of their dress appears to the best advantage for it obviously appears to answer some useful purpose. He stared at me for some time, and then upon recollection dropp'd the subject as he well knew that paint and the dancing master were as essential to the distinctions of a fine lady at Geneva as they are at Paris where a female's skin never sees the light of day.

Geneva has its passing as well as its permanent peculiarities. The meteor of the present hour is Prince Edward, the fourth son of our wise K. who displays a brilliancy of character worthy the fountain from which he sprang. – His mistress, his houses, his contempt of his tutors, and his royal extravagance afford the town no small diversion. He presents the inhabitants with splendid concerts. But he generally sends them away most compleatly fatigued. For he has either been deceived by the flattery of others or by his own conceit, into the opinion that he is a first rate singer. His royal bounty, therefore, seldome presents the company with less than 20 songs, and it is a common thing to hear his guests pride themselves on their dexterity by which they have diminish'd their burden and escap'd hearing more than 12 or 13 Songs in a night. He will soon join the concert at Carleton House, and I dare say give full satisfaction to the wishes of his elder brothers.[87]

On Friday 14th we set out on our way to the Glaciers. Amidst mountains burried in clouds and mists and threatening us with bad weather, we travell'd to Bonne Ville which nastiness and poverty taught us very soon to place within the limits of the Sardinian King's dominions. In a few minutes the door of our inn was block'd up with phaetons & coaches. While in possession of the best room we saw a train of ladies crammed into a dirty bedchamber. Our gallantry hastened us to propose an exchange which was received with seeming reluctance, but with real eagerness & pleasure. We soon learnt that our politeness had kindled the glow of thankfulness in breasts no less elevated than those of the Count and Countess of Boust.[88] Their train consisted of ten servants, and every one of the poor creatures seemed to be a fatigue to themselves, what must they be to the Master and Mistress on whom in these mountainous regions they were to depend for food and other conveniences.

An English company in a short time join'd our procession to the Glaciers, whose providence secur'd all the horses – and left us the poor choice of staying some days in the Alpine hovels or of proceeding on foot. We were now 18 miles from Chamougny, the object of our destination.[89]

It was 3 o'clock in the afternoon and fatigue had already intended upon the strength of our limbs. We paus'd like the great Hannibal in similar circumstances, and, like him oppos'd the spirit of resolution to the scowling front of danger and difficulty.[90] Like the mightiest children of enterprise our first steps were those of speed and a mile pass'd off in an instant as one of our guides who was a shoemaker amus'd us with his good sense and his heresy. He had read Voltaire, and he took some pains to assure us that there was no such thing as the Devil. Alas, the heat of his argument was soon quench'd, for a cloud as black as the Devil pour'd his contents upon us and continued its fury till we were almost compleatly drench'd. We bow'd under the weight of our cloaths, and ⅔ of our journey seperated us from Chamougny, when the whole company displayed a most forlorn spectacle. I blew like a porpus, Mr. Boddington's lameness became more and more visible and for his decreasing speed he referr'd us to a most seizing headach.[91] Olyet Woodhouse, for once in his life, walk'd directly forward, and Mr. Rigby, alas poor Rigby, how he grunted and groan'd and curs'd the fashions of the world. For his coat had been made in the fashion of 1786 when it was not right that a coat should button. A linen waistcoat therefore was all he had now to protect his belly. Another rain had render'd this covering as tight as the parchment of a drum. For a whole hour we were loaded by a most weighty shower and during the whole time Rigby railed against fashion, and wished in vain for the possibility of buttoning his coat. The sun smil'd upon us when he was soon to leave us and before we had crawled to the halfway house the night was at hand. We stopp'd half an hour, and when we reassum'd our march we found no other light shining upon us than that of the stars.

By the clatter of a mule's feet we very soon discover'd an approaching object, which was one of the English company who had join'd us with one of Count Boust's female servants mounted behind him. We had now enter'd a forest and as I was foremost of the company was the first to be surprized by something like a human being amongst the bushes. I approach'd nearer the object and found another of the English company hawling most strenuously at the bridle of his mule who would not stir one step, but bade defiance to all the powers of the whip and spur. "Sir," said I, "Shall I help you?" "It is in vain," said the poor traveller. "Some of our party are still in the rear and I must wait till they come up." "Why did not your friend stay with you?" said Mr. Rigby, "It is terrible to be left in this dark place all alone." – "O," said the young man, "that's my Lord Gillford,[92] he could not stay as he had one of the female servants with him." – A very curious reason, thought I, so near the frigid regions of Mont Blanc. The climate is a dreadful one for gallantry and the road will not allow his Lordship to gallop long. My prophecy was true, for in less than a league, we found the loving couple returning most piteously. A torrent had stopp'd their progress, and his Lordship had very considerately shrunk from the danger of fording it in the dark. He gladly courted our company, and I verily believe liked our guides much better than his mistress during the remainder of the journey.

Indeed, nothing could be altogether more gloomy than our progress for twelve miles together. We were scarcely ever out of a forest. Fatigue had closed our lips in silence and we knew that we were together only by the clatter of our feet. At ½ after 10 we saw the lights of Chamougny but our joy was damp'd by assurances that every lodging was engaged and that we had not the least hope of a bed.[93] We entered the inn and threw ourselves on the benches which surrounded the kitchen fire. I was asleep in an instant and continued so till I was awaked to eat some broth in the next room. My hunger and thirst would have made this potion a most delightful feast, had not I shiver'd with the wet and the cold. A neighbouring farmer pitied our condition and allowed us a room where I slept the remainder of the night in the straw. The Count, the Countess, and their English companions were greater sufferers than ourselves. Their mules brought them to Chamougny about one in the Morning and tho' almost dead with fatigue they were obliged to lie on chairs and on the stone floors of the inn till some of the beds became vacant by the early departure of some of the lodgers.

The fleas in the straw allow'd me but little rest, and my limbs were aching with fatigue, when we were all summon'd to rise by our Guides. The day is clear; you may wait a month and not meet with such another. The very summit of Mont Blanc is now visible. This oratory kindled new strength in our limbs and before 7 we were again on the march.[94] We ascended over rocks and along the roots of trees for 3 hours with scarcely any intermissions of rest, and when we had reach'd the height of 2000 yards above the level of the sea we commanded a full view of what they call Le Mer du Glace or the Icy Ocean.[95] To conceive of this singular appearance you must paint before your mind 10,000 billows piled one above the other by a furious storm, and while in this agitated state congealed into perfect solidity. Between each frozen billow is generally a gaping fissure, whose depth in some instances exceeds that of 500 feet. This sea extends for 30 Miles and is in most places about ½ a mile wide. The cause of so wonderful a Phaenomenon must be obvious at first sight. It exists in a deep valley, and the surrounding mountains are all bare. From their sides immense precipices of snow have fallen and fill'd the cavity where they exist in a temperature which disolves the surface in the day, and in consequence of this dissolution wears the frozen snow into its present Romantic form. A thousand cascades tumbling from the neighbouring summits wash the basis of the glacier and make it hollow. The mass at top therefore is crack'd by having no weight to support it, and thro' these cracks deluges pour off the thaw'd surface. In consequence of this accumulation of waters, a most amazing torrent gushes from the extremity of every glacier. That of Le Mer du Glace is very singular. An amazing arch of ice yawns upon the spectators. It is not less in size than the largest arch of Black Friars Bridge. From every part of the disolving concavity a perpetual shower of very large drops is perpetually falling and discovering to the observer what takes place under the whole lower surface of the glacier. The torrent which bursts forth under this arch is not less than Yarmouth River, but we were stunned by its roar and terrify'd by its rapidity.[96] I should have told you that the abundance of these waters is by no means extraordinary when we consider that on a very elevated part of this Icy Sea the Therm. rose to 52°, and that the air near the surrounding Rocks was up to 56°.

From the sight of these wonderful appearances we returned home so well pleased that we scarcely felt the fatigue of having walked 21 miles, emaciated by all the bruizes and languors of the preceding day's journey. We were in bed before 7 o'clock but were retarded in our next day's excursion by the absence of our Guides who were obliged to attend mass and a procession as it was a day sacred to some part or other of the blessed Virgin's operation. This mumery delay'd us till 12 o'clock, when we set off for the Glacier of the Boissons.[97] There the weight of the fallen snow had impell'd the ice further than the Mer du Glace into the warm air of the valley. The thaw was therefore more powerful and instead of frozen billows the fissures were such as to give the whole the appearance of congealed ruins whose turrets rose some 100s of feet into the air and whose walls and battlements were all constructed of crystal. Between those Romantic edifices the melting waters tumbled in most beautiful cascades. We heard the roar of their descent from very far below the congeal'd surface. The ice of this glacier was much more clear than that of the Mer du Glace as it protruded into the valley, and was not cover'd with the dirt and stones which the snow in its fall generally tore from the surrounding precipices.

In our departure from this Glacier we passed thro' a wood where rocks weighing thousands of tons now and then lay across our path. I observed vast trees almost crushed to atoms lying under them. To one of the largest our Guide claim'd our notice. "I saw it torn," said he, "last year from yonder precipice by a fall of snow, it bounded over an intervening cavity several yards in width and levell'd the forest in its descent. Its roar was heard like that of thunder at the distance of 4 miles." "This was the rock," said I, "or perhaps a much greater, to whose headlong downfall Homer compar'd the impetuous devastation of the greatest amongst his heroes."[98]

I cannot quit the valley of Chamougny which contains so many wonders without giving you some picture of itself. The lower parts are extremely fertile and consequently the aspect is made cheerful by the scatter'd appearance of several villages. This vale is the residence of 3000 happy beings. Every peasant is freeholder of his own farm. He pays a 20th of his produce to the King and nothing to the Priests which in a Roman Catholic country is a wonderful singularity. They owe their exemption to their having purchased the valley from a neighbouring monastery. The Guide assur'd us that they owe all their happiness to the English whose money has absolutely given a new aspect to the vale. The Government is republican or rather Aristocratic.[99] A self chosen Council and three Chief Magistrates possess all the power. Of these magistrates our Guide was next year to be one.[100]

A long day's journey on the morrow hurry'd us to bed which we quitted by two in the morning to enjoy one of the finest sights that can gratify the eyes of man.[101] The moon was in the meridian glittering like crystal. The blue vault of the heavens seem'd to have purged away all its vapours. Every star darted its effulgence with unusual brightness. Mont Blanc rais'd his white summit almost to the zenith and reflected the rays of the moon from un-number'd surfaces. The shades of his prominences were projected into all the varieties of the most fantastic forms. The ice of the glaciers dazzled the eyes, & a thousand falling cascades added theirs to the general lustre. A phalanx of surrounding mountains cover'd with snow supported the sides of Mont Blanc and here and there open'd a view into the vast heavens whose stars glitter'd on the very edge of their summits. To this scene of glory was contrasted that of the sable mountains below. They were black as death itself and from their forests they roar'd aloud with the voices of numberless cataracts, each one of which seem'd to have a tone of majesty peculiar to itself.

We walked along the vale for some leagues admiring this scene of beauty and greatness before the twilight announc'd its approach by changing the sober hue of Mont Blanc's highest summit into a gleamy white. While we were yet gazing on this early messenger of day we saw the verge of the new light descend. Its shadows mingled with those of the moon, and were as distinctly mark'd by their different colours as any amongst the various objects we beheld. The twilight was just shewing itself on the neighbouring mountains of snow when the golden summit of Mont Blanc declar'd that the sun itself was not far below the vast horizon which he surveyed. The succession was very rapid. The yellow rays of the rising day was intercepted

by other summits just as Mont Blanc began to reflect the golden light of the
sun itself, whose glories, as it mounted, were answer'd by the brightening
glories [of] this stupendous height. In a short time we beheld the blaze of a
surface perfectly white on the loftiest snows, below these a milder diffusion
of yellow splendor which spread from the glaciers to some of the highest
rocks. But still clouds far above us were in all the darkness of night, and
when we saw the meridian day crown the upper regions in the valley we
wander'd amongst objects that were still waiting the dawn.

I was attentively watching this change of delightful appearances when I
saw a bright cloud bursting from one of the snowy precipices. It descended
with vast fragments of ice and rock. Our Guides shouted, and desir'd us to
mark what followed. In a few moments our ears were assail'd by a roar to
which that of thunder is trifling. This was one of those falls from the sides
of the mountains which form the Glaciers. We have but one thing now,
said I, to wish for and this scene of sublimity would be compleated. Let
Mont Blanc open wide his jaws and disclose the horrors of his entrails. Let
him belch forth a torrent of fire and whirl into the air his concealed stores
of combustible matter. Let a destroying lava dissipate the snow and combined
torrents of liquid fire & ice pour into the valley. Let the surrounding rocks
shake and totter and the ground below us undulate. Add a Volcano to our
views, and we shall then see what the world's greatest sublimities cannot
surpass.

I was thus finishing the picture I wished to gaze upon, when I was awaked
from the dreams of imagination by the danger of one of our mules, who
had tumbled from one of the wooden bridges into a foaming torrent, whose
fury bore down the poor animal.[102] The skill of the muleteer saved him. I
had now walk'd 9 miles, and I found that I had still a league to ascend before
we breakfasted. We had left the common road and for the sake of seeing
the country preferr'd a more arduous one over the mountains.[103] At length
we reached a wretched collection of huts on a summit a mile high. On the
dewy grass we devour'd the bread and milk and cheese which they placed
before us;[104] we soon proceeded on our ascent and with much panting,
reach'd a summit a mile and a half high. Here we took breath, and admired
the possible perturbations of Nature. The heavens and the mountains seem'd
to be blended in the same confusion. We saw nothing but stupendous
hollows, distorted precipices, unbounded regions of ice & snow, and piles
of clouds which appear'd as much below the mountains in some places as
they were below the heavens in others. Our contemplation & rest on the
highest elevation of our lives was succeeded by a tedious descent into a
distant valley. – But I begin to suspect that the length of my journey must
weigh your eyelids down. I will therefore defer the continuation of my rout

to Lausanne where I now am, till I have reach'd Basle. You see I am returning fast homewards. My journey is shortening daily. It has cost me a deal of trouble, but it has rewarded me with a world of new ideas.

THE END

Summary of contents[105]

Letter I: Lisle, July 5, 1789
Calais, walls, children, soldiers, street shrine, temperance, swarming villages, famine.

Letter II: Paris, July 9, 1789
Lisle – "Slavery, mummery and folly", Sunday. Church service. Soldiers hearing mass. Sunday afternoon.
Douai – University. Fenelon's monument. Ninety miles of cultivation. A French village. Prince of Condé's forest, park, stable, palace, &c.

Letter III: Paris, July 13, 1789
At Versailles. Paris mob night of July 13. "No play" at theatre. "Aux armes." Barriers in flames. Mob hunting for guns.

Letter IV: Dijon, July 21, 1789
Approach to Paris. Paris barrier. Lodgings. Palais Royal. Scene, the ladies & gentlemen &c. Architecture, Numedee Gazon at theatre playing Blue Beard!
Versailles – National Assembly, Gallery, King and Queen. Turned back by mob.

Letter V: Lyons, July 24, 1789
Forest of Fontainebleau. Land of vineyards; every hill top cultivated. Villages, people, more than ever. Banks of the Seine. Joigny – Telling the story to the people. Aux[err] – Hill country. Dijon – Citizens in arms. Boys and girls' dress. Bugs and fleas.

Letter VI: Marseilles, July 29, 1789
First sight of the Alps. Tracer cut by mob. Chalons. The river Soane. Wheel on fire. Macon – Approach to Lyons. Mt. Blanc: Lyons – its wonderful site and smells and river Rhone and antiquities. Theatre. The merchants' country seat.

Letter VII: Nice, Aug. 2, 1789
Fleas and bugs. Lofty Lyons houses. Outdoor life. The burnt barrier. By boat down the Rhone, – swift! Vienne – The grave digger. "Toujours le tiers Etat!" Wild mountains and old castles. Pont St Esprit. Avignon and its antiquities, and noise. Olive trees blasted. Pont du Garde. Nismes. Aix. 4,000 Marseillese releasing prisoners. The Mediterranean! View of Marseilles.

14,000 citizens enrolled. The released prisoners carried in triumph. Romantic, rough road to Toulon. That city. [F]rejus. The Governor after news. At Antibes. Nice.

Letter VIII: [V]evey, Aug. 17, 1789
Geneva and its Lake. The judges' seat, trinkets, ladies. Prince Edward of England. To the Glaciers. The crowded inn at Bonneville. The night-walk to Chamougny through the storm. Mer de Glace. Glacier of the Boissons. Rock-falls. People of Chamougny Valley. Mt. Blanc by moonlight and sunrise. An avalanche. Now for a volcano. The mountain chalet.

Notes

[1]   In late June and early July 1789, during the stand-off between the Estates General, the new National Assembly and the Palace, and in response to increasing popular unrest, Louis began calling in troops from northern frontier towns and further afield. The movement of soldiers into the Paris area – some 30,000 soldiers encamped around the Ile de France by the 12th, many of them foreign mercenaries – was seen as confirmation of an 'aristocratic plot', and, by putting further pressure on food supplies, proved a major factor in the unrest which would boil over into action on the night of 12 July. See Godechot, *The Taking of the Bastille*, pp. 169–78, and especially 179–87 on troop build-up; Samuel F. Scott, *The Response of the Royal Army to the French Revolution: The Role and Development of the Line Army* (Oxford, 1978), pp. 51–3.

[2]   At least one letter is missing from the beginning of the journey; it may never have arrived, or GCM may have decided to leave it out of his fair copy. Details of this part of their journey can be found in 'Rigby Letters', Letter 1, 2–3 July 1789, which includes the interesting vignette of a moonlit walk along the beach and 'Morgan's admirable remarks on the formation of the earth, the changes which this globe has undergone, the constant fluctuation of the sea, and such other subjects'. Paul Frame is currently exploring the significance of these remarks for the history of geology.

[3]   Calais, first stop for many on the Grand Tour, was thoroughly geared towards tourists from Britain; see Black, *The British Abroad*, pp. 16–17. Several British writers passed through it. A year after GCM, the student Wordsworth 'chanced to land' there 'on the very eve of that great federal day', the first anniversary of the fall of the Bastille (William Wordsworth, *The Prelude* (1805), Book 6, lines 345–6). In 1792 Thomas Paine was elected to the National Convention as member for the Pas-de-Calais; see Moncure D. Conway, *The Life of Thomas Paine* (2 vols., New York, 1892), I, pp. 347–50. According to Boddington and Rigby, our travellers stayed at the Lion d'Argent, Rue Neuf.

[4]   By the eighteenth century, under the influence of Locke, swaddling was much less common in Britain; for the constant comparisons made by travellers on the

relative informality and comfort of English styles compared with the Continent, see Aileen Ribeiro, *Dress in Eighteenth-Century Europe 1715–1789* (London, 1984), pp. 160–2.

[5] This is, inevitably, a leitmotiv in many British travel journals. See Black, *The British Abroad*, pp. 261–76. GCM's attitude to Catholicism is discussed on p. 22.

[6] Sarah Price Morgan, GCM's eldest child and only daughter, was aged five or six at the time of writing; see pp. 143–5 and 184–5 for more details of her life.

[7] Pudding cart: a cart for offal or refuse.

[8] GCM's constant references to the apparent fertility of the land and its people are discussed on p. 10.

[9] The terrible harvest of 1788, exacerbated by severe hailstorms in the Paris region, meant that bread prices soared throughout 1789: by mid-July the cost of bread and grain had reached their highest point since 1715 and hunger was a major factor in the country's political unrest (Doyle, *Oxford History*, p. 86; Godechot, *The Taking of the Bastille*, pp. 119–23). Cf. Rigby: 'We were told at Calais that there is now a very great scarcity of Corn in France, & we found this confirmed here, not by our finding any scarcity of [? –] &c. but by the Information of those around – to behold the Face of the country one would suppose that a scarcity could never take place here – but when we came into the Towns, the crowds of People are so immense, that a prodigious quantity $^{of\,corn}$ must be consumed' ('Rigby Letters', Letter 3, 5 July 1789).

[10] The modern spelling is Lille; the town was noted for its textile industry, and its marked Catholicism.

[11] For Ollyett Woodhouse and Samuel Boddington, both in their early twenties, see p. 9.

[12] British astonishment at the informality of mass extended to Versailles itself, where several commentators note the king chatting and laughing through the service; see John Lough, *France on the Eve of Revolution: British Travellers' Observations 1763–1788* (Chicago, 1987), pp. 273–4.

[13] Douai University, founded in 1559, was home to many British Catholics during the Reformation, including prominent Welshmen Richard Gwyn (who was martyred) and Owen Lewis (1533–95; bishop of Cassano in Italy); it closed in 1795 and the university was transferred to Lille. See further Bernard Ward, 'Douai', *The Catholic Encyclopedia, Vol. 5* (New York, 1909), at *http://www.newadvent.org/cathen/05138a.htm*.

[14] Our travellers here met up with 'Master Pitchford', the son of John Pitchford, a radical and Catholic Norwich friend of the Rigbys: 'Tell Mrs Pitchford,' writes Rigby, 'that Mast P. looks very well & I think him a very sweet Boy' ('Rigby Letters', Letter 4, 6 July 1789). John Pitchford appears several times in Godwin's diary: he is present with Rigby at a dinner on 29 June 1794, where they 'talk of the punishment of kings'. See Myers, O'Shaughnessy and Philp (eds.), *The Diary of William Godwin*. Pitchford is also mentioned in C. B. Jewson, *The Jacobin City: A Portrait of Norwich in its Reaction to the French Revolution 1788–1802* (Glasgow, 1975), pp. 54, 59, 116.

15   The principal of the English College from 1781 to 1790 was William Gibson, 'a
      very polite and sensible man' ('Rigby Journal', p. 11ʳ). The establishment did
      not survive the Revolution, and the author of a 'Tour in France in 1818', notes
      that the 'English College . . . is now converted into a cotton manufactory': *The
      Gentleman's Magazine*, XC (January–June 1820), 295.

16   The theologian François de Salignac de la Mothe-Fénelon (1651–1715), archbishop
      of Cambrai, was employed as tutor to the grandson of Louis XIV. He fell from
      the king's favour with the publication of his utopian *Les Aventures de Télémaque*
      (1699), written for his royal charge, but critical of the divine right of monarchy.
      The work influenced many who went on to play a part in events in Revolutionary
      France; Fénelon is cited by Richard Price in his *Discourse on the Love of Our Country*
      (London, 1789) as one of those great thinkers who 'sowed a seed which has since
      taken root, and is now growing up to a glorious harvest' (*Discourse*, p. 16). See Antoine
      Dégert, 'François de Salignac de la Mothe-Fénelon', *The Catholic Encyclopedia*,
      Vol. 6 (New York, 1909), at *http://www.newadvent.org/cathen/06035a.htm*.

17   The tomb in Cambrai was destroyed, along with the cathedral itself, in 1793; the
      English tourists of the 1818 'Tour' went to quite a lot of trouble to find out what
      had become of it (Anon., 'Tour in France in 1818', 295).

18   This is probably Pont-Sainte-Maxence, noted in Rigby's 'Journal' (p. 114ʳ), and
      mentioned as a stopping point before Chantilly by Thomas Nugent, *The Grand
      Tour* (4 vols., London, 1749), IV, p. 353.

19   At the time of the group's visit the occupant of the Condé estate was Louis-Joseph
      de Bourbon, cousin to Louis XVI; he fled France with his family in 1789 and
      helped organize a counter-Revolutionary army at Coblenz. He was responsible
      for the construction of a guest chateau in the grounds at Chantilly, and for the
      fashionable 'English' gardens which left our tourists less than impressed; see the
      picture by Jean-Baptiste Lallement, *Le chateau de Chantilly au XVIIIe siècle, après
      les travaux effectués par les Condés* (Musée Condé).

20   This theme is developed at some length in Morgan's *Address to the Jacobine Societies*;
      see pp. 93 and 109. During the summer of 1789 some peasant communities did
      in fact attempt to reclaim local hunting grounds from their aristocratic owners,
      those of Chantilly included; see Godechot, *The Taking of the Bastille*, p. 131.

21   *jets d'eaux*, water fountains.

22   Rigby found the fountains 'unnatural & very ill placed' and the gardens 'laid out
      in a very bad Taste' ('Rigby Letters', Letter 6, 8 July 1789); Boddington refers to
      the 'savage despotism of the shears' and found 'the formal disposition of the Jet
      d'Eaus without any apparent utility . . . all very disgusting' ('Boddington Letters',
      Letter 3, 8 July 1789). For other British reactions to the magnificence of Chantilly,
      see Black, *The British Abroad*, pp. 18–20.

23   Jacques-Christophe Valmont de Bomare (1731–1807), naturalist and mineralogist.
      His *Dictionnaire raisonné d'histoire naturelle* (1764) went through many augmented
      editions and was translated into most European languages. See Boddington's
      account of their encounter on p. 10.

24   These lost letters to Richard Price are of crucial importance for the perception of
      the events of the Revolution in Britain; see the discussion on pp. 11–12.

25 For a detailed discussion of this letter see pp. 15–16 and 28–9.

26 The Genevan-born Jacques Necker (1732–1804) was Louis XVI's director general of finance from 1776. He became generally popular for measures which included poll-tax reform and advocating the use of loans and higher interest rates rather than direct taxation to finance the national debt. He was responsible for the first ever public account of royal finances, the *Compte rendu au Roi* (1781), which though flawed in its figures, encouraged people to consider governmental income and expenditure as their direct concern. With many enemies at court, he was made a scapegoat during the deepening financial and political crisis of 1789, dismissed and reinstated by popular demand in June; his second dismissal on 11 July was, as is clear from this text, a contributory factor in sparking the revolt in Paris. Doyle, *Oxford History*, pp. 108–9; Schama, *Citizens*, pp. 317–18; Godechot, *The Taking of the Bastille*, pp. 184–8, and the Necker-related bibliography, ibid., p. 336.

27 This was probably the Théâtre Français du Fauborg St Germain ('went to the Theatre Francaise – no Exhibition', 'Rigby Journal', p. 23'). The play not performed that night would have been Corneille's *Le Cid* or Poisson's *Le Procureur arbitre*; see the online database of plays performed during the Revolution at *http://cesar.org.uk*. Now the site of the Odéon, the building was completed in 1782 to house the Comédie-française. In 1784 Beaumarchais's controversial *The Marriage of Figaro* was performed there; later in 1789, after a political split amongst the actors, the Théâtre de la République was established in the Rue de Richelieu. See Schama, *Citizens*, pp. 118–23.

28 For the 'people at the door of the theatre' see p. 13, and Farge, *Un épisode de la journée du 12 juillet*, pp. 21–6.

29 Between 1781 and 1784 the Palais-Royal was completely redesigned by Louis-Philippe II d'Orleans, who would become known as 'Philippe Egalité' for his espousal of republicanism under the Revolutionary regime (he would sign his cousin's execution warrant); see Tom Ambrose, *Godfather of the Revolution: The Life of Philippe Egalité Duc d'Orleans* (London, 2007). For the atmosphere of the Palais, see Mercier, *Tableau de Paris*, I, pp. 257–60; Isherwood, *Farce and Fantasy*, pp. 217–50. For the mood on the 12th, see Schama, *Citizens*, pp. 314–18.

30 'About seven last night an alarm was spread that some soldiers had attacked a party of citizens. This was unfortunately believed . . . ' ('Rigby Letters', Letter 7, 13 July 1789). See discussion on pp. 14–15.

31 Le Grand Hôtel du Palais Royal is still *in situ*, 4 Rue de Valois.

32 The *barrières* or tollgates were a recent development in the city, having been completed in 1787–8. They were widely hated as the mechanism by which government controlled the price of flour and grain. According to George Rudé, 'forty of the fifty-four customs posts were destroyed by fire in the course of four days' rioting', idem, *The Crowd in the French Revolution* (Oxford, 1959), p. 49.

33 For rumours of massacres of citizens by royal troops, see Spagnoli, 'The Revolution Begins', and pp. 15–16 .

34 For the raiding of gunsmiths on the night of 12–13 July, see Rudé, *The Crowd*, pp. 48–9.

[35] The *Garde française* or National Guard that formed during these first days of revolt was by now composed of soldiers who had refused to fight against the people, but defection was a huge problem even in the regiments supposed to be loyal to the king. In the end, it appears that the officers' lack of faith in the reliability of their men led to the general retreat during the night of the 12th–13th, leaving the streets to the rebels, large numbers of soldiers amongst them; see Scott, *The Response of the Royal Army*, pp. 59–60; and Clifford, 'The National Guard'.

[36] These letters are now lost; see p. 11.

[37] A buggy was a light vehicle for one or two people, usually two-wheeled, with one horse; a phaeton was a light four-wheeled open carriage usually pulled by a pair of horses. Arthur Young was equally baffled by the relative scarcity of vehicles close to the city gates: Young, *Travels*, p. 8. See also Lough, *France on the Eve of Revolution*, pp. 20–2.

[38] See p. 81 n. 32 .

[39] A hackney coach was larger, with two horses and seating for six, usually for hire.

[40] For the costs of accommodation and travel, see Black, *The British Abroad*, pp. 83–110.

[41] See p. 14.

[42] Louise-Rosalie Lefèbvre (1755–1821), Madame Dugazon, was a mezzo-soprano and star of the Comédie Italienne.

[43] *Raoul Barbe-Bleue*, by Sedaine and Grétry, played at the Théâtre Italien (salle Favart) on 9 July 1789 (*http://cesar.org.uk/cesar2/index.php*).

[44] 'Saturday Morning went to Versailles – was in the Salle des Etats – a glorious Sight – every one admitted – Heard Mirabeau, Target, Fayette & Lailly – Marquis de Fayette moved for a Bill of Rights – Lailly supported it both spoke in a very animated manner' ('Rigby Journal', p. 23ᵛ). The National Assembly had reconstituted itself a mere two days earlier as the National Constituent Assembly; for its dramatic evolution from the original *Tiers état* (Third Estate, or Commons) of the Estates General of 5 May into a representative legislative body, see the account in Doyle, *Oxford History*, pp. 86–111.

[45] Morgan speaks of 'one attempt to leave', but a lengthy and dramatic account of their various attempts to get past the *barrières* can be found in *Rigby-Eastlake*, pp. 71–84 (although not, unfortunately, in the surviving manuscripts).

[46] The royal palace at Fontainebleau was developed by the French monarchy from the twelfth century, but had, as GCM's description suggests, fallen into some neglect. Most of its assets were sold off during the Revolutionary period until Napoleon I revived it for his own use. The palace and park are now a UNESCO World Heritage Site.

[47] J. M. W. Turner would sketch this view as 'Joigny from the Yonne' in 1802: see his 'France, Savoy, Piedmont Sketchbook' at *http://www.tate.org.uk*.

[48] Cockades indicating political allegiance (rosettes or ribbons, usually pinned to a hat) were widespread after the fall of the Bastille. The very earliest Revolutionary cockades, from the first moments of protest at the Palais Royal, were green (on the suggestion of Camille Desmoulins, to symbolize hope: see Farge, *Un épisode de la journée du 12 juillet*, pp. 12–13, and note Rigby: 'The Bourgeois wore green

Cockades – it was wonderful with what Stillness their Meeting was conducted – & how soon afterwards so many thousand green Cockades appeared' ('Rigby Journal', p. 27ᵛ)). Very rapidly, however, blue and red (the colours of Paris), with the later addition of the king's white, became the norm. See Doyle, *Oxford History*, p. 112.

49 It was quite a trek: 'We did not reach Auxerre till 11 at night it is 107 miles from Paris we were 17 hours upon the road 16 of which were passed in the carriage' ('Boddington Letters', Letter 7, 21 July 1789).

50 Morgan is wrong about the river; Auxerre lies on the Yonne, which divides from the Seine several miles further north. The travellers stayed at 'Les Trois Couronnes' and sampled the local Burgundy ('Rigby Journal', pp. 46ʳ⁻ᵛ).

51 The Benedictine abbey of Saint-Germain dates from the ninth century and (although they were undiscovered at the time) houses some very early Carolingian murals; the Gothic cathedral of Saint-Etienne was largely constructed between 1215 and 1233 over an eleventh-century Romanesque crypt. See Kenneth John Conant, *Carolingian and Romanesque Architecture 800–1200* (3rd edn., Harmondsworth, 1973), pp. 27–8.

52 See Baker, 'The French Revolution as Local Experience'.

53 'I never saw any thing of this Kind so very pleasing'. For a fascinating description of the hospital at Dijon, see 'Rigby Letters', Letter 11, Friday 24 July 1789; 'Rigby Journal', pp. 49–52.

54 George Cadogan, junior was the second of the Morgan children.

55 A bagwig is a wig with the back hair encased in a small silk bag. For children dressed as little adults, see Ribeiro, *Dress in Eighteenth Century Europe*, pp. 160–2.

56 As Samuel Boddington would write from the English-themed 'Hôtel du York' in Nice, 'Mr Morgan in particular has recruited himself here as the French ragouts have not suited him at all & he has been most terribly molested by the vermin' ('Boddington Letters', Letter 11, 2 August 1789). See the chapter on 'Food and Drink' in Black, *The British Abroad*, pp. 149–65.

57 'I last night was attack'd by a new ennemy fleas of enormous size they have used me most cruelly & they are such an active foe that there is no escaping from them' ('Boddington Letters', Letter 8, 24 July 1789). Cited in Black, *The British Abroad*, p. 146.

58 This is a typical episode for the period known as the 'Great Fear' (la Grande Peur), which swept the country in three weeks in July and August. See Lefebvre, *La Grande Peur*; Timothy Tackett, 'La Grande Peur et le complot aristocratique sous la Révolution française', *Annales historiques de la Révolution française*, 335 (Janvier–Mars 2004), 1–17; and p. 21.

59 The little town was St Albin, where they arrived 'hot, dusty and cross, and were set down to rest our weary limbs when Scheilds came with a grave face to inform us that the blacksmith had done his utmost and was now "au desespoir"'. Finally, 'Mr Morgan and myself attended the Blacksmith for the first time turned Coachmaker and by our skill and his labour we got out of our difficulties much better than expected.' Boddington's detailed and highly entertaining account of the whole episode ('Boddington Letters', Letter 8, 24 July 1789) is cited at length in

Black, *The British Abroad*, pp. 184–5. Coach mishaps form an inevitable sub-genre within travellers' narratives at this period.

[60] This is Mâcon, Saône et Loire.

[61] Lyons was the second largest city in France, and famous for its manufacture of silk; by the late 1780s war, changes in fashion and the general economic crisis had crippled the industry, causing high unemployment and extreme poverty. Unlike in Dijon and Paris, however, the social composition of the town, and in particular the presence of a class of hugely powerful merchants, meant that the events of July 1789 did not initially give much of a voice to the very poorest. The fortnight before the arrival of GCM and his companions had seen popular rioting and the burning of the customs houses, as in Paris, but this was swiftly followed by the summoning of royal troops and the restoration of order: 'in both Paris and Lyon the events of early July led to the formation of militias to defend bourgeois interests, but while in Paris it was, in the first instance, to defend them against the court, in Lyon it was to defend them against the people' (Edmonds, *Jacobinism and the Revolt of Lyon*, p. 44).

[62] The tall houses were characteristic of the silk-weaving industry, whose workers needed light; for their conditions, see Edmonds, *Jacobinism and the Revolt of Lyon*, pp. 10–15; D. Longfellow, 'Silk Weavers and the Social Struggle in Lyon during the French Revolution 1789–1794', *French Historical Studies*, 12 (1981), 1–40. The particular problems facing the female workers (Morgan's 'dirty individuals of your sex') are discussed in Daryl Hafter, 'Women in the Underground Business of Eighteenth Century Lyon', *Enterprise and Society*, 2 (March 2001), 11–40.

[63] This jokingly refers to the theories of Aristotle and to other beliefs held from antiquity through the middle ages, that putrefied matter mixed with rain water could generate new life; see Eugene S. McCartney, 'Spontaneous Generation and Kindred Notions in Antiquity', *Transactions of the American Philological Association*, 51 (1920), 101–15.

[64] GCM may have in mind the comments of Strabo in Book Four of the *Geography*, 'The navigation of the Rhone being difficult on account of the rapidity of its current, the merchants prefer to transport in waggons certain of their wares, which are destined for the Arverni, and the river Loire, notwithstanding the vicinity of the Rhone in some places' (trans. H. C. Hamilton and W. Falconer (London, 1854), p. 281).

[65] This presumably refers to the Christian Martyrs of Lyons, whose massacre under Marcus Aurelius in AD 177 is recorded in Eusebius's *Ecclesiastical History*. The number of dead ominously prefigures those killed in the Terrorist reprisals after the siege of Lyons in October 1793. See Edmonds, *Jacobinism and the Revolt of Lyon*, p. 280; Paul Mansfield, 'The Repression of Lyon, 1793–4: Origins, Responsibility and Significance', *French History*, 2, no. 1 (1988), 74–101.

[66] Mr Rey was one of Boddington's contacts, and helped the group negotiate the next stage of their journey, by boat down the Rhône. He and his brothers had 'lately purchased about 100 Acres of Land' a mile or so out into the country; their country house in its extensive grounds, shared with his mother and 'three or four' sisters, receives admiring comments from everyone, and Morgan is not the only

one to fantasize about settling in the area: 'Rigby Journal', pp. 67–9; 'Boddington Letters', Letter 9, 29 July 1789.

[67] The word is written clearly as 'prion' but I have been unable to trace its use elsewhere.

[68] This perception may not be entirely accurate; see p. 84 n. 61.

[69] These boats ('neither handsome nor commodious', notes Boddington) were equipped to take both travellers and their carriages; for Boddington's description of the journey, and for the experiences of other travellers on the same stretch of water, see Black, *The British Abroad*, pp. 123–4.

[70] This odd episode is explained more fully by Rigby. They were reading an inscription on 'a Monument just erected to the Memory of an young Englishman who died about a year ago' – the journal names him as 'Dr Stark a Scottish Physician aged 24' ('Rigby Journal', p. 70) – when his friend appeared and explained that, not being a Catholic, Stark had been buried in unconsecrated ground. His friend had applied 'for leave to have a piece of ground consecrated and appropriated to the Interrment of Strangers who should die professing a foreign religion', and was planning on reburying the body that evening ('Rigby Letters', Letter 13, 27 July 1789).

[71] This stop was Tain-l'Hermitage, on the eastern bank of the Rhone: 'arrived at 9 – situated most romantically at the Foot the Hermitage Mountain which produces the celebrated Wine of that Name – on the opposite shore is another large Town, Tournon, the Wine on that side not so good' ('Rigby Journal', p. 73ʳ).

[72] The Pont Saint Esprit was commissioned by the Abbey of Cluny, and begun in 1265. See Marjorie Nice Boyer, *Medieval French Bridges: A History*, Publications of the Medieval Academy of America, 84 (Cambridge, 1976), pp. 126–7.

[73] Avignon was a papal possession from 1348 (and the seat of seven popes during the fourteenth century) until 1791, when it was reincorporated into France. See Martin Garrett, *Provence: A Cultural History* (Oxford, 2006).

[74] The cicada.

[75] The devastation of the olive groves was one of the many effects of the appalling weather conditions in 1788. See Doyle, *Oxford History*, p. 86.

[76] Morgan may have in the mind here the exuberant passage from Rousseau's *Confessions*: 'The reverberation of my steps on these immense vaults made me believe I heard the strong voices of those who had built them. I lost myself like an insect in that immensity. While making myself small, I felt an indefinable something that raised up my soul, and said to myself while sighing, "Why was I not born a Roman!"', *The Confessions and Correspondence, including the Letters to Malesherbes*, trans. Christopher Kelly, ed. by Christopher Kelly, Roger D. Masters and Peter G. Stillman (1995; paperback edn., Hanover, 1998), p. 214.

[77] See p. 37 n. 69.

[78] This is most likely a reference to Ann Yearsley (the 'Bristol Milkwoman'), whose *Poems, on Several Occasions* came out in 1785 under the auspices of Elizabeth Montagu and Hannah More.

[79] The population of Toulon was largely royalist, and in the summer of 1793 surrendered the port to a multi-national taskforce led by the British under Lord

Hood. They were repulsed some months later by the young commander Napoleon Bonaparte. See Malcolm Crook, *Toulon in War and Revolution: From the Ancien Regime to the Restoration, 1750–1820* (Manchester, 1991). Rigby comments on the difference in mood here: 'This City being inhabited principally by Officers & others holding Places under the King, did not exhibit so many of the outward Signs of Patriotism as all the other Places we had passed through; . . . at Toulon there were no Cockades to be seen, no Acclamations to be heard' ('Rigby Letters', Letter 18, 2 August 1789).

[80]   The group stay at Nice, which was then part of the kingdom of Sardinia.

[81]   They were already booked to take a sea trip around the bay, where the 'Sea was beautifully blue – and not rough' – although 'it heaved a great deal – Mr M. was sick' ('Rigby Journal', p. 92ᵛ).

[82]   There is most probably a letter missing here, as the manuscript has no account of the journey from the Mediterranean coast through the mountains to Turin, and from thence (with their carriage disassembled and carried by mule) over Mount Cenis to Geneva, described in detail in letters by both Rigby and Boddington.

[83]   Rigby was equally distraught: 'I really scarcely know how to bear the Disappointment – a thousand painful Reflections crowd into my Mind, the Possibility of what may have happened in five Weeks to those I so much love makes me almost tremble' ('Rigby Letters', Letter 21, Geneva, 11 August 1789).

[84]   The Republic and Canton of Geneva is part of the Swiss Confederacy, and was established in 1541.

[85]   Caesar defeated the largest tribal group, the Helvetii, in Geneva in 58 BC.

[86]   Rigby says he is 'a Barber, & his Time is much devoted to his Business, but notwithstanding this, we found when we breakfasted with him, that he had not neglected the Improvement of his Mind' ('Rigby Letters', Letter 23, Vevey, 17 August 1789).

[87]   Boddington relays further anecdotes about the prince's bad behaviour: see Black, 'On the Grand Tour', p. 351.

[88]   Boust is a town in the Moselle, north eastern France.

[89]   From Rigby's account they appear to have stopped at Sallanches, which is about 18 miles from Chamonix. For the rapid growth of tourism and scientific discovery at this period, see G. R. de Beer, *Early Travellers in the Alps* (London, 1930); *idem, Alps and Men: Pages from Forgotten Diaries of Travellers and Tourists in Switzerland* (London, 1932). Richard Bevis has a section on various literary responses to the Chamonix region in *The Road to Egdon Heath: The Aesthetics of the Great in Nature* (Montreal, 1999), pp. 151–4.

[90]   The Carthaginian general Hannibal famously crossed the Alps with an army that included trained war elephants in 218 BC on his way to invade Rome.

[91]   Cf. Boddington's earlier reference to this injury: 'My Ancle has been much less trouble than I expected it gets stronger daily & I hope will be quite well before I return' ('Boddington Letters', Letter 8, Lyons, 24 July 1789).

[92]   This character has not been positively identified but may perhaps have been one of the Clanwilliams of County Down, some of whom took the title Lord Gillford;

or (following the spelling given by Boddington) one of the three sons (all of them born between 1757 and 1766) of Francis North, second earl of Guilford, who was prime minister between 1770 and 1782.

[93]   For the growing popularity of Chamonix as an Alpine centre see de Beer, *Alps and Men*, pp. 27–31.

[94]   They were not the only early risers: 'We set off with two Guides & each of us a long Staff like so many Foresters; as there were many others besides ourselves going the same Journey, making in all more than forty Persons, you would have thought it a pleasant sight to have seen us marching along' ('Rigby Letters', Letter 23, Vevey, 17 August 1789).

[95]   The name (correctly, La Mer de Glace) may have originated with William Windham, who visited in 1744: 'The description which travellers give of the seas in Greenland seems to come the nearest to it. You must imagine your lake put in agitation by a strong wind, and frozen all at once, perhaps even that would not produce the same appearance.' See de Beer, *Early Travellers*, p. 107. J. M. W. Turner's journey through Switzerland in 1802 resulted in some extraordinary sketches and paintings of this landscape – see, for example, the 1812 print 'Mer de Glace' at *http://beta. tate.org.uk/art/work/A01011*, and the 1802 St Gothard and Mont Blanc sketchbook at *http://beta.tate.org.uk/art/sketchbook/65724?pg=1*. For a richly illustrated account of the tour itself, see David Hill, *Turner in the Alps* (London, 1992).

[96]   By 1857 the Arveyron no longer burst forth under an 'amazing arch', but issued 'laterally from the glacier at the summit of the rocks called *Les Motets*': John Tyndall, *The Glaciers of the Alps, being a Narrative of Excursions and Ascents, an Account of the Origin and Phenomena of Glaciers, and an Exposition of the Physical Principles to which they are related* (London, 1860), p. 38.

[97]   The Glacier des Bossons is just south of Chamonix. The 1838 guidebook promises 'immense blocks broken or melted into fantastic forms, and so impending, that they excite a shudder': *A Hand-Book for Travellers in Switzerland and the Alps of Savoy and Piedmont*, John Murray editions (London, 1838), p. 291.

[98]   Book Thirteen of the *Iliad* contains the following description: 'The Trojans came on in a mass, with Hector in the van sweeping forward like a boulder bounding down a rocky slope, when a river swollen by winter rain has washed its supports away and thrust the misbegotten thing over the brow of the hill. Leaping high in the air it hurtles down through echoing woods and then runs on unchecked till it reaches level ground, where it stops rolling, much against its will' (Homer, *The Iliad*, trans. E. V. Rieu (London, 1963), pp. 237–8).

[99]   This sentence reads oddly now, but prior to the French Revolution the term 'aristocratic', meaning 'government of a state by its best citizens', was often used to express a type of republican government, and regularly contrasted with 'monarchial' (see *OED*). Thus, when referring in these letters to the upper classes, Morgan consistently uses the term 'Noblesse'. By his *Address* of 1792, however, he is moving towards a more modern usage: 'The vast Circumference of your Aristocratical Domains, what are they but the ample Measure of Monarchial Profusion, squandering upon its Creatures the Property of the People?' I am grateful to Mark Philp for his thoughts on this subject.

[100] This may have been one M. Simond, 'a very intelligent Man, who was not only our Guide to the Glaciers, but attended us over the Mountains to Biex' ('Rigby Letters', Letter 24, Lausanne, 17 August 1789).

[101] It is clear that 'Mont-Blanc by sunrise' was already part of the Alpine tourist experience, and there are many descriptions of its spectacular effects. One of the best known is Coleridge's 'Hymn, before Sun-Rise, in the Vale of Chamouni' (1802), which is based on a German poem by Friederike Brun. Coleridge was never in Chamonix, but his poem became itself part of the 'experience', cited approvingly by travellers *in situ* (e.g. Tyndall, *The Glaciers of the Alps*, p. 39).

[102] Rigby, who rides one of the mules in the early stages of this journey, does not mention this incident, but marvels instead 'with what Care & apparent discernment those Creatures pick their Way' ('Rigby Letters', Letter 24, Lausanne, 24 August 1789).

[103] The nine-hour journey on foot between Chamonix and Martigny via the Col de Balme provides a superb panoramic view of Mont Blanc flanked by other mountains: 'at the summit one of the finest scenes in the world bursts upon the traveller': *A Hand-Book for Travellers in Switzerland*, pp. 301–2.

[104] Rigby explains in more depth how the inhabitants of these 'hovels' made a living: 'It is the Business of these People to tend the Cattle, to milk them & to convert the Milk into Cheeses, for which they are paid by the Owners so much per Head. Our faithful Guide, M. Simond, had three Cows here, so that through his Means, we got some very good Milk, which with Bread & Cheese we brought from Chamouny, afforded us a very good Breakfast' ('Rigby Letters', Letter 24, Lausanne, 17 August 1789).

[105] This text follows on from the final letter in the manuscript.

George Cadogan Morgan
Address to the
Jacobine Societies (1792)

Introduction

In late summer or early autumn 1792 an anonymous pamphlet was printed, addressed to the 'Jacobine and other Patriotic Societies of the French'. It bears no mark of a place of publication or of a publisher, and its author styles himself simply 'a Native of England and a Citizen of the World', but there are good grounds for thinking, with D. O. Thomas, that it is the work of George Cadogan Morgan.[1] There are some clues in the body of the work itself, most notably a familiar obsession with the barrenness of land sacrificed to the pleasures of royal hunting, and the claim to have been an early eye-witness to the 1789 uprising: 'I was at Paris during the first Moment of your Revolution – I saw you burst from your Chains'. A rare copy of the pamphlet held at the National Library of Wales strengthens the case for authorship. It was bound at some point after 1798 together with the obituary of Morgan which appeared in *The Monthly Magazine* in that year; and the obituary itself refers to his authorship of 'a pamphlet, abounding with profound remarks and powerful eloquence', which set out to:

> explore the conduct of the French legislators, and to direct the attention of the people of France to those principles, on which alone he conceived that they could establish a permanent system of rational liberty. This pamphlet, as it had no reference to England, was not published in this country, but it obtained extensive circulation in France.[2]

The National Library of Wales copy bears a label with the name 'John Ashburner': this is almost certainly the son of William Ashburner who, with his siblings William and Mary, became part of the Morgans' extended family in the 1790s.[3]

The pamphlet was written in the second half of August 1792. An 'Advertisement' explains that it was a response to the motion put before the National Assembly on 11 August, the day after the invasion of the Tuileries and the suspension of the king, 'that a Governor to the *Prince Royal* be appointed'.

Concerned that this proposal indicated a strengthening of feeling in favour of the monarchy, Morgan composed his diatribe almost at once, as various references within the text (the advance of the Duke of Brunswick, for example) make clear. It is not clear how long it took to get it printed, and once again the rapidity of Revolutionary time complicates our reading of the text: by the admission of the Advertisement (added, one presumes, shortly before printing) the pro-monarchy faction has not in fact been successful, and the urgency of the moment of writing already requires an explanation, a context. Nor is it possible to tell from the laconic phrase: 'subsequent Events, have seemingly proved, that his Apprehensions were wrong' whether 'Subsequent events' include the September massacres and the battle of Valmy, or even (though this is perhaps less likely) the decision on 3 December to put the imprisoned monarch on trial. In any case, this furious tirade urging the immediate extirpation of 'the most destroying Pestilence that ever desolated the Universe' must have read rather differently after the execution of the king on 21 January 1793.

Morgan's *Address*, divided into ten brief chapters, is a detailed exploration of the evils of monarchy. An energetic, overblown piece, it revels in the rhetoric of the genre, outdoing even the 'uncharacteristic flamboyancy' of the congratulatory address to the Jacobin Society sent by the London Society for Constitutional Information in the same year.[4] As Thomas has noted, it marks a significant change in Morgan's political beliefs from his speech on parliamentary reform made eight years earlier; it also, he suggests, diverges from the position held by his mentor, Richard Price, at the end of his life. Price, though critical of the institution of monarchy, more pragmatically accepted the notion of a 'balanced constitution', involving the curtailment of the powers of the Crown; Morgan on the other hand is an entirely committed republican.[5] Yet they may not have been so far apart; it seems quite likely that Price himself is the 'eminent Political Character' referred to in one passage, who, on receiving letters from worried members of the Patriotic clubs in Paris, clearly states the dangers of maintaining any kind of system involving a king.[6]

Morgan's message to the French is a simple one: abolish monarchy. The very notion of a king, after all, violates their own Declaration of Rights, which states that 'all Men are born equal'. Had the 'God of Nature' intended a single family to rule over thirty million people, he notes drily, he would 'most probably have fixed some expressive Mark on Lewis the 16th and his Progeny' to indicate his inherent superiority. The presence of a king and the entourage of a royal court cause the inevitable flow of the nation's wealth and real political power into the hands of a greedy, scheming few: briefly 'interrupted' in its feast by the Revolution, this 'voracious and insatiable

Herd' is even now gathering strength on the borders of France. 'Their Howl,' he says, 'is not silenced':

> The boisterous Hero of Brunswick, having placed himself at the Head of Priests, Pimps, Parasites, Strumpets, Princes, and all the vagrant Train of a routed Court, is marching forward to re-establish the Empire of Riot, Waste, Wantonness, Injustice, Profligacy, Plunder, and Assassination, upon the Ruins of Paris, deluged by the Blood of its Citizens.

Monarchs themselves, he admits (and he casts a scathing eye over the stock of the various royal dynasties of Europe), may not be the most culpable schemers, being often too congenitally stupid, too bred-out, to be capable of complex thought. But their loyalties are always to those of their blood and class, and it is folly in the Assembly to imagine that systematic re-education, even under a 'Prodigy of Virtue and Wisdom', could alter the nature of 'a Stalk of the most poisonous Trunk that ever grew on the earth':

> Yet in Defiance of all Probability, they hoped to change the Tygers into Lambs. They sagely expected, that a carnivorous Kind, which had fed on Blood and Plunder from their earliest Appearance in savage Life, might be continued in their old Dens, and yet cease to devour.

Waste and war are powerful and intertwined themes. Following the argument made by Paine a year earlier, Morgan argues that the conspicuous consumption of the courts is funded by punitive taxes, themselves justified by an endless round of deliberately 'fomented' wars: 'in what former Reigns of your Kings,' he asks, 'could half the Money be raised, which Louis the 15th and 16th have squandered upon their Wars and Favourites?' Courts bloat the metropolis, and create a desperate imbalance of wealth, starving the peripheries, which render up their produce and receive nothing in return. As in the letters from France, he is particularly incensed by the 'enormous waste' of land given over to 'Hunting Forests, from which their Sport has driven the Spirit of Agriculture, and the consequent Life of Thousands'.

While it seems likely that Morgan intended this work to be read in France, the declaration in the obituary that this work 'had no reference to England' requires a pinch of salt: it undoubtedly takes a double aim. A stated target audience can, after all, act as a kind of rhetorical camouflage, and the pamphlet has much to say about the failings of the British government. Certain factions in the French Assembly are taken severely to task for idealizing the British system of representation. The notion that it is a model of balanced power is nothing less, he claims, than delusional – it masks, in fact, exactly the same kind of corruption:

> This famed Balance of Powers – This celebrated System of imaginary Checks – This theoretical Neutralization of unruly Forces, has, in Reality, displayed one continued Succession of Royal Inconstances and Versatilities.

As in Britain, a royal court would swiftly work its corrosive power on any new government: 'you may rest asured, that your Court, if established, in a very few Years, will manage your Biennial Representatives with as much Ease as we manage our Septennial Hirelings in England.' No matter how noble the proposed aims of the Assembly, therefore, ministers in the pocket of the royal entourage will push to revert to the old ways of profligacy and war: 'under our *glorious* Constitution,' he points out bitterly, 'we have had, in the last Century, three Civil Wars, and five or six Foreign Wars – Above Half the Time has been consumed in destroying'.

Concluding the first part of his *Rights of Man*, Paine wrote of the British mixed constitution that 'the moving power in this species of Government is Corruption'.[7] For Morgan, as for Paine, the only solution to corruption is constant replenishment: the body politic must be kept flowing 'to make it in its several parts changeable, but as one whole, firm, and permanent'. The Assembly should be chosen 'for a year only', and committees should be 'rendered changeable, by the Addition of a certain Number of new Members every Month'. To further avoid the formation of cliques and cabals, the members should be chosen from all over the country. Also Paineite is Morgan's insistence that the role of government itself should be kept 'as simple as possible'. It is not its job to direct, educate or restrain people in the minutiae of their daily lives, but to ensure, through a more equal division of wealth and opportunity, that they all have a chance to thrive physically and intellectually. Only then, says Morgan, perhaps with his Voltaire-quoting Swiss mountain guide in mind, will we see 'the Elevation of the Labourer into a Peasant, and of the Peasant into a Sage or a Philosopher'. To those who insist that strong government is the only way to prevent people committing crimes and harming each other, he replies that most members of society are inherently decent, and when they do behave badly there are obvious reasons:

> I am still not afraid to maintain, that the Evil proceeds from a most shameful Inequality, and that Aristocracy and Courts give Birth to those Excesses in the lower Order, which call for Law and Punishment from those who are their Superiors in POWER more than CHARACTER – When there are Thousands,

perhaps Millions, in your Nation, who lose their next Meal, if Sickness, or a Dearth of Opportunity interrupts their Labour – When the perpetual Provocations of Want are thus urging War against the general Peace – When Nature itself inflames in Man the Ferocity of a hungry wild Beast, then, indeed, the Power that controuls must be great – Chains and Prisons become necessary, and the STRENGTH of your RULERS must grow with the MISERY and WANTS of the MULTITUDE.

The *Address to the Jacobine Societies* lacks the devastating restraint of *Rights of Man,* but Morgan's huge debt to Paine – intellectual, if not stylistic – is significant. Most of the substantial points in the *Address* can be found in Paine's influential work, the second part of which had come out in February that year. We know, moreover, that the two men had met a few weeks before Morgan wrote his pamphlet, in June 1792, when Paine was guest of honour at a Republican Dinner held in New College, Hackney.[8] Since this was held at the height of Paine's fame – or notoriety – very soon after his indictment for seditious libel, feelings would have been running high. It seems likely that Morgan's republican stance, already evident in 1789, was strengthened and emboldened by the energetic presence of Thomas Paine in print and in person.

Yet if the language calling for the 'extirpation' of the institution of monarchy is extreme, the practical solution to the problem of what to do with Louis XVI and his ilk is not. A lengthy response to the question, 'How I should dispose of the present King?' argues against 'an Example of Severity', since, stripped of his royalty, Louis must be considered 'too contemptible an Individual to gratify the Vengeance of a great People'. He is, after all, likely to be a valuable hostage during the period of war. And when peace comes, suggests Morgan, drawing once again on his classical education:

the Descendant of the Bourbons should enjoy the Fate of Demetrius Poliorcetes – In some distant, but safe Enclosure, he should sport and fatten amongst his Stags – He should indulge all his natural Propensities, and display to your infant republic the full Brutality of his Species.[9]

In February 1792 Thomas Paine confidently gave the institutions of monarchy and aristocracy no more than 'seven years' to run their natural course in 'the enlightened countries in Europe'.[10] As people began to question the basis for their existence, he assumed, common sense would dictate that they be abolished as an illogical hangover from a previous age, and an unnecessary drain on their nations' resources. George Cadogan Morgan sounds rather less sanguine; and although, two centuries on, we appear to have arrived at a version of his theme-park monarchy, it is doubtful that the 'instruction' derived therefrom is quite what he had in mind.

Editorial note

The text is given here exactly as it was published, with capital letters, emphasis, and division into chapters intact.

Notes

1   See Thomas, 'George Cadogan Morgan', pp. 61–3. Thomas does not explain his attribution of authorship.
2   Anon., 'Account of the Late Mr George Cadogan Morgan', p. 477.
3   Besides the one in the British Library (available digitally through ECCO) I have not traced further copies. The NLW copy contains one handwritten correction on p. 15, where 'Austides' is amended to 'Aristides'.
4   See Carl B. Cone, *The English Jacobins: Reformers in Late 18th Century England* (1968; paperback edn., New York, 2010), p. 125.
5   Thomas, 'George Cadogan Morgan', p. 62.
6   See p. 118 n. 7.
7   Thomas Paine, *Rights of Man,* ed. by Gregory Claeys (Indianapolis, 1992), p. 106.
8   Burley, *New College, Hackney*, p. 9.
9   Plutarch relates that Demetrius I, king of Macedon, became notorious for his excessive lifestyle and was eventually defeated and confined to the Syrian Chersonesus: 'There he was kept, indeed, under a strong guard, but Seleucus sent him a sufficient equipage, and supplied him with money and a table suitable to his rank. He had also places of exercise and walks worthy of a king; his parks were well stored with game.' After a while 'he sank into indolence and inactivity' and 'took to drinking and play', dying after three years of captivity. John Langhorne and William Langhorne (ed. and trans.), *Plutarch's Lives* (revised edn., Baltimore, 1836), p. 632.
10 Paine, *Rights of Man*, ed. by Claeys, p. 119.

An ADDRESS

to the

Jacobine *and other* Patriotic Societies

of the

F R E N C H

urging the

Establishment of a Republican

Form of Government

———————————

By a Native of England

and

a Citizen of the World

————————

1792

Advertisement

Lewis the 16th was suspended on the 10th of August. On the 11th, a member of the National Assembly moved, "That a *Governor* of the *Prince Royal* should be appointed". From this Circumstance, the Author apprehended, that a Spirit, strong in the interest of Royalty, was still prevalent in France. He, therefore, wrote the following Address. – Subsequent Events, have seemingly proved, that his Apprehensions were wrong. – But he still flatters himself, that his effort may not be superfluous. The faintest voice adds something to a general Cry – And Powerful is the Language of every Mind, the Purity of whose motives cannot be doubted, whose enquiries can have been directed by no local interests, and whose zeal can have no other stimulant, than the general Happiness of Mankind.

ADDRESS, &c.

CHAP. I.

FELLOW CITIZENS OF THE WORLD:

THE Spirit of Philosophy and Heroism has at length raised you to the grandest Opportunity ever enjoyed by Man-kind – Seize and improve it, and convince the Human Race, that to banish Kings and Courts, is to extirpate the most destroying Pestilence that ever desolated the Universe. You cannot doubt this Truth. The last Sufferings of a thousand Years Torture are now convincing you. Louis the 16th, emulating his Forefathers, has filled and finished his Day with Perfidy and Blood. He is still before your Eyes a monstrous Figure in that hateful Pageantry which has displayed all the possible varieties of Royal Folly and Wickedness: Nay, though you have dispersed the voracious and insatiable Herd which followed his Steps, and joined in his Devastations, their Howl is not silenced: They are yet heard at a distance, marking out thousands of your best Citizens for the Scaffold, and menacing your Millions with all the Woes of their old Tyranny, and with the new havock of Vengeance and interrupted Appetite. The boisterous Hero of Brunswick,[1] having placed himself at the Head of Priests, Pimps, Parasites, Strumpets, Princes, and all the vagrant Train of a routed Court, is marching forward to re-establish the Empire of Riot, Waste, Wantonness, Injustice, Profligacy, Plunder, and Assassination, upon the Ruins of Paris, deluged by the Blood of its Citizens. The passing Moment is exhibiting these Characters of Royalty, or of that Prodigy in Evil to the Sport and Riot of whose Excesses, you have been subject for ten Hundred Years. But it is not one destroying Swarm that has thus consumed the very Pith and Marrow of your Existence: Your Blood and Treasure have fattened the Vermin of Foreign Courts. Every Country has some awful Story to tell of their worst Men, confederated in Schemes of Wickedness with your Kings and Oppressors. Where have they not fostered the most perfidious Intrigues? Where have they not fomented the most horrid Wars? In short, your own Annals, and those of all Europe, speak but one Language – that French Courts have been the Worst of all Courts – and that of the whole Host of Royal Plagues yours has been the most calamitous and destructive. The Ruins of your Prisons, what are they but Vestiges of your Kings in the Plenitude of their Grandeur, or of enthroned Brutality, in the Days of its greatest Indulgence and Triumph? The vast Circumference of your Aristocratical Domains, what are they but the ample Measure of Monarchial Profusion, squandering upon its Creatures the Property of the People?

Have you peopled the Deserts, which their Wars have spread over your Country? or, when you see the Palaces they have raised – or the Hunting Forests, from which their Sport has driven the Spirit of Agriculture, and the consequent Life of Thousands – when, moreover, this enormous Waste has reduced near 20 Millions of your Citizens so as scarcely to earn a Meal by their Labour. – With all these Evidences of his voracious Appetites before your Eyes, will you keep the Monster? The Eggs of the devouring Brood are in your Hands, will you still expect to hatch from them any thing that is not poisonous and fatal?

C H A P. II.

YOUR Constituent Assembly[2] knew all that you have suffered, and well, very well knew the Cause. The History of the World was before them, and in the History of Kings they could see but one common Picture of what was delineated more strongly in the Records of France. Yet in Defiance of all Probability, they hoped to change the Tygers into Lambs. They sagely expected, that a carnivorous Kind, which had fed on Blood and Plunder from their earliest Appearance in savage Life, might be continued in their old Dens, and yet cease to devour.

To gratify their wild Expectation of effecting Impossibilities, your Constituent Assembly began with violating boldly, and immediately after they made it, their own Declaration of Rights.[3] It is one if ITS first ARTICLES, that all Men are born equal; and it is one of THEIR first DECREES, that one Man by Birth is above all the rest, or that he his [sic] born with Rights belonging to none but himself. Now had the God of Nature designed what your Assembly decreed – Had he intended that the Power of ruling Thirty Millions of Men should belong to one Family, he would most probably have fixed some expressive Mark on Lewis the 16th and his Progeny: And as he has done in other Instances, he would, by some exttraordinary [sic] Appearance, have distinguished the King Bee of his Hive.

I was at Paris during the first Moment of your Revolution – I saw you burst from your Chains – and from the Intelligence and Magnanimity of your first Proceedings, anticipated great Events to Mankind – The tumbling Edifices of Superstitions and feudal Tyranny declared the proper Antipathies of your Minds – and when I saw the Pillars shaken, I hoped that the great Mass itself would soon fall to the Ground – When Tythes, Game Laws, &c. were demolished, though Monarchy was still alive, I yet enjoyed its Convulsions as Symptoms of approaching Death – Your motley Legislators, however, made up of Shreds and Patches,[4] of Priests and Nobles, and new

Patriots, came in as Physicians, they swore the Animal was useful, and that he would never bite or kick when he had once been purged by their Medicines, and placed under their Regulations. You have Reason to rue this Quackery and Presumption. The Devourer recovered his Strength. His Doctors became fond of him – and in their future Labours they scarcely thought of any thing but him. For to your whole Constitution what has given its Character, but the supposed Necessity and the consequent Dread of a King, whom they placed at its Head? – In this intricate Complication of Movements and Forces – In this System of Checks – In this Chaos of contending Jealousies, if you put your Finger on each One out of unnumbered Decrees, and ask, Why is this made? You are answered, "We feared the Court. We have empowered a King to corrupt us, and we must not trust ourselves. There are Men, likewise, who wish to be near him, for the Sake of his Pleasures and his Purse; and if such Decrees are not passed, these Men will buy us." – But say that you have no King, no Court, no rich Places, and who is to buy you? Make your Government as cheap as it ought to be, and as it may be, and you have nothing to watch, nothing to fear, no Bone to quarrel about. Amongst yourselves, the Trade of governing will be at an End, and with the Trade away goes the Mystery – Every requisite of Government will appear simple, and you will stand astonished, that the World has been so long desolated by so contemptible a Craft.

C H A P. III.

I MUST confess to you, that when I heard the Constituent Assembly begin their career with *declaring*, and *contradicting*; with establishing Monarchy, and yet with Pretensions, high sounding, in Favour of Liberty, I fully expected that the Struggles of the Day would end with the Attainment of a Phantom, or with the Exchange of a CORRUPT for a VIOLENT Tyrant. – When you had proceeded with the Work of your Constitution for near two Years, I conversed with several Members of your Society, and found no Relief to my first Apprehensions.[5] In Defiance of the most splendid Parts of History, you urged the Necessity of Kings for extensive Nations – You acknowledged them to be dreadful Nuisances, and though you were shocked at the daring Corruption with which your Court had begun its Career, yet Perjury and a most impious Renunciation of all that was awful in Promise and Profession, did not wean you from the Partiality you felt for your dangerous Bawble – Selfishness mixed with and strengthened the Fondness of your Constituent Assembly and they forced you all to swear, that whatever Calamities your King heaped upon you, whatever Evidences you might have of his Corruption or Perfidy, you should, notwithstanding, keep him and obey him for many Years.

During this Interval of Rest and passive Obedience on the Part of the People, not one Power favourable to a thriving Despotism was witheld from the Tyrant – His Means were exorbitant – His Situation the best possible – His Circumstances those of the most inviolable Security. – He had Money enough to carry on his Plans – He was the Controller of all your Laws – The Director of all your Powers – And with these terrible Arms in his Hands, he was placed where he could best serve his own Friends, and your determined Enemies – He still loves his Brothers, his Cousins, and his former Favourites – But what could his Head, or Hands do for them at Coblentz?[6] What could he not do for them at Paris? – He could disunite you – He could tell them all your Plans – He could stop or embarrass every wise Decree of your Representatives – He could starve and wither your Armies – And he could counteract your Generals. – Millions might stand up in your Favour – but vested with the Omnipotence decreed by your Constituent Assembly, he might blast all your Efforts, and give you up to the Havock of your Foes. – You have Reason to thank God, that your Court had more Wickedness than Wisdom – For a larger Portion of Art in their Characters – A winning Spirit of Compliance in small but showy Things – Patience in their dark Proceedings – A few Lessons from the Treasury of England concerning the Management of Senates – A Plan for doing in Seven, what they have wished to accomplish in one Year, and a Series of Measures directed by such a System, would have blinded the Multitude, and foiled the discerning Few. The French Nation would have been managed completely, and, like the English, you would have had the Boast of a glorious Constitution in Speculation, and the Disgrace of being really enslaved by Intrigue and Corruption. You have Reason, I say, to thank God for the Madness of your Court – Violence is an admirable Quality in a dangerous Enemy. It has been the Character of your Tyrants. They have, therefore, acted so as to be understood by all, and at length you have opened your eyes, I hope, never to shut them again.

C H A P. IV.

WHEN you experienced your earliest Apprehensions of the Intrigues of your Court, and the Powers vested in it by the Constituent Assembly, several of your Patriotic Clubs expressed their Fears, and applied for Advice to one of the most eminent Political Characters in England.[7] The Directories They described as particular Objects of their Terror, in whose Establishment they expected, that of so many distinct Tyrannies, as soon as the first Vigilance and Zeal of the Revolution began to slumber.[8] I was present when these Letters were read; and this was the Language they called forth:

"Let the French take away their Court, and all their Danger is dissipated. Let them withdraw the Million that will certainly be employed to corrupt their Representatives, and they will have a pure Body of Legislators, who will always correct subordinate Evils. But every inferior Tyranny is formidable, when there is a King to take the lead; for, depend upon it, that he will have a common Interest, with all that resemble and support his Character." – It appears to me, that the late History of your Directories has sufficiently verified this Observation.

It was the strange Idea of some in your Constituent Assembly, that a King of Wood, or of Wax, might do for the Throne of France, and that such a King was the Monarch they had established.[9] – What! Can that Composition of Feelings, Appetites, and Passions, which form the Human Being, be vested with Royal Prerogatives, and bear no Character? Can Man be placed in Circumstances the most stimulating to Pride, Ambition, and Avarice – the most seducing to brutal Propensity, and the most unfavourable to every natural Talent and Virtue, and yet continue a Nothing? Is there one harmless Nothing to be found in the whole Catalogue of Dead or of living Kings? or, if you take out of the Swarm, all those who are declared Fools, open Rogues, and deluded and vicious Devotees, how few will remain to justify the Hopes of the Constituent Assembly?

It was the Language of your Legislators, "We will establish sure Means, and such as were never used before, for making our Kings innocent at least, perhaps worthy. We will ourselves appoint a Governor, who will teach them all that is right."

Then the Happiness of the Nation is to depend upon the Governor, who is sagely expected to be perfect, whatever Intrigues his Passions may be exposed to from the Men and the Women of a corrupt Court. The Parents, likewise, are sagely supposed to have no Influence; and to make the King a compleat Monster, you forbid him the Exercise of all domestic Care and Affection. But if the Governor is to do so much, or if that Prodigy of Virtue and Wisdom can be found, who is qualified to do, what was never done before, or to make a good King, why take two Steps, when one only is necessary – or, why not make the Governor himself, King?

Now, had you selected a Family from all the Families of the Earth, to supply you with Royal Masters, nothing appears to me more extravagant, from a View of every Obstruction arising from the Court, the Parents, the Dangers of the Governor, and the probable Defects, of the Prince, than the Possibility of rearing a King so as to be a harmless Character. But this was not the Case with your Constituent Assembly: They made no Selection, but thought their Purposes would be answered by a Stalk of the most poisonous Trunk that ever grew on the Earth. They expected to form a perfect Innocent in the vilest and most profligate Court that ever disgraced the Annals of Mankind. The Son of Marie Antoinette was to be changed into a Favourite of the People. The first Cousin of every Conspirator in the Royal Concert of Kings was to become the Cato or the A[ri]stides of France![10]

But let us allow that you could mould your Kings into mere Men of Wax. Still the worst Curse of Monarchy would flourish with full Domination. Have a King, and you must have a Court. Have a Court, and you must have a profligate Aristocracy; pampered by all that there is in Royal Luxury to debase the Character, and to hatch Poison for the Infection of your Metropolis, and thence of your whole Community. But the happy Moments are now passing – The glorious Power is in your Hands – Free yourselves from an Influence more pestilential and destructive than the worst Plagues of Ægypt – You have Slavery to no Purpose – if it beget not the Hatred of all Kings and Courts.

C H A P. V.

IT will be asked, But how is the Executive Power to be managed – and to whom is it to be confided? I will answer, that if you look for Parade and Magnificence, restore it to your King, and he will spend your money most gorgeously. If you wish for a new Aristocracy, restore their Power to your Kings, for they *will* have Courts, and Courts will soon collect into one Spot, and then transform into one Character all the rich Men of your Land. If you wish for bad Manners, extravagant Fashions, Profligacy, and whatever there is in Vice, to distress a Community, let Royalty take the Lead. For its Wives, its Brothers, its Cousins, its Favourites, its Creatures, and ITSELF, will have nothing to do, but to be wicked, to give you an Example of Excess, and then to spread that Excess, by selecting, for its Companions in Power and Office, those who are its Companions in Waste, Peculation, Prostitution, and Adultery.

If, moreover, you look for a Government that will grow worse, and that will certainly in a few Years degenerate into something execrable, by all Means chuse a King. Degeneracy in every respect is the essential of Royalty, and of every Thing that belongs to it – surrounded as it is by Men who are Favourites only in Proportion to their Invention of new Crimes, new Indulgences, new Poisons for the Court, and new Plagues for the Nation. The last Race of Kings in Europe were degenerating fast into a Race of Fools. The present is a contemptible Set of Idiots. Francis the First of Austria is famous for leading Processions, and kissing Relicts.[11] The Successor of Frederic falls asleep with a full Stomach on the Lap of his Mistress, and then sees Visions.[12] The House of Orange seems to have concentrated all the DULLNESS, as well as the POWER, of the Nation into its own Family.[13] What the House of Hanover has at length produced, the English can testify – and you have before your Eyes the setting Brightness of the House of Bourbon. Nature is kind in making the Situation of Kings so favourable to the Production of Fools – for nothing could be more terrible to Mankind than the frequent Union of Talents with the growing Wickedness of a Throne.

It may be here said, perhaps, that a Degeneracy in the Character of Kings is not necessarily followed by a Degeneracy in the Character of their Governments. *Then it follows, that* powerful Causes may exist in Circumstances the most favourable to their Energy, and yet produce no Effects. A Multitude of unforeseen Exigencies and Events, requiring the immediate Exercise of discretionary Power, are continually occurring in a great Kingdom. All these are so many Opportunities propitious to the Increase of every constituted Power; which Opportunities will frequently take place during those Intervals of Torpor and Sleep, to which all Communities are subject; and while the Inclinations of the King stand ready to grasp and accumulate, he will never want auxiliary Parties, whose wicked Interest will co-operate with his own. Experience proves that Constitutional Checks can only retard the Evil; and you may rest assured, that your Court, if established, in a very few Years, will manage your Biennial Representatives with as much ease as we manage our Septennial Hirelings in England. Under a firm Conviction of what I have urged, the Tools of our Court are at this Moment loud in execrating the Impatience of your King and his Junto. "Had he taken a little Time (say they) he would have discovered the right System; he would have hit upon the effectual Method of buying what he wanted. The Nation had given him Money enough; and, with a little Skill, every necessary Power might have been his own."

Besides, where has the Monarchy yet existed which has not changed its Character in a very few Years, and which would not continue till the very Vitals of the People were consumed, if its Prodigality did not grow faster than its Power – In what former Reigns of your Kings could half the Money be raised, which Louis the 15th and 16th have squandered upon their Wars and Favourites – Or would you now have been free, if your present Court had been contented with ten Times the Tax which satisfied preceding Tyrants?

Soon after our Revolution in England, a Profusion of Three or Four Millions would have provoked a Civil War – But George III has squandered

140 Millions Sterling – He has lost Thirteen Colonies – He has more than doubled our Taxes and our Poor; and yet, because the Power of Corruption has kept Pace with his Prodigality, he is more absolute than ever; and even the younger Branches of his Family can spend more with Impunity, than would have satisfied the most voracious of the Stuarts or their Predecessors – What presuming Folly then was it in your Constituent Assembly, to expect the Atchievement of that which the whole Experience of Mankind proved to be impossible; and more particularly the Experience of that very Constitution, whose Character they were eager to copy.

Once more. Let me ask you, Whether you wish for the Reign of Poverty in your lower Orders, and of enormous Wealth in your higher Orders; of Luxury amongst the Few, and of Misery amongst Millions? Then restore your old, or establish a new King – Place him at the Head of a Court, and near the delusive Splendour of his Palace, you will raise an overgrown Metropolis, which will starve the Extremities of the Kingdom to support its Luxuries and Pleasures. Let the Example of England warn you, whose Pride is, at this Moment, inflated by the increasing Magnitude of a Metropolis, which, in time, will certainly eat up our whole Country. Its present Consumption is dreadful. The Income of above Half the Landed Property of the Kingdom is spent in it – So, likewise, is all the Wealth that comes from the East and West Indies, all that the Gentry and Aristocracy of Ireland can squeeze out of their oppressed Country; nor does the Barrenness of Scotland refuse near the Half of its Produce to our Metropolis – Be it added, that in London, the Nursery of all that is foolish, excessive, and profligate, the Fortunes of our wealthiest Tradesmen are squandered; and our Manufacturers in the Country, likewise, are no sooner rich, than they hasten to unite in, or to imitate the Prodigality of the Court – In short, whoever thrives under the partial Liberty we enjoy, mixes precipitately with the Crowd which riot at St. James's and Carleton-House.[14] A Monarchy will produce the very same Evils in France – The Communication of the Kingdom, with the Luxuries of your Court, will be increased by the perpetual Intercourse of your Representatives, who will be seduced by its Splendours, and will imbibe its Follies; and the Power of your Metropolis to corrupt and desolate will be great, in Proportion to the extensive Greatness of your Kingdom. General Washington is now laying down the first Stones of a Royal Palace – He is building a Federate City.[15] What he calls the Seat of Power, will, in a few Years, become the Seat of Luxury, or the Nursery of those Evils which begin with the Depravity, and end with the Slavery and Misery of the whole Nation. This great Man has now been King four Years – I wish he may not be infected by the Passions belonging to his Office – The Period of his Reign has been much too long for the Security of his

Virtue – He certainly does not despise the show of a Court, for he is taking the most effectual Means to establish and spread its Influence.

C H A P. VI.

I HAVE now enumerated a few of the several Effects that must inevitably follow, if you restore your King, or if you vest any ONE MAN with the Executive Power. Do not then suppose that you finish your Work, when you dethrone Louis 16th, or that you ensure Liberty to Posterity, when you confer the Government on his Son. If this be your Remedy, the Necessity of purging the Thuilleries will soon recur;[16] for while the office lives, the Race of Tyrants will never die. TO him then that asks you, Where is the Executive Power to be placed? Let this be your Answer, "We know certainly where it ought not to be placed; and if we err again, we cannot do so much mischief as we did before – We will have something that we can change, without the Effusion of Blood, or the Danger of a Civil War – We will have nothing permanent, but that which Experience proves to be good. The Civil List is annihilated, and our National Convention will at least be pure: And if they abolish Monarchy, by REMOVING THE WORST OF ALL POSSIBLE THINGS, They will remove the greatest of all Obstructions to political Improvement."

To this general Answer to the proposed Difficulty of managing the Executive Power, may I think be added, the Recommendation of a more specific Measure – Let your National Assembly be chosen for a Year only, and do not be afraid of giving it too much Power. The Nomination of your various Ministers of State cannot injure a Legislative Body, who at the End of Twelve Months, give up their Place, mix again with the People, and become subject to their own Decrees.[17]

No Application of Money, no Execution of Laws, can be managed better than under the Controul of such an Assembly, or a Committee selected from it, provided that Committee be rendered changeable, by the Addition of a certain Number of new Members every Month. Your Representatives, congregated from all Parts of a large Kingdom, cannot possibly be seduced by any particular Interest of their own into Cabal and Intrigue – Even a rich Court could hardly make it worth their while to be unfaithful for so short Time. But when there is no Court, I know not what is to corrupt them.

It appears to me, that the great Object to be aimed at in forming a Constitution is this – To make it in its several Parts changeable, but as one whole, firm, and permanent. The System of the human Body will explain my Meaning – All our Fluids and Solids are continually dissipating, but continually succeeded by new integrant Parts. The Body is, notwithstanding, still the same, nay, its Strength, Activity, and Health depend upon its incessant Changes; for when any Part is stopped in any Place, Disease and Corruption are sure to follow.

Whether you could establish a Rotation in your high Offices of State, I know not – The Object deserves your Consideration – The successful Example of the Roman State may instruct you – Nor should you be without Apprehension from the Resemblance of a Court, in case your first Officers and their Connections and Dependents should always reside near your Representative Assembly – Certain I am, that a great Reduction of their Parade and Power may take Place without Danger to the State; and that your public Concerns may be very well managed, without bestowing so much Consequence to your Servants as will render them at all formidable.

It is observed with Truth, that the essential Movements of the English Government are altogether guided by a few subordinate Secretaries; and if these Men were removed, so little would be known by those who are the ostensible Men, and who enjoy the cast Honours and Emoluments of the State, that the whole Machine would become inactive. Indeed, if the Intrigues of the House of Commons, and of the corrupt Boroughs which chuse it; if such a dexterous Disposal of all Places in the Army, the Navy, the Church, the Custom-House, the Excise-Office, the India Company, &c. &c. as may best serve the ruling Faction, be a Part of Government, then what I have said is not true; For such Purposes, a very complicate System must be adopted; a large Portion of Craft is necessary; and an honest Man is, of all others, the most unqualified for the Business – He succeeds best, who has most of the Hypocrite in his Character – and hence we learn, why Mr. Pitt is the most powerful and prosperous Minister that ever lived.

C H A P. VII.

I TRUST that you have Philosophy enough in your Nation to perceive, that the sole End of Government is Protection, and that Rulers and Legislators must continue to be mischievous, while they direct their Attention to other Objects – Your Constituent Assembly was too much possessed by this Spirit of Impertinence and Usurpation – They have pretended to foster Trade by the monopolizing Restraints of a Navigation Act –[18] They have planned Systems of Education, together with many other systems, which, as Society improves, will be found to operate as so many Hindrances – The human Being, if left to himself, or if left to cultivate what the infinite Bounty of Nature has given him in a most ample Abundance, without any Molestation from Superiors or Tyrants, will never fail to do well. Injury should prescribe the Limits of Law; and whenever the Legislator think of any Thing but the Repulsion of Injury, he violates his Duty, and becomes a Nuisance to Society.

It should then, I think, be your general Principle, to be as simple as possible, and to remember, that as the Circumstances of your Nation improve, as the Embarrassments accumulated by your old Government are gradually extirpated, as the Necessities imposed by an infernal System of War and Intrigue in foreign Courts, become less and less urgent, you may very much improve in the Simplicity and the consequent Ease of governing. Indeed, it is but a moderate Share of Justice and Humanity, dispersed amongst the several Individuals of a Nation that is requisite, to take away the Necessity of Law and Officers altogether. Let any one reputable Person judge from himself. Let him look to the History of his own Life, and he will not find the Moment in which Government was necessary to keep him in order; consequently, if his own Character were that of all Individuals, THAT VERY STATE of Society would take place, in which Legislators and Rulers would have little or nothing to do. Perhaps this is the Case with Twenty-eight out of the Thirty Millions which people France at this Instant. Indeed, in every Country that Portion of Men is small, whose Violation of Property and Person have introduced the Necessity of Controul, and the consequent Usurpation of Tyranny.

But should all this be denied, and the Majority of Society, represented as naturally disposed to plunder and destroy, I am still not afraid to maintain, that the Evil proceeds from a most shameful Inequality, and that Aristocracy and Courts give Birth to those Excesses in the lower Order, which call for Law and Punishment from those who are their Superiors in POWER more than CHARACTER – When there are Thousands, perhaps Millions, in your Nation, who lose their next Meal, if Sickness, or a Dearth of Opportunity interrupts their Labour – When the perpetual Provocations of Want are thus urging War against the general Peace – When Nature itself inflames in Man the Ferocity of a hungry wild Beast, then, indeed, the Power that controuls must be great – Chains and Prisons become necessary, and the STRENGTH of your RULERS must grow with the MISERY and WANTS of the MULTITUDE. But, suppose the Sum of Three Hundred Millions Sterling, which the Wars of two Reigns only have cost you, had been employed in peopling and cultivating your Waste Lands – Or, suppose the Hunting Forests of your Princes had been let out in small Leases to your distressed Peasants – Or, suppose that, instead of $^{19}/_{20\text{ths}}$, only Half the Produce of your Lands had been consumed by the Pleasures of your Nobility, and the rest enjoyed by the Labourer – Such a State of Society must have taken Place, even from this partial Diffusion of good, as the Minds of Men, like yourselves, cannot conceive of; I say like yourselves, for your Views must be those of a Nation immersed in the Dregs and Darkness of a Thousand Years Slavery. But you have a numerous Body of Sages and Philosophers amongst you – It is indeed a glorious Scene of Happiness, that must animate them to the wise and vigorous Direction of those Powers which you have now at your Disposal – Give them Confidence, and doubt not the Reality of those great Things which they hold forth to your Expectations – Liberty and Equality!* They are the Attributes of an omnipotent Society – They imply Leisure and Opportunity to Thirty Millions of intellectual Beings – They imply Advantages to your vast Nation, which have hitherto been confined to a few only, in a few large Towns – They imply the Banishment of Luxury, the Exclusion of Want, and the peopling of your Deserts – They imply the Elevation of the Labourer into a Peasant, and of the Peasant into a Sage or a Philosopher. Who, seeing the general Wealth they produce, will not learn how amply bountiful, Nature has been to Man? And who seeing their powerful Influence in meliorating and raising the Character, will not testify, how partial Man naturally is to Virtue?

C H A P. VIII.

ATHENS was raised on a barren Rock, and was fed from Infancy to an Hour of Strength and Independence, by the Industry which enriched a small Surface of the surrounding Desert. Athens was partially free, and Equality was enjoyed by the eleventh Part only of its Inhabitants. Its Government was imperfect; it was disturbed by the Intrigues of neighbouring

---

*   The Abettors of Tyranny in England, and other Countries, have an Interest in the Misinterpretation of the Word Equality, as it is now used by the French. They assert, that the Multitude expect a general Division of Property, or that an agrarian Law will soon reduce all the French to a Level. The wealthier Members of Communities are thus reduced into a Dread of all Political Changes, and the avaricious Fears of Mankind are made the Advocates of Tyranny. By Equality, the French mean only an Equality of Rights and Privileges; in other Words, that all French Citizens are equal in the Power of Chusing their Representatives, and in the Capacity of being chosen. That no Difference of Rank is to sway the Decisions of public Justice, and that no Superiority is to be vested with Power, but that of Merit and Talents. The Philosophical Legislators of France must perceive, that if their Constitution be good, a gradual Approximation to a general Equality must be its Consequence. They have already adopted very powerful Means for this Purpose; and, if they attend rigorously to the Law which divides the Property of every Parent amongst his several Children, the Bulk of large Fortunes and Estates will soon be reduced, and the most fertile Cause of Aristocracy exterminated.

Monarchies, impoverished by frequent Wars, desolated by numerous Plagues, and frequently tormented by its own Disorders and Tumults; but 20,000 Freemen thus struggling and fighting, thus exposed to Alarms and Calamities, thus unquiet in the interupted Enjoyment of Liberty, have furnished the World with all that is excellent in Art and Philosophy. The whole Produce of the World in intellectual Excellence and Greatness, is a Trifle compared to that of this single City. The Powers which were possessed in this Instance, are possessed by you in a greater Degree. The Equality of 20,000 amongst them, may be that of 30,000,000 amongst you – Their Famines cannot assail you, and their Plagues cannot desolate you – The Barrenness of their Soil is the Contrast of your Fertility; and the Greatness of your Power is a sure Protection against such Neighbours, as perpetually disturbed, and [at] length utterly destroyed them. Be it added, that their Feuds and Animosities were the Consequence of a Government subject to the Passions of a Multitude – But you will govern by Representation – And when the first Storms and Dangers of your Revolution are over, I trust you will govern with perfect Calmness and Tranquility – Remember, however, that with all these Circumstances of Superiority, you may, by one Variety, fall far below them – They had NO KING, THEY had no COURT – They loathed the very Name of a Monarch – They watched his Appearance with a Jealousy that was frequently unjust – And they never failed to thrive during the Absence of this Pestilence.

Had one of the Bourbons lived within their Walls a Year, he would have swallowed the whole sustenance of their Country. A single Payment of His Civil List would have purchased the Fee-simple of their Territories; nay, all that went to the Support of their Artists, to the Nurture of their Philosophers and Philosophic Schools, and to the Erection of those Edifices which are the Admiration and Instruction of the World, would not supply your Court with the Pleasures of a few Month; or with a Pension to satisfy one of the Prostitutes of your Kings, or the Favourites of your Queens.

C H A P. IX.

IT has, however, been urged, that the Splendour of Republics very soon vanishes; but that the Glories of Monarchy are stable and permanent; in other Words, that the HAPPINESS of Nations is fleeting, but that their CALAMITIES are durable. To shew that Monarchy is a LASTING Evil, is a curious Mode of defending it; but the Falsehood equals the Absurdity of this Defence – The Roman Republic proves, that the Powers of Man, when free, will go on for Centuries, adding one stupendous Display of

Greatness to another, The Grecian States flourished a longer Time, and their History testifies, that the same Power of Liberty which enabled one Republic to conquer the World, when directed towards the Cultivation of Art and Science, is equally astonishing in its Effect. Nay, it is probable that they would have advanced in the vast Progress of intellectual Improvement to the present Day, if, instead of being several, they had formed one Commonwealth, united by a common Interest, and governed by a general Representation. Their combined Powers would have stopped the Inundations of neighbouring Tyrannies – Nor would the martial Prowess of Rome have finished the Ruins which others had begun. But why should you appeal to these remote Instances? You have, almost within your Sight, a small Republic, which has afforded Happiness to Thousands, on a snowy Surface of Crags, for near Twelve Hundred Years. – The free Citizens of St. Marino, surrounded by Precipices, have defied the Invasions of every neighbouring Potentate; and they are thus preserved as an Evidence, that where there are no Wars, no Kings to corrupt, divide, and destroy, good Governments are always lasting – Their Representatives are chosen frequently, and their Executive Power is CHANGED EVERY SIX WEEKS.[19] In short, they are raised on high, to give the Advocates of Monarchy the Lie; and to tell you what is possible, if you hate Military Carnage, and take Care that the Power which governs shall never engender Corruption, by RESTING LONG IN THE SAME HANDS. Let it be recollected, that on a few Miles of barren Surface, bounded by the Ice, and chilled by the Winds that blow over it, their Inhabitants are more numerous than those which the Area of a Thousand Leagues spread below them, and forming the most fertile Country in the World, has produced under the blasting Influence of Monarchies – Nay, the Fifty Millions of enlightened Citizens, which even the Martial Republic of former Times had nourished in these exuberant Regions, are now, by a destroying Confederacy of Nobles, Priests, and Kings, reduced to a few Thousand Wretches and Assassins. Who will deny, that the Glories of Monarchy are of a lasting Nature, when it impresses such Marks of its tremendous Greatness? or, who does not see that it is always enthroned amidst increasing Ruins and spreading Deserts?

To those, however, who maintain, that the Governments of Kings are always stable and permanent, in Opposition to the Restlessness of Republics – It may be answered, that the NAME, indeed, continues unaltered for Centuries – But that of all versatile Things, the Character of a Court and its Measures is the most capricious and inconstant.[20] Every new Minister is a Tyrant of a new Construction; and every distinct reign displays some new Variety of Woes and Calamities. While the same Individual continues on the Throne, he is perpetually shifting his Favourites; and in all Countries, but more particularly in your own, the Government has altered not less frequently than the King's Appetites, which, when sated with one Mistress, have required the Provocatives of a new Strumpet before they could be gratified. Take the List of your Civil Wars and Persecutions, of your external Wars and Oppressions, and examine whether your Monarchy has been uniform in any Thing but a varied Contrivance of Means to harrass and plunder, and desolate the People. But what is true of France, and of all the other Domains of Kings, is not less true of the English Monarchy − This famed Balance of Powers − This celebrated System of imaginary Checks − This theoretical Neutralization of unruly Forces, has, in Reality, displayed one continued Succession of Royal Inconstancies and Versatilities. It has been frequently observed, that so busily have our several Kings been employed in devouring each other, or in worrying the People, till they have devoured them − That Four of the same Family have never yet reigned successively on the British Throne − For near Five Hundred Years our Country was incessantly the Prey of contending Nobles − An Empire might almost have been peopled by the Multitudes which perished on the Scaffold during our Civil Wars − In a single Reign, Sixty Thousand are said to have been dispatched by the Executioner alone − What must that Deluge be, which our Royal Masters have poured on the Field of Battle, or spilled by the Hands of the Assassin? The long Reigns of Murder and Carnage, which preceded the Time of the Tudors, do not speak less in Favour of the steady Tranquility belonging to our finely-balanced Monarchy, than the stormy Periods which followed. You well know the bloody and perfidious History of the Stuarts, their Wars, their Massacres, their own miserable Fortunes, and the SANGUINARY VENGEANCE WHICH MARKED THEIR RETURN TO POWER − The Revolution was by no Means the Commencement of Peace − Under our glorious Constitutions, we have had, in the last Century, three Civil Wars, and five or six Foreign Wars − Above Half the Time has been consumed in destroying, and the other Half in forming Plans for carrying on future Schemes of War with less Molestation − In short, our Court, under the Mask of Forms, and with the delusive Fascination of high-sounding Language concerning our *glorious* Constitution, have kept Pace in the Paths of Waste and Destruction with your wicked Court; but with Mischief infinitely greater, for it has loaded Eight Millions in this Northern Region with that Burthen, which is intolerable to Thirty Millions in your fertile Country. Yes, in truth, PERMANENCE DOES BELONG TO MONARCHIES, for we find, that our Taxes never change but for the worse, that our Debts are never lightened, that our Wars never cease, that our Corruption is still growing, and that the Reign of Squandering Favourites, and Hypocrites, is more absolute and extensive than ever. In delineating, however, the steady and permanent Mischiefs of Monarchy in France and England, we have given a Picture which suits, in its leading Features, all the Kings of Europe – Nor in the Contemplation of so durable and dreadful a Calamity, can you doubt the Justice with which Philosophers have deplored over the actual, compared with the possible, State of this Quarter of the Globe.

"Europe (say they) is peopled by Two Hundred Millions of Inhabitants, of which about $^1/_{100th}$ Part are rich, corrupt, luxurious, ignorant, and oppressive – A Few Hundreds are Men of improved and exalted Minds – The rest are Wretches and Slaves."

Europe (say they) is capable of supporting, in the Exuberance of Enjoyment, above Two Thousand Million of Inhabitants, of whom there are but few who have not Faculties equal to those of our greatest Men – Millions of them at least might be raised, by moderate Leisure and Education, to look down upon the highest Philosophers of the present Day – But what might they not be when these future Advantages prevail, which must arise from the Employment of an unnumbered Multitude, in hastening the Perfection of Art, and extending the Boundaries of Science – But Kings and Courts have ruled for Centuries – And this Possibility is still looked to as the Dream of Speculatists – Our Rulers take away the Opportunities of Cultivation, and then scoff at the possible Bounties of Nature – They make the Desert, and then say that God ordered it – But let the first Nation in the World, be the first to declare War against these Blasphemers of Heaven's Benevolence, against these pestilential Harpies, who breathe Mildew, and blast the fair Countenance of the World.

C H A P. X.

AGAIN and again I urge you to remember, that under the Reign of Kings, the Good has always withered, and the Bad grown worse – The Multitude are Labourers and Slaves, and the Few are Profligates and Tyrants. Men of Letters are Flatterers and Sycophants; the Artist is the Tool of his Patron; and the brightest Efforts of Fancy are employed to hide or adorn the Monster which desolates Mankind – Under Republics, even indifferently formed, the most renowned Characters for Virtue, the greatest Philosophers, the most eminent Artists, and the most enlightened Multitudes, have always flourished – But your Republic may be far more perfect than any that have yet been established – You have but one Thing to keep in View – A Provision for the Adoption of Improvements, without the Danger of fatal Animosities. Experience will be abundant in its Discovery of new Things;

and your happiest Power will be, that of returning fast from the Path of Error and Abuse, and of crushing nascent Tyrannies in their Infancy, before they have Strength to resist, and by their Resistance to shock the whole Community.

In Republics these Things are easy – In Monarchies impossible. The Factions of a King are always formidable, and can be destroyed by no other Means, than the PERILOUS STRUGGLE OF AN UNWIELDY MULTITUDE. In Republics, a general Equality will soon discover the upstart Ambition of one or a few Individuals, who may be easily crushed, when there are no hereditary Prejudices and Attachments to support them.

Besides, a National Convention of Representatives, which is now convoked for your Relief, may be always assembled with Expedition and Effect – But under the enlightening Influence of a Republic, each successive Convention will be distinguished by increased Wisdom and Virtue, and of course by greater Abilities to improve and perfect your Government – From your next you will gain every Thing you can wish for, if you gain the Exclusion of Monarchy; or, in other Words, if you chuse Deputies who do not resemble the Members of your Constituent Assembly in their Opinions and Prejudices. THEY were deluded by a Fondness for the *English Form*, which has never yet been tried by Experience; and while this Delusion continues, you will be always changing one refined System of Corruption for another. May this Truth be regarded as an Axiom by your new Legislators – That TYRANNY IS the SURE OFFSPRING OF HEREDITARY OFFICE –[21] That every Man, born in the privileged Circumstances of a Ruler, is born out of the Course of Nature – His first Distinctions are a Violation of the Rights of Man – His Education is necessarily directed by Views and Expectations destructive to Character – And, sooner or later, his Ignorance or his Wickedness will punish the Folly which gave him his Power. – But what is peculiarly calamitous and execrable in EVERY HEREDITARY OFFICER, is eminently so in HEREDITARY KINGS AND GOVERNORS – They are generally the Produce of Debauchery and Impotence – They come into the World formed, diseased, and cursed by the Profligacy of their Royal Parents – Their Cradles are surrounded by Fawners and Sycophants – The first Language they hear, is that of Deceit; and the first Nourishment they take, is mixed with Poison to their Manners and Habits.

As they go on, through the various Scenes of a Royal Existence, what a Host of Powers, fatal to Character, invade them on all Sides – Their Servants indulge them, their Creatures flatter them, their Parents fill them with Prejudices, and multiplying Gratifications, subject them to

the Tyranny of the most destructive Passions.[†] Nor is it possible that any
Infusion of Knowledge can mitigate their evil Properties, or check their
sad excesses — The Probabilities are great, that they are naturally weak,
and *can* learn nothing; but the Probabilities are much greater, that if they
have Talents, they *will learn* nothing. — They have no Equals to stimulate
their Emulation and Industry, and they have no Superiors to enforce
Attention and Perseverance — They are secluded from the World and its
Intercourse, and their Minds must be narrow and barren. — They are
confined to the Society of a Court and its Minions; and how can their
Minds be otherwise than bad and profligate?

What a Prodigy must a good Prince be, when thus born, reared, and
educated — Or can it seem strange, that the WORST MEN in the World
have been HEREDITARY PRINCES, and that three or four only of
Thousands and Thousands would have escaped the Block, or the Gallows,
if they had received their Deserts. While Circumstances continue the same,
the Characters they produce will never vary — Consequently, while you
have Kings by Birth-right, it will be Folly not to expect a Succession of the
same Royal Enormities, which have hitherto disgraced and depopulated
Mankind. May the Wisdom of your National Deputies save you from the
Restoration of such Calamities — But if their Prejudices depress you once
more under the Domination of King, or expose you again to the Perils of
their OPEN Perjury and SECRET Treason, the Freedom you have struggled
for is a Phantom only — It may be soon blown away by some successful Plot,
or it may gradually vanish before the Breath of Intrigue and Corruption. If,

---

[†] Were I a Member of the National Convention, and were I asked, How I should
dispose of the present King? — My Answer would be regulated by the general
Question: Whether Monarchy or a Republic is to be established? — In case a
Republic is to be established, an Example of Severity would answer no Purpose,
as no similar Officer would succeed to derive Benefit from his Calamities. When
stripped of his Royalty, I would consider Louis the 16th as too contemptible
an Individual to gratify the Vengeance of a great People. Besides, during the War
he is a valuable Hostage. During this Period, in which every Object will be
estimated by the Folly and Prejudices of Tyranny and its ideot Adherents, Things
the most insignificant in themselves, may become of Importance to you — It
may happen, that the Existence of a valuable Officer, or a capital Patriot, or of
some City Obstinate in its Valour, may be secured, by making it the Price of
Security to the Royal Family. But when the Season of Peace commences, the
Descendant of the Bourbons should enjoy the Fate of Demetrius Poliorcetes
— In some distant, but safe Enclosure, he should sport and fatten amongst his
Stags — He should indulge all his natural Propensities, and display to your infant
Republic the full Brutality of his Species.

however, by the Voice of your Convention, you shew yourselves worthy of a free and manly Commonwealth, the vast Good you obtain will be lasting, and the Evils you chase away will never appear again. That Moment of Greatness will soon be at Hand, in which the Wisdom and Virtue of your Exertions will be testified, by the Magnitude of every known Blessing, and by the Birth of unnumbered Blessings hitherto unfelt by Mankind.

The oppressed World calls upon you – The Power is in your Hands – Give their Death Blow to the Desolators of God's Family – Overturn the Monarchies of the Earth. You have already shaken their Pillars – Already, you are the Terror of all Courts and Courtiers – The very Sound of your Name strikes a Panic into their Hearts. From the Story of your Enterprizes and your Victories they fly as from a Recital big with Woe and Horror – They see a flaming Sword of Vengeance hang over their Heads, and they see the small thread which suspends it – You have taught every injured slave how easily it is cut through, and you have given the oppressed a Lesson of Instruction, most awful to their Oppressors – you have shewn the People their Strength, and you have proclaimed the weakness of their Tyrants – Go on with the Cause of Mankind, and to the Example of bursting from your Chains; add the more seducing Example of multiplying in Numbers, and improving in Happiness, under the government of a FREE and EQUAL REPUBLIC.

Notes

1. Karl Wilhelm Ferdinand, duke of Brunswick and commander of the forces allied against France, published a proclamation on 25 July 1792 urging the citizens of Paris not to resist to his counter-Revolutionary army, and threatening vengeance if any harm came to the royal family. It was intended to intimidate the Parisians but had the opposite effect, leading directly to the storming of the Tuileries and the overthrow of the monarchy on 10 August.

2. The National Constituent Assembly evolved from the original meeting of the Estates General, and held power until 30 September 1791, when it dissolved and reformed as the Legislative Assembly. This body ruled for exactly a year before becoming the National Convention.

3. George Cadogan Morgan was present when the first of many drafts of the Declaration of the Rights of Man was put before the National Assembly by Lafayette on 11 July. It was adopted on 26 August 1789, and substantially extended in 1793. See p. 12.

4. *Hamlet*, III. iv. 103: 'a king of shreds and patches'.

5. There is no record of Morgan returning to France after 1789, but this conversation (*circa* 1791) could have been with visitors to London.

⁶ From 1791, especially after the flight of the royal family to Varennes, Coblenz became the seat of a large part of the French court in exile, and the headquarters of counter-Revolutionary activity. Doyle, *Oxford History*, pp. 302–3.

⁷ Given Morgan's close association with this person ('I was present when those letters were read'), we take this to refer to Richard Price. There remains some doubt, however, in that the position of the 'eminent Political Character' seems more extreme (or is recalled as such by Morgan) than that usually attributed to Price, who, after 1790, was obliged to defend himself vigorously from the charges of republicanism levelled at him by Burke. Similar sentiments do, however, appear in earlier works: 'let the united States continue for ever what it is now their glory to be – a confederation of States prosperous and happy, without LORDS – without BISHOPS – and without KINGS', Richard Price, *Observations on the Importance of the American Revolution* (London, 1785), p. 72. For Price's complex attitude to monarchy and republicanism, see chapter eighteen of Paul Frame's forthcoming biography, *Liberty's Apostle*.

⁸ For the use of 'directories' (more usually associated with the 'Directoires' which governed France 1795–9), see, for example, the 1792 translation of Jacques Necker's *An Essay on the True Principles of Executive Power in Great States*. Explaining that in France, no lucrative posts are now directly in the gift of the king, he writes, 'Every part of the interior administration is entrusted to councils, to directories of districts and departments, the members of which are elected by the people'(p. 227).

⁹ This is likely to refer to the position of the Feuillant party, or constitutional monarchists, who were in the ascendancy in the latter half of 1791. See further Doyle, *Oxford History*, Chapter 6, on the 'Breakdown of Revolutionary Consensus'.

¹⁰ Marcus Porcius Cato (234–149 BC), or Cato the Elder, was renowned for his wisdom and his plain living and became censor in Rome in 184 BC; Aristides 'the Just' (530–468 BC) was an Athenian statesman and famous strategist, praised by Plato for his good leadership. The typing error 'Austides' has been corrected by hand in the NLW version.

¹¹ Francis I of Austria (1708–65), Holy Roman Emperor; he was married to Maria Theresa of Austria and was the father of Marie Antoinette.

¹² Frederick William II (1744–97) was the nephew of Frederick the Great of Prussia and succeeded him in 1786. Inclined to mysticism, he joined the Rosicrucians in 1781. He was much influenced by his mistress, Wilhelmine Enke.

¹³ Willem V (Prince of Orange; 1748–1806) was the last stadtholder of the Dutch Republic; his aspirations to kingship were among the causes of the quashed Patriot rebellion of 1787.

¹⁴ St James's Palace was the principal London residence of George III; Carlton House was the town residence of the Prince Regent from 1783 and was substantially redeveloped by him between then and 1796.

¹⁵ Washington D.C. was founded as the national capital in 1791. Morgan's suspicion of George Washington's hold on power is one of the few points of contrast with Paine's *Rights of Man*, which is dedicated to the American leader, whom he knew personally. Morgan's comment echoes earlier anxiety about Washington's leadership

of the Society of Cincinnati, which Jefferson, Franklin and Mirabeau all denounced for its 'hereditary' potential. See Adams, *The Paris Years of Thomas Jefferson*, pp. 147–8, and Frame, *Liberty's Apostle*, chapter 14.

[16] The 'purging' of the Tuilleries refers to the attack on the palace on 10 August.

[17] This is what Paine calls a 'state of constant renovation': *Rights of Man*, ed. by Claeys, p. 162.

[18] This must refer to the proposal for a Navigation Act, on the British model, put forward in 1791 by the deputy Delattre on behalf of the Committees of the Navy and Agriculture and Commerce. See Jeremy J. Whiteman, *Reform, Revolution and French Global Policy 1787–1791* (Aldershot, 2003), pp. 160–3. A later Act proposed by Barrère was passed in 1793.

[19] The Republic of San Marino, on the Italian peninsula, is the oldest surviving consitutional republic in the world. It became a point of reference for discussions of the nature and practicability of republican government after Joseph Addison devoted several pages to the subject in his *Remarks on Several Parts of Italy &c. in the Years 1701, 1702, 1703* (London, 1705), pp. 130–40. Morgan may well be responding to its appearance in a recent publication by John Adams, *A Defence of the Constitutions of Government of the United States of America* (London, 1787), which is itself a response to earlier works by Richard Price and the French politician Turgot. Adams (pp. 8–16) argues that San Marino is not in fact a full republic, and that its size makes it worthless as a model for government in America. Both Adams and Addison claim that the executive changes every six months, not six weeks.

[20] Cf. Paine: 'Today it is one thing; to-morrow it is something else. It changes with the temper of every succeeding individual, and is subject to all the varieties of each. It is government through the medium of passions and accidents', *Rights of Man*, ed. by Claeys, p. 135.

[21] 'All hereditary government is in its nature tyranny', ibid.

Richard Price Morgan
A Journey Across America

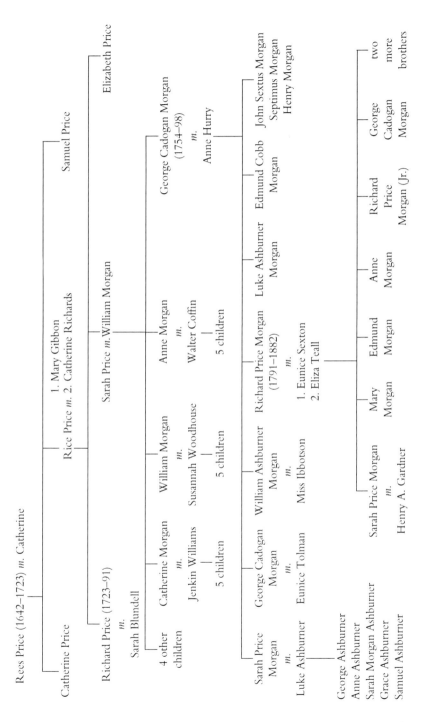

Figure 3. Price/Morgan family tree – abridged

Introduction

During the nine years that separate the 1789 Paris adventure of George Cadogan Morgan from his death in 1798, events occurred in France and Britain that we might expect to have undermined, as they did for many others, his radicalism, his republicanism and his support for the revolutionary route to change. Not only had his acquaintance Tom Paine been outlawed from Britain for writing the seditious tract *Rights of Man* (1791–2), he had also been imprisoned in Paris, under sentence of death, for advocating the banishment rather than the execution of Louis XVI (a policy advocated also by George Cadogan Morgan). The same period saw the execution of the king, the rise and fall of Robespierre, the Terror, and the start of a war between France and Britain. In Britain itself, Pitt the Younger began curbing homegrown radicalism by suspending Habeas Corpus in 1794 and passing the Treasonable Practices and Seditious Meetings Acts in 1795. A French invasion of Ireland was attempted in 1796 and another into west Wales in February 1797. There followed fleet mutinies at the Nore and Spithead, and in the spring of 1798 a major rebellion erupted in Ireland. Yet, despite all this, George Cadogan Morgan remained committed to his radical opinions. That we know this is due, in part, to the 'Autobiography' of his son Richard Price Morgan (1791–1882), which constitutes the final text in this volume. Part memoir, part travelogue, it encompasses the history of the Morgan family up to George Cadogan Morgan's death in 1798, the family's subsequent life in Britain, their emigration to the United States in 1808 and Richard Price Morgan's own travels in the American west and his later life as a farmer and canal and railroad engineer.

Another recently discovered voice from the Morgan family is that of Sarah Morgan Ashburner, the daughter of George Cadogan's eldest child, Sarah Price Morgan. Her unpublished memoir gives much additional information on the Morgans' life in Britain, their decision to emigrate to America and their early life at Stockbridge, Massachusetts.[1] There are, however, significant differences of tone and content between the two texts. As Sarah indicates, her memoir relies on 'the conversation of a Miss Sharpe' and her 'details are few and not sufficient'.[2] Generally, therefore, priority has been given here to factual details in Richard's 'Autobiography', which were after all written by someone who was present at the events described. The difference in the two writers' evaluations of the emigration itself is very striking, however, suggesting considerable conflict within the family at the time.

The last years of George Cadogan Morgan 1791–8

Evidence for George Cadogan Morgan's continuing radicalism in his last years comes from three sources. The first is the praise given to republican government in his publication, *An Address to the Jacobine and other Patriotic Societies of the French* (1792), reprinted above. The second is another of his published works, the two-volume *Lectures on Electricity* published in Norwich in 1794, the year Pitt began his repression of British radicalism. The 'Introductory Lecture' in volume one of this work contains an enthusiastic and, at a time of revolution in nearby France, potentially dangerous endorsement of the rebel and founding father of that more distant American republic, Benjamin Franklin. 'No tyrannicidal hero,' wrote Morgan, 'had ever proved more beneficial to his species, than the Republican, who, when he had disarmed the clouds of their fury, armed his countrymen on the very same spot in the cause of freedom and humanity.' That 'very same spot' was Philadelphia, on the Delaware River, where America's Independence had been declared in 1776. He continues:

> will not eminence belong to the example and intellectual greatness of Benjamin Franklin, who, when he had wrenched the thunder bolt from the grasp of tyranny and fraud, enrolled himself amongst the heroes of his country, chased away the minions and mercenaries of oppression, and amongst the ruins accumulated by despotism in the fury of its dying hour, established the first free community that ever blest the eyes of men?[3]

Morgan got to know Franklin in London through his uncle Richard Price (1723–91). Originally from Llangeinor in south Wales, Price was a London-based Dissenting minister who spoke and wrote on many issues, including moral philosophy, mathematics, demography, political and electoral reform, religious toleration, civil liberties, old age pensions, annuities, life assurance and the dangers of a national debt (on the subject of which he was consulted by Pitt).[4] Price supported the Americans in their revolution and, in his last public sermon *A Discourse On The Love of our Country*, given in November

1789, he also supported the opening events of the French Revolution, igniting what is now known as the 'Revolution Controversy' and spurring Edmund Burke to publish his *Reflections on the Revolution in France* (1790) in answer to Price's 'wicked principles'. Richard Price died on 19 April 1791 and his funeral cortège included more than fifty coaches, the pall being carried by, among others, Joseph Priestley. Many Jacobin Societies in France expressed their sorrow at the demise of a man they called the Apostle of Liberty; Horace Walpole, though, viewed Price's death as fortunate for all those who hoped to die peacefully in their beds.[5] It was after this radical uncle that George Cadogan Morgan named his son – Richard Price Morgan – who was born in 1791, the year Richard Price died. And it is in the son's autobiography that we find the third line of evidence confirming Morgan's continuing radicalism.

One of the earliest memories recollected by Richard is of sitting on his father's knee as a five-year-old in 1796 and hearing him sing the Revolutionary song 'Ça Ira', which had first appeared in 1790, quickly accruing new lines, including those advocating the hanging of aristocrats from lamp-posts. We do not know which version the boy heard, but the fact that it was sung to him *circa* 1796, after the execution of Louis XVI, certainly suggests that his father had not lost his republican spirit. Richard also recalls the political meetings held at his family's house in Southgate, near London, and his father's involvement with radicals such as Thomas Hardy, whom he describes as a 'particular friend'.[6] Though deeply unsettled by the Treason Trials of 1794 and Pitt's regime, Morgan did not change his opinions; even a few months before his death in October 1798 he was writing to his mother telling her of the horrific consequences of the Irish Rebellion in May that year and of what he called 'aristocratic opinions' of such events. Yet, while evidence of Morgan's post-1789 radicalism constitutes a major part of the importance and interest of his son's work, the account also provides us with an insight into the aftermath of the French Revolution and its continued influence on the lives of this family of Anglo-Welsh descent.

Morgan family life in Britain after 1798

Following George Cadogan Morgan's death in November 1798 his family entered on a life of peripatetic though always genteel poverty. As they moved from one set of relatives to another, including George Cadogan's brother, the actuary William Morgan, at Stamford Hill,[7] the family began gradually to break up. Richard's sister, Sarah Price Morgan, married and left for India with her husband Luke Ashburner, while one of his brothers, George Morgan, set off to scout out prospects in America – a 'first foolish step', according to Sarah Morgan Ashburner, for George 'knew no business . . . was kindly . . . and about as fit as Moses Primrose[8] to go forth among men and into the great greedy world'.[9] Though we might also expect that with the death of their father and the gradual break-up of the family the Morgans would now lose touch with their roots in south Wales, this was not the case and Richard's account describes in some detail a visit to south Wales and the birthplace of his father, grandfather and namesake Richard Price. While there he visited numerous cousins, aunts and uncles, some of whom were destined to become prominent figures in the early nineteenth-century industrial development of south Wales. It would also be to Llandaff in Cardiff that his mother, Mrs Anne Morgan, would return to tend her dying daughter, Sarah Price Morgan, on her return from India.[10]

As the family moved around the country the French situation continued to impact on their lives in various ways. Exiles from France came to live with and teach the Morgan children, among them a French governess and a French Catholic priest: the presence of the latter suggests a continuation in this Dissenting family of the religious tolerance exhibited by their father and his uncle Richard Price, despite both men's Protestant dislike of Catholicism. In 1802 Anne Morgan's youngest brother, the shipping merchant Ives Hurry, was taken prisoner in the English Channel: he would spend the next few years 'under circumstances of peculiar severity and injustice' at Verdun in France.[11] Remarkably, 'he escaped in disguise, made his way through France to the shores of the Mediterranean, and got safely home'; an adventure which was, according to the family memoir, 'the more wonderful because Mr Ives Hurry was a man upwards of six feet in height and large in proportion'.[12] Prisoners of war must have been much in mind, therefore, especially when the family moved to live in a house near Gosport which backed onto Forton military prison, a place housing many French prisoners, as it had Americans during an earlier revolutionary war. From Gosport the family's last journey in Britain would be to the docks at Clifton in Bristol, there to await a ship to take them to a new life in the United States.

In 1773, prior to the American War of Independence, Richard Price had written: 'America is the country to which most of the friends of liberty in this nation are now looking; and it may be in some future period the country to which they will be all flying'.[13] He could hardly have expected that this would be the fate of his own descendants. As we have seen, there is evidence that the family considered emigration to the United States as early as 1794,[14] at the time when George Cadogan Morgan was expressing his enthusiasm for Benjamin Franklin, and the British government was clamping down on radicalism. 'In the days of Pitt,' noted Sarah Ashburner Morgan, when 'the Priestley riots were still fresh in people's minds . . . many independent liberal people were greatly alarmed at the progress of arbitrary government, and talked much of migration.'[15] One member of the Morgan family deeply impressed by this 'prevailing talk' of emigration was Sarah Price Morgan's new husband Luke Ashburner and it was he who advised Anne Morgan, in the wake of her husband's death, 'to emigrate, to remove her eight fine boys to a land where the world was all before them – an open field for talent and industry – noble institutions – no blight of aristocracy – nothing to check the ardour of enterprise – the advantages of education and knowledge.' Luke, indeed, apparently considered Europe 'a barrel of gunpowder' waiting to explode.[16] By the time the Morgan family came to leave Britain in 1808 Europe had witnessed the extraordinary rise of Napoleon who, in Richard's words, went from being the 'champion of freedom and progress' hailed by 'true republicans' to a 'recreant to the cause, by making himself Emperor of France' in 1804.

In such circumstances, emigration to America in the hope of a new and improved life clearly seemed the best option; but from within the family there was considerable opposition. According to Sarah Ashburner, not only were her grandmother's sisters, her relations and her friends all against it, but so was her late husband's brother, William Morgan of Stamford Hill, who 'was indignant and so angry at the suggestion that his opposition did no good'.[17] Selling a valuable house in London left to them by Richard Price the Morgans realized 'all the money they could command preparatory to investments in the New World' and began their journey.

Departure for the New World 1808

In 1808 Richard Price Morgan and his family embarked at Bristol on the American ship *Anne Elizabeth* and set sail for a new life in the United States. But even as their ship began its journey the French situation intruded itself once again, this time in the shape of a flotilla of British ships assembling in a convoy for mutual protection. The 'Yankee captain' of their own vessel was also worried at the prospect of being boarded by French privateers, despite America's neutrality in the war between Britain and France. With their transatlantic connections, the Morgans would certainly have been aware of the dangers of an Atlantic crossing at a time of war, or indeed any other time. During the years leading up to the American War of Independence Richard Price had entertained a number of eminent American visitors to London, among them Henry Marchant, the attorney general of Rhode

Island. Following his return to America in 1772 Marchant wrote to Price vividly describing the onboard dangers of an Atlantic crossing and what might await even those travellers who reached their final destination:

> I arrived at Boston after Eight Weeks Passage. The latter part of it we had very disagreeable Weather, and once were in Great Danger of being consumed by Fire, thro' the Carelessness of the Carpenter who had left a Pot of Pitch on the Fire, which boiled Over, catched into a Flame and set on Fire the Caboose [ship's galley], but we were so happy as in a few Minutes to extinguish it. Upon my Landing I had the melancholy News of the Death of my Third and only Son about three years old. He died of the Measles, my two Daughters had it very ill, but are happily recovered. Mrs Marchant, from Her great Affliction, and Trouble, I found very low in Health and Spirits, but I hope She is getting better.[18]

Transatlantic crossings with tragic endings would be the lot of Anne Morgan in future years, but not this time. Despite a scare when their captain spotted 'a suspicious looking vessel', the Morgan family escaped interference by the French navy. They did, however, face ferocious 'head winds and rough seas', and 'a sudden squall, which took [their] sails all aback', and the experience of being 'in utter darkness' listening 'to the fury of the storm which howled over us'. Their compensation, according to the indomitable Richard, was 'the grand sight' of 'the ocean under the influence of such a gale'. With some of the crew sick, Richard was 'proud to distinguish [his] sailor-like qualities' and climbed the rigging to help set the sails. The entire journey took forty-seven days.

Beginning life in the New World

Following this stormy crossing to Philadelphia the family made their onward journey, via New York and the Hudson Valley, to a new home in Stock-bridge, Massachusetts. The seventeen-year-old Richard Price Morgan seems to have quickly settled into his New World life; unlike some of his brothers he does not appear to have ever returned to Britain nor hankered to do so. One who did make that journey again was his mother Anne. She made at least two return trips across the Atlantic in order to be with several of her other sons and daughters as they returned to Britain from India, journeys marked by tragedy as some of her children died in America while she was away and others while with her in Britain. If the hero of Richard Price Morgan's writing is his father, then his heroine is certainly his 'excellent' mother, who was 'always ready to encounter any hardships or submit to the severest sacrifices'. She appears all the more remarkable when we consider that, according to her grand-daughter's memoir, Anne 'had been brought up in the midst of easy abundance, without habits of economy or thrift such as might have fitted her for the wife of a poor Unitarian clergyman'.[19] At one point she looked after a family of nineteen including herself, servants, tutors, her own children and those of a number of widowed friends and relatives.

Before they left for America George Morgan, who had gone ahead of the family, reported back that he had secured 'a habitation for his mother' at Stockbridge, but when the family finally arrived there, it proved to be a small and 'horrid farmhouse'. Ever resourceful, and clearly with enough capital at this time, Anne Morgan took 'a nice, large, clean farmhouse'. Some time later Richard, who had trained as an architect before leaving Britain, designed and built a spacious family home on their land, which 'lay along the shores of the pretty river and [included] the lovely meadows called the Oxbow'. Ultimately, however, this house had to be sold and the family were obliged to live in a much smaller 'farmhouse, near the former dwelling'.[20]

Once settled in Stockbridge Sarah Ashburner implies that the family remained largely isolated from their American neighbours on account of their declaring themselves to be Unitarians: 'a sect held in great horror and unknown in that retired little village'. They also ran into problems by advancing ideas of democracy that were better suited to life in the old anti-democratic and monarchical regimes of Europe than openly republican America:

> When the boys were led into conversation or expression of opinion, it was that of the extremest Democracy. Parties ran very high in those days, and to ally yourself with the Democrats was a very different thing from democracy and popular opinions in England. They knew nothing of the great questions at issue and took up the badge, as they thought of it, of the cause they had left at home.[21]

Richard (who experienced it at first hand), however, paints a rather more sanguine picture of life in Stockbridge, where he 'readily joined the lively parties of farmers sons and pretty courting girls who frequently assembled' in the neighbourhood. Certainly he notes that the townspeople were 'punctilious in attending religious services' and that there was 'a general sense of respectability which every family strove hard to maintain'. If there was a degree of aloofness it emanated mostly from 'the family of Judge Sedgwick and their connections' who 'maintained their exclusiveness to a moderate extent, constituting thereby a circle of polished and agreeable people'.[22] A degree of snobbishness is clearly detectable in Sarah's account; for Richard, though he became acquainted with the Sedgwicks and was invited to visit them, it was 'a foolish bashfulness' that actually led him 'to prefer the freedom and manners that prevailed among our plainer neighbours'. Both writers note the visits made to the family by Catherine Maria Sedgwick (1789–1867), who would become one of the earliest female authors of note in America. Yet, while Sarah suggests that Catherine Sedgwick remained 'quite shy' of the Morgan family, Richard claims that she visited his mother 'frequently'. Catherine Sedgwick later converted from her family's Calvinism to the Unitarianism espoused by the Morgans, suggesting that either the sect was better known in Stockbridge than Sarah would have us believe, or else that she fell under the spell of the Morgan family's example.

A less immediate problem in the family's life in America after 1808 is the continuing war between Britain and France. Its consequences do, however, provide a leitmotiv to Richard Price Morgan's early travels in his adopted country, mainly through the British and American war of 1812–14 whose origins lay, at least in part, in the continuing conflict between Britain and France. By the summer of 1812 a French victory in the war with Britain seemed at least possible and there was confidence among some in the United States that if they too went to war with Britain they would be on the winning side. The US Congress declared war that same year, just as Richard Price Morgan set out on his first American river journey.[23]

Richard Price Morgan's early travels in America

In 1812, 'desirous of seeing the wonderfully fertile country in the far west', Richard Price Morgan began the first of his three journeys to the frontiers of America's early settlements, whose border then encompassed the Mississippi and Ohio rivers and the Great Lakes. Travelling with a companion by foot, wagon and stage-coach through Philadelphia and Lancaster he eventually reached Pittsburgh. There the two young men purchased a small boat and headed down the Ohio River to Cincinnati and Louisville, Kentucky (see map, Fig. 4). At Louisville, having worked for a while at a saw mill in New Albany to replenish their funds, they turned for home following an overland route northward which eventually brought them to Sandusky, at the western end of Lake Erie. Here they viewed the scene of a recent battle in the war of 1812–14 before travelling eastward and overland to Buffalo, which they found to have been burnt by the British a few months earlier. From Buffalo Richard took a stage-coach home to his family in Stockbridge.

A second journey was quickly decided upon but undertaken this time in company with two of his brothers and with the aim of making some profit from the enterprise. This involved buying timber at the town of Olean on the Allegheny River and using it to supply settlements along the Ohio River. Once the timber was sold they would use the profit to purchase flour to be taken onward to New Orleans via the Mississippi (see map, Fig. 5). Purchasing the timber proved expensive because of demand from 'a large crowd of emigrants' and even when purchased, made into rafts and sailed down the river they found 'an unusual supply of lumber offered for sale at every village'. Their selling price was consequently low. After various misadventures and miscalculations which resulted in the loss of 'our entire profits', Richard ended up working his way on another raft back up the Mississippi to Louisville. From there, having shrunk from a man who weighed 175 pounds in New Orleans to a mere 158 in Louisville, he bought a horse and returned home overland.

His third river journey would also have a profit motive but this time with timber purchased at 'a different point on the head of the Allegheny River' (see map, Fig. 5). Once again the sale of the lumber 'barely paid our expenses' and if the French Revolution forms a leitmotiv to Richard Price Morgan's early life, then a lack of a hoped-for profit from an assortment of beguiling enterprises is the depressing accompaniment to his years in America; this lack of fiscal skill seems to be a trait shared with his father, whom Sarah Ashburner declared to be 'no economist'. Nevertheless, on this last river journey Richard did manage to turn a profit of $500 after he bought a freight boat in Louisville and transported fifty hogsheads of tobacco to New Orleans. From there he sailed for New York and home.

Richard Price Morgan as farmer and engineer

With the completion of his three American river journeys Morgan's story enters a new phase as he involved himself first in farming and then, from about 1828, in a career as an apparently self-taught civil engineer working on America's early canals and railroads. Improvements in agriculture had been one of his father's interests, and at Stockbridge Richard was determined to try his hand at 'improved agriculture'. At this he was initially successful: 'By manuring my land highly I succeeded in raising several remarkable crops, which gained me premiums [from] agricultural societies.'

Unfortunately, at a time when money was needed in his family as never before (he had recently married) 'no immediate profits were . . . realized' and despite his achieving improved productivity from the soil, 'without capital to carry out this mode of improvement [further] the greatest efforts were ineffectual.' In 1828, therefore, nearing his fortieth birthday, he hoped to 'advance' his 'interests as an expert in the construction of railroads'. From this time on he was heavily involved in the surveying and construction of many new railroads in the area of New York, Boston, and Chicago, as well as work on the Croton Aqueduct designed to supply New York with a secure fresh water supply for the first time.

This phase of his life as a civil engineer is a paradigm of the change described by the historian E. J. Hobsbawm as that from the 'Age of Revolution' to the 'Age of Capital'.[24] It was a brutally competitive world, and Richard Price Morgan suffered grievously from the underhand dealings of the directors and boards of the various railroad companies for whom he worked, and the unreliability of men he trusted as partners. We see too the consequences of broader economic collapse, as in the so-called Financial Panics of 1873, '74 and '75, and the inexorable rise of the money men and robber-barons that characterize some of the early railroad developments in the America of this time. Yet, despite the fact that he faced an almost continuous lack of a secure income, a worry compounded by family tragedies including the death of his first wife and a son, he maintains an extremely positive outlook on life and, in the true spirit of his adopted homeland, displays an unwavering determination to achieve. What he does not appear to manifest is the radicalism of his forebears.

Although there is nothing in America akin to the revolutions that periodically convulsed Europe between 1820 and 1848 this does not mean that radical, even revolutionary opinions like those that reverberated through the earlier French Revolution were not a part of the American scene. In New York in 1829 for example George Henry Evans[25] bought the *Free Enquirer* newspaper from Fanny Wright[26] and Robert Dale Owen,[27] the son of Welsh utopian socialist Robert Owen.[28] Evans relaunched the paper as the *Workingmen's Advocate* and its first edition in 1829 carried the headline: 'All children are entitled to equal education; all adults to equal property; and all mankind to equal privileges'. Dale Owen would also be elected secretary of the Workingmen's Party, which supported an end to tax breaks for ministers and church properties, urged 'the wider community to 'destroy banks altogether,' and declared 'we have nothing to hope from the aristocratic orders of society'.[29]

Although Sarah Ashburner claims that in their early days in America all the Morgan boys expressed opinions 'of the extremest Democracy', there are reasons why Richard may have been less radically inclined – or at least less politically active – than his forebears. The life he found in the New World was, after all, one where religious discrimination was less evident and where there already existed a republican system of government and a constitutional division of church from state. But above all, one senses, Richard's own character was far from militant: his memoir shows him to be neither a natural radical, motivated by ideals or theories of social justice, nor indeed a natural capitalist, motivated by the potential acquisition of money or power. He is, if anything, a pragmatist. Perhaps, therefore, it is in the building of his own boat as a young man in order to take his 'Dulcinea' (an early flirtation) along the river Itchen in Hampshire, or in his later sailing of rafts down the Ohio and Mississippi rivers that we see his true character revealed: a practically inclined doer rather than a bookish theorizer and, in that respect, every inch the American pioneer he claimed to be. Dogged, good-natured, loyal to his family, he is also (perhaps fortunately, given his poor business sense) a man immune to the glamour of great wealth. In that sense at least he seems every inch the son of a man who once wrote:

> Make a man rich, and you make him lazy, luxurious, the slave of his own passions, and altogether the reverse of that busy self-denying agent which both Christianity and Philosophy point out as the only individual who can rise to moral excellence. Make a man rich and he is the slave of the times, the interested friend of every established abuse, and the most obstinate supporter of all religious and civil tyranny. Make a man rich, and you expose him to all the arts, the intrigues, the flatteries, the delusions, and all the poisonous frauds by which the worst characters in society rise on the idleness and passions of the most foolish.[30]

A last echo from the past

There remains one other thread linking Richard Price Morgan's auto-biography to his Welsh roots and to the French and American Revolutions. It was his namesake Richard Price who in his *Observations on the Importance of the American Revolution* (1784) argued: 'The negro trade cannot be censured in language too severe. It is a traffick which, as it has been hitherto carried on, is shocking to humanity, cruel, wicked and diabolical.'[31] Till the Americans abolished slavery, Price argued, they would not deserve 'the liberty for which they have been contending. For it is self-evident, that if there are any men whom they have the right to hold in slavery, there may be others who have a right to hold them in slavery.'[32]

In France in 1794 the Convention of the First Republic abolished the evil in the French colonies (although Napoleon as First Consul reinstated it in 1802 and it then continued until 1848). In the British Empire the slave trade would be outlawed in 1807 and slavery itself abolished in 1833. In America, however, its continuation is another leitmotiv haunting, albeit more faintly, the pages of Richard Price Morgan's journal. Not only did he visit places that formed part of the 'Underground Railroad', along which escaped slaves moved north toward Canada, but in Stockbridge, where the Morgan family settled, there resided the freed slave Elizabeth Freeman, of whose story they must have been well aware. As a slave she had escaped from her master because of the cruelty of his wife. In 1781 Theodore Sedgwick of Stockbridge had pled her case under the new Massachusetts constitution of 1780. This constitution (which had been partly written by Richard Price's friend John Adams) declared in Article 1 that 'All men are born free and equal'. The court found in her favour and she was declared free. Adopting the name Elizabeth Freeman she took up paid employment in the home of Theodore Sedgwick, whose son would later marry Sarah Morgan Ashburner, Richard's niece. Elizabeth's freedom, of course, did not mark the end of slavery in general. That would be left to a later American generation, one that included Richard Price Morgan, junior who, as the reader will see below, adds an elegiac postscript to his father's 'Autobiography'. Richard Price Morgan, junior became a friend of Abraham Lincoln and, as Colonel R. P. Morgan, would fight for the North in the Civil War of 1861–5 that finally brought to fruition the 1784 appeal for an end to slavery made by his Welsh namesake, Richard Price.

Editorial note

Unlike the diary of George Cadogan Morgan the handwritten text of Richard Price Morgan's 'Autobiography' could not be copied because of its fragile state. Instead, the Newberry Library in Chicago supplied the editors with a typescript. American spellings as well as some original quirky spellings have been left as originally written. Wherever possible blank spaces in the typescript, representing illegible words in the original text, have been filled following suggestions made by the editor and a perusal of the relevant page of the original manuscript by the library staff. In some cases photocopied sheets of the original were then sent to the editor for confirmation.

Square brackets [. . .] have occasionally been used to supply missing or uncertain text. Extremely long paragraphs have been broken up, and some very short paragraphs have been conflated. Richard Price Morgan's enthusiasm for commas has been somewhat curbed, and other obvious errors in punctuation in the typescript have been silently corrected.

Notes

[1] We are extremely grateful to Ginger Smith and Ben Coogle for permission to use Sarah Morgan Ashburner's unpublished typescript of twenty-four pages: it is cited hereafter as SMA, 'Memoir'. The constant repetition of Christian and family names in succeeding generations can be confusing and so the main branches of the various families discussed have been outlined in Fig. 3 and in the Index to the main families.

[2] SMA, 'Memoir', p. 11.

[3] George Cadogan Morgan, *Lectures on Electricity* (2 vols., Norwich, 1794), I, pp. xxxv–xxxix.

[4] In his first published book, *A Review of the Principal Questions and Difficulties in Morals* (London, 1758), Price outlined a moral philosophy that prefigured by more than twenty years Immanuel Kant's *Critique of Pure Reason* (1781); see Paul Frame and Geoffrey W. Powell, '"Our First Concern as Lovers of Our Country Must Be to Enlighten It": Richard Price's Response to the French Revolution', in Constantine and Johnston (eds.), *Footsteps of Liberty and Revolt*. He summarized his life assurance and annuities work in *Observations on Reversionary Payments* (London, 1771), which Franklin described as 'the foremost production of human understanding that this century has afforded us' (Benjamin Franklin to Richard Price, 11 February 1772, in Peach and Thomas (eds.), *The Correspondence of Richard Price*, I, pp. 125–6). Price's *Observations on the Nature of Civil Liberty, the Principles of Government, and the Justice and Policy of the War with America* (London, 1776) set out his thoughts on the American Revolution.

[5] See also D. O. Thomas, *The Honest Mind: The Thought and Work of Richard Price* (Oxford, 1977), and D. O. Thomas, John Stephens and P. A. L. Jones, *A Bibliography of the Works of Richard Price* (Aldershot, 1993). Price's collected correspondence, a veritable *Who's Who* of eighteenth-century Britain, France and the United States, is in W. Bernard Peach and D. O. Thomas (eds.), *The Correspondence of Richard Price* (3 vols., Durham, 1983–94).

[6] Thomas Hardy was a boot-maker who founded the London Corresponding Society in 1792. In 1794 he attempted to establish a convention in London along the lines of an earlier General Convention of the Friends of the People, which had been broken up in Edinburgh. Arrested on charges of treason, Hardy spent time in the Tower of London and Newgate before a nine-day trial that ultimately saw him acquitted.

[7] Although William Morgan was 'the natural friend and admirer of his brother's widow', Sarah Morgan Ashburner did not think that 'he got on with his sister-in-law' (SMA, 'Memoir', p. 5).

[8] The son of Dr Primrose in Goldsmith's *The Vicar of Wakefield* who swapped a good horse in exchange 'for a gross of worthless green spectacles, with copper rims and shagreen cases': E. Cobham Brewer, *Dictionary of Phrase and Fable* (Philadelphia, 1898).

[9] SMA, 'Memoir', p. 12.

[10] Named after Sarah, the wife of Richard Price, Sarah Price Morgan would be laid to rest in Llandaff Cathedral churchyard in 1820.

[11]   *The Monthly Repository of Theology and General Literature*, II (1808), 215.

[12]   Hurry-Houghton, *Memorials of the Family of Hurry*, pp. 69–70.

[13]   Peach and Thomas (eds.), *The Correspondence of Richard Price*, I, p. 164.

[14]   See p. 31.

[15]   SMA, 'Memoir', p. 8. During the Church and King riots of 14–17 July 1791 in Birmingham a loyalist mob ransacked and burned Joseph Priestley's house, laboratory and chapel because of his continuing support of the French Revolution. Priestley had been one of Richard Price's closest friends and he felt sure that if Price had not died in April that same year his house and chapel would have suffered the same fate. See Jenny Graham, *The Nation, The Law and The King: Reform Politics in England, 1789–1799* (2 vols., Lanham, 2000), I, p. 238 and n. 104. Joseph Priestley himself emigrated to America in 1794 and died there in 1804.

[16]   SMA, 'Memoir', p. 8.

[17]   Ibid., p. 9.

[18]   Henry Marchant to Richard Price, 21 November 1772: Peach and Thomas (eds.), *The Correspondence of Richard Price*, I, p. 151.

[19]   SMA, 'Memoir', p. 2.

[20]   Ibid., pp. 13–14, 20–1.

[21]   Ibid., p. 15.

[22]   Judge Theodore Sedgwick (1746–1813) was a Federalist and fifth speaker of the US House of Representatives between 1799 and 1801. He also served in the Massachusetts Supreme Court from 1802 until his death.

[23]   For the 1812–14 war, see N. A. M. Rodger, *The Command of the Ocean: A Naval History of Britain 1649–1815* (2004; paperback edn., London, 2005), pp. 564–5.

[24]   E. J. Hobsbawm, *The Age of Revolution 1789–1848* (London, 1962) and *idem, The Age of Capital 1848–1875* (London, 1975).

[25]   George Henry Evans (1805–56) was an English-born Paineite radical and sometime atheist, opposed to all forms of slavery and a champion of Indian Rights. His major concern was Land Reform. He published *The Workingmen's Declaration of Independence* in December 1829. In 1834 he became vice-president of The Working Men Opposed to Paper Money and in 1841 declared 'Property is any thing produced by labor. Therefore, I say, land is not property.'

[26]   Fanny Wright (1795–1852; 'the female Tom Paine'). Born in Scotland and from a wealthy background, she came to America in 1818. A woman of unconventional and radical opinions on sexual matters and religion she was called 'the Red Harlot of Infidelity' by her enemies. She stayed for a time at the Robert Owen colony of New Harmony. In 1825 she became the first American woman to publicly oppose slavery and she founded a colony in Tennessee to encourage racial equality. See Celia Morris, *Fanny Wright: Rebel in America* (Chicago, 1992), pp. 1–25.

[27]   Robert Dale Owen (1801–77) was a social reformer, abolitionist and editor of the liberal *Free Enquirer* with Fanny Wright. He served in the Indiana State Legislature (1836–8) and US House of Representatives (1843–7).

[28]   Robert Owen (1771–1858) was a Utopian Socialist born in Newtown, Wales. He bought the New Lanark cotton mills in Scotland and there began his experiment

in community building which continued with the New Harmony community in Indiana. He believed character to be made by circumstances and that 'all religions were tainted with error and that men could not live in peace and harmony until they recognized this fact'. He later returned to Newtown and was buried there. See *DWB*.

[29] See Edwin G. Burrows and Mike Wallace, *Gotham: A History of New York City to 1898* (New York, 1999), p. 519.

[30] Cited in Williams, *A Welsh Family*, pp. 125–6.

[31] Richard Price, *Observations on the Importance of the American Revolution* (London, 1784), p. 83.

[32] Ibid.

Autobiography of Richard Price Morgan, Senior

Family and early years

The Morgans and their ancestors dwelt for a long period in South Wales, in the County of Glamorganshire, which derived its name probably from their number and influence.[1] My Grandfather was a physician in Bridgend, a beautiful village in that county, a few miles from the Bristol Channel.[2] His family consisted of three sons, William, John and my father, George C[adogan] Morgan, and three daughters, whom I knew only by their names as married women, Mrs. Williams, Mrs. Coffin and Mrs. Huddy, and as the parents of numerous, highly esteemed cousins.[3]

My Father was born in 1754, and at a suitable age was sent to the celebrated University of Cambridge, in England, where his progress as a classical scholar and mathematician was highly creditable.[4] At the age of about twenty-five years, he was settled as a Unitarian minister, in Norwich, the county-seat of Norfolk, on the Eastern coast of England. Being called occasionally to preach to a congregation in Yarmouth, one of the five great seaports where many of the ships of the British Navy were frequently stationed, he became acquainted with the Hurry family, who were prominent as merchants and ship owners in that city.

There were three brothers, Thomas, Samuel and William Hurry, well known for their liberality in politics, as well as in their religious principles, and highly respected for their sterling integrity.[5] My Father soon gained their esteem and married Ann, the daughter of William Hurry, who was about five years his junior. She had two brothers, Edmund Cobb Hurry, the eldest, and Ives Hurry,[6] the youngest of the family, also three sisters, Hannah, Elizabeth and Priscilla, who afterwards became respectively, Mrs. Tolme, Mrs. Goodeve and Mrs. Morris.[7]

The descendants of these several families were consequently my contemporaries and occasionally the companions of my boyish days. As I may have occasion to speak of them in these memoirs, I subjoin a list of all my first cousins. The Tolme's consisted of one son and two daughters, Charles, Hannah, and Isabella. Edmund Cobb Hurry's children were, William Cobb, Anne and Edmund. Elizabeth Hurry, who lived single for many years as a companion to my Mother, eventually marrying Mr. Goodeve, a widower with three children. She had only one child, consequently the family was composed of William, John and Eliza Goodeve and Henry her own son. The children of Mrs. Morris were two daughters, Elizabeth and Mary, and an only son Frederick, afterwards distinguished as an Episcopal minister and for his great literary abilities.[8] Ives Hurry married a Miss Michel, who acquired some reputation as an authoress, their family consisted of two children, Maria and Samuel.[9]

Of the Morgan race, there were five of the Williams family, John, Richard, Mary, Kitty and Anne, and five of the Coffins, Walter, Mary, William, John and Anne. The children of William Morgan,[10] my Father's only surviving brother, at the time within my remembrance, were, Sarah [b. 1784], Susan [1788–1855], William [1791–1818], John [1797–1844], Cadogan [dates not known] and Arthur [1801–70]. In addition to these my Father's family comprised the total list of first cousins. These were Sarah Price Morgan, George Cadogan, William Ashburner, Richard Price, Luke Ashburner, Edmund Cobb, John Sextus, Septimus, and Henry.

My earliest recollections were in relation to my Father's residence in Southgate, a small village eight miles Eastward from London.[11] The building was commodious for a seminary as well as for the pursuit of his philosophical studies, and was selected probably, for those purposes, as at that time, having given up his position as a clergyman, he devoted himself exclusively to those objects.[12]

Before attempting however to describe his mode of life and the impressions I received at that period, it may be interesting to know that previously his pursuits had been closely identified with those of his Uncle, Dr. Price, who was also a very extraordinary man, possessing abilities of the highest order, whether as a clergyman or a philosopher.[13] His sermons and treatise on morals will compare favorably with any works of the kind that have ever been published. As a mathematician he had few equals, having originated the most perfect system of equitable life insurance, which is the basis of calculation up to the present time, and his financial works in reference to the national debt, gave him a high reputation in every part of Europe and eventually in the United States.

His philanthropy and disinterestedness, however, were the most remarkable features of his character and at the commencement of the American Revolution he boldly uttered his sentiments, as the friend of civil liberty, uniting with Dr. Franklin in warning the British Government of the consequences of the war and their injustice towards the colonies. He engaged the friendship of Dr. Franklin, John Adams, Dr. Rush[14] and many of the great statesmen and patriots of his day. He was looked up to even by his opponents in public affairs and appealed to for advice on subjects of the first national importance. Among his best friends was Lord Shelborn, who was prime minister when peace was concluded with the United States and their independence acknowledged. His death, which occurred in 1792[15] at the age of sixty-eight was deeply regretted by a large circle of friends and although he had manifested a strong desire to have a private burial, his funeral was almost without precedent in the magnitude and respectability of its attendance.

No one was more sincerely attached to Dr. Price than my Father. Associated with him in his ministry, emulating his virtues, with the ability to join him in his mathematical researches and enthusiastically devoted to the cause of freedom, the warmest friendship existed between them. It was, however, subsequent to the death of Dr. Price, that the interest and excitement caused by the French Revolution, had aroused the republican feeling in England to its highest pitch. In this my Father participated enthusiastically, and owing to the high esteem in which he was held, many of the friends of a free government shared his sentiments in relation to it.

A short time previous to this period, he had, in company with some of his friends made the ascent of the celebrated Mont Blanc and on his return from Switzerland, spent a few days in Paris, where he witnessed some of the terrible scenes then in progress, and was present at the taking of the Bastile, one of the most extraordinary achievements ever effected by a mob, but the people had risen with an irresistable determination to throw off the yoke of tyranny with which they had been so long oppressed, and was ready to sacrifice their lives in the effort.[16] Although only five years old, I well remember the eloquent description, given by my father, of the heroism displayed in the attack. It is not surprising, therefore, that some of my first recollections were the patriotic songs of the period. For while trotted on the knee, I was frequently entertained with the 'Marseilles Hymn', 'Ca ira' and a variety of lively French national tunes.[17]

My Father's pupils, although the sons of aristocratic families, fully imbibed his republican sentiments, and acquired under his instructions that fund of knowledge that afterwards made them useful citizens. It was not merely elementary studies that they were placed with him to pursue; their friends preferred providing for them the benefits and opportunity of expanding their minds under his effective teaching, rather than to subject them to the influence of vicious associates at Oxford or Cambridge. His schoolroom was his study, an immence apartment, not less than sixty feet in length, and twenty-five feet wide, and proportionably high, with book shelves requiring a step ladder to get access to all the valuable works in his extensive library.[18] Considerable space was appropriated to his philosophical apparatus, specimens for the study of natural history, anatomy and mineralogy, occupied the shelves of large glass cases, while a broad table supported electrical machines, jars and other experimental models, as well as globes and a grand telescope, manufactured by Dolland, which had been a legacy from Dr. Price.[19]

This room was strikingly characteristic of the great mind that furnished it. It was well organized, in every sense, for the acquirement of useful knowledge and its application to that purpose was faithfully carried out. If family pride was ever commendable, the descendants of a man possessing the wonderful attainments and excellence of character, for which my Father was so generally respected, have reason to acknowledge it. If they inherit any of the noble qualities which rendered him eminent, let them emulate the indefatigable industry and love of virtue, which gained the admiration and esteem of his numerous friends.

Under the circumstances in which I was placed, while we remained in Southgate, although very young I learned to appreciate his superiority of mind by the strongly marked admiration of all that were intimate with him. The same wonderful influence which he exercised over his pupils was directed to improve the minds of his children, with a love of knowledge and admiration of what is truly noble in the conduct of men.[20] It was not, however, in mental acquirements alone that he excelled. He cultivated the physical powers of his scholars as well as their classical and scientific tastes. He joined with all the enthusiasm of his character in their daily amusements, and particularly in fencing, practicing constantly with them to aid the instructions they received from a Mr. Goddard, a very remarkable man who had distinguished himself in the art even in Paris, and came once a week (eight miles from London) to give them the benefit of his skill, and to form one of a club meeting every Saturday afternoon, to discuss the political condition of the world, and the interesting events daily occurring on the continent.[21] Napoleon was then marching his army across the Alps and achieving his memorable victories, and as the champion of freedom his progress and successes were hailed with delight by these true republicans.[22] So freely did they express their feelings that Mr. Hardy, a particular friend of my Father's, was arrested and tried for *high treason*, but the spirit of the times, supported by the eloquence of Lord Erskine, obtained his *triumphant* acquittal.[23] My Father's scholars also partook of the surrounding enthusiasm, which would have ultimately established a republic in England, had not Napoleon proved recreant to the cause, by making himself Emperor of France.[24]

The superiority, however, of my Father's character did not merely consist of the bold political eloquence with which he electrified his hearers; his love of science, his exquisite classical taste, his moral rectitude, his amiability and practical benevolence, endeared him to all who knew him. Among his friends were the best men of the period, Dr. Price, Lord Landsdown,[25] Dr. Franklin, Professor Porson[26] and many other persons of superior intellect. It is not difficult to understand how much the sudden death of such an excellent man, at the early age of forty-four, was felt by his friends, or how generally his loss was lamented by both rich and poor. He left a family of one daughter and eight sons. The eldest, Sarah Price Morgan, was scarcely fifteen years old at the time of his death. She inherited much of his intellect and ability, and by his teaching acquired a love of knowledge which at a future period raised her to eminence in the highly cultivated society of Bombay to which place she had accompanied her husband, Mr. Luke Ashburner, immediately after her marriage.[27]

I well remember some of my Father's pupils, in consequence no doubt of my being at the right age to attract their notice. Sir George Cayly took my attention by his remarkable agility in jumping and fencing, and more particularly by a great exhibition of fire works when he was married.[28] Those, however, in whom I took particular interest, in after life, left my father's house when I was too young to remember much of them. Of these were Mr. William Ashburner and his brother Luke, who had left for India several years before my Father's death. Their only sister, Grace, when very young was married to Mr. Samuel Boddington, a rich West Indian merchant, residing on a beautiful estate in Southgate near my Father's residence, where he became acquainted with her.[29] The match was considered a most excellent affair. They lived together till she became the mother of two children, but under circumstances of great temptation, she eloped with her husband's cousin, Benjamin Boddington, who fell desperately in love with her, and availing himself of his relationship to become an inmate of the family, and the opportunity afforded by the daily absence of the merchant to his counting-house in London, eventually overcame her scruples.[30] A divorce was the necessary consequence, producing of course a great sensation. So much so that it gave rise, as was asserted, to the celebrated tragedy entitled 'The Stranger'.[31]

The two children, however, were placed under my Mother's care; the eldest, Grace, who subsequently married the Hon. Mr. Webster, son of Lady Holland,[32] and Samuel the youngest child, both of them constituting part of our family for many years. Three of the children of Mr. William Ashburner were also added to it soon after.[33] His brother became their guardian and sent them to England to receive their education. He had taken them out of the hands of their mother, who owing to her ungovernable temper had lived very unhappily with her husband. She had acceded very willingly to this arrangement, her motives becoming very plain from the fact that she married Sir Charles Forbes within five months after the death of Mr. Ashburner.

Soon after my Father's death we removed from Southgate to Stamford Hill five miles nearer to London, and not far from the residence of my Uncle, William Morgan. We occupied an old fashioned house, with a moderate rent, on what was called Bell's Lane, a little back from the great public road, but well adapted to the wants of our large family, consisting of fourteen children, for it had numerous rooms and extensive play grounds with a large garden. My Mother's sister, Miss Elizabeth Hurry, took charge of our elementary instruction, and we had masters, who came to teach Latin, French, and geometry, as well as fencing and dancing. There were many French emigrants at that time in England, one of these a Monsieur B[. . .], a Catholic priest, proved to be a very excellent teacher for us.[34] My Father's old friend, Mr. Goddard, came twice a week giving lessons in fencing and drawing, as well as in dancing. I had consequently the best opportunity for improvement, but while my brother William, two years older and with much greater natural abilities, made rapid progress in his studies, I was fully conscious of the great distance between us.

My Father had been so much devoted to scientific pursuits, that his valuable library and philosophical apparatus constituted the greater part of the property he left, and as my Mother's income was quite limited it became desirable that the elder boys should fit themselves for productive employment. My sister having manifested much taste and skill in drawing, determined to become an artist, and pursued the preparatory studies with great spirit and industry, under the guidance of Mr. Goddard, who was a perfect enthusiast on the subject. We were not in a position to go much into society, but Sarah and William received marked attention from our wealthy neighbors.[35] I was too young to join in their visits, and when allowed to go out, spent much of my time at my Uncle William Morgan's, who resided with his family at Stamford Hill. Sarah Price Morgan, my sister and Sarah Morgan, her cousin, were decidedly the belles of the neighborhood and had numerous admirers, but Sarah Price was too much devoted to the arts to indulge in flirtations.

My Father's Saturday afternoon visitors after his decease assembled for a while at Mr. William Morgans, but the moving spirit was no longer present, the survivor was too much of a conservative and too timid to suit these radical politicians, and when Napoleon ascended the throne of France, republicanism died out in England.[36] After we had lived at Stamford Hill about three years, Mr. [Samuel] Boddington, wishing to have his children nearer to him, induced my mother to move to a pleasant situation called

Craven Hill, only a mile and a half from his elegant residence in Brook St., near Hyde Park in the fashionable part of London. At Craven Hill, Sarah had far better opportunities for improving herself in drawing and painting. We were nearer the Royal Academy, and visited several celebrated artists, among whom were Benjamin West,[37] Mr. Opie[38] and the famous sculptor and draughtsman Flaxman.[39] On application being made to Lord Landsdown, he readily offered the niece of Dr. Price free access to his magnificent palace in Berkly Square, to copy the splendid paintings which ornamented its walls, works of some of the great masters; an opportunity which she accepted with no small degree of delight. My brother William was at that time employed as a clerk in one of the offices of Government and it devolved upon me to accompany my sister in her visits to this grand old house, to copy the pictures and statues, many of them in the library, one of the finest collections in England.[40] In the anteroom the old Marquis had placed a large portrait of General Washington and no other picture, deeming it the noblest memorial, he could select.[41]

The arrival, however, at that period of Mr. Luke Ashburner, from India,[42] soon revolutionized all our proceedings, he came, of course, to visit his old friends and to see his nieces and nephews, but soon learned to appreciate the superior qualifications of my sister [Sarah Price Morgan], and before the expiration of many weeks, became her husband. Much as my mother approved of the match, in other respects, the idea of a separation from a daughter, on whom she doted, to spend many years, perhaps, in India, required all her strength of mind to endure, but a plan was proposed, which in some degree reconciled her to this severe trial. As the rest of the family were all boys, it was Mr. Ashburner's opinion that the chances to get forward in life were better in the United States than in England and advised my mother to emigrate, promising to meet her there with his wife, in a few years.[43] The wedding had taken place in the autumn, but as the India fleet did not sail till December, the intervening time was spent among our numerous relations and friends, who vied with each other in showing attention to the bride and bridegroom. Mr. [Samuel] Boddington, who had married Grace Ashburner, my new brother-in-law's sister, although it awakened many sorrowful associations, threw open his house to his old friend, where the guests who assembled were of the fashionable order, many very intellectual individuals, however, were prominent among them.

Early in the ensuing winter I was invited to visit my cousin William Cobb Hurry at Holly Hill, a beautiful country residence his father had recently purchased in Hampshire, between Portsmouth and Southampton, where I remained till the departure of Mr. and Mrs. Luke Ashburner for Bombay.[44] The India ships lay at anchor for weeks before sailing, almost in sight of

Holly Hill, and my sister persuaded her husband to leave her there with us and several of my mother's sisters, till they were signalled to go on board. These were the last days I ever spent with her, and when I parted from her, although naturally very hopeful, I could not avoid the impression was almost irresistible that I should never see her again. The presentiment proved too true. A victim of the climate, after remaining in Bombay ten or eleven years she [was] unable to reach the United States, and having brought her young family of five children to England, survived only long enough to spend a short period with her mother, who at the age of seventy, recrossed the Atlantic to meet her.

Soon after the sailing of the India ships I returned to Craven Hill, where for a brief period we continued our studies as usual. My brother George in pursuance of Mr. Ashburner's plans embarked for the United States, very soon afterwards, to find a suitable situation to which the rest of the family might eventually move. My brother William had previously gone to France by the invitation of a Monsieur Mascelet, a friend of my father who had been appointed Prefect of Boulogne by Napoleon.[45] He returned home, however, at the close of the short peace between England and France under the treaty of Amiens,[46] with the intention of studying law and of following his sister to Bombay. At that time no professional men could go out to India excepting by permission of the East India Company, and lawyers could not practice in their country without passing through a certain routine in England, which occupied five years. William, however, by his extraordinary natural abilities and the friendship of Mr. Boddington and other influential friends, who gained for him the influence of some of the Directors of that immensely powerful Company, eventually obtaining leave to go out to Bombay with a good appointment. He remained in England, however, till he was twenty-one years of age, occupying a room in the Equitable Life Assurance office of which my Uncle William Morgan was Actuary, and availed himself of the best masters London could afford, to fit himself for his future duties in India.[47] During the period of two years, which he spent in that great Metropolis he was distinguished among his associates for his fine personal appearance and physical strength as well as his intellectual superiority.

In the meantime George had located himself on a farm in Stockbridge Massachusetts, and wrote favorably of the United States, but my mother was unwilling to leave England as long as William remained.[48] My Grandfather Hurry also invited her to come and live near him and her sisters, Mrs. Tolme and Mrs. Morris, till she should feel prepared to embark for the United States. He had removed from Great Yarmouth to a small town ten miles South of it, called Loestoft, where he could have a view of the German Ocean, across which, in early life he had made numerous voyages.[49] A country home was, consequently, found for us called Mutford Hall,[50] an easy two hours drive from Loestoft, passing midway an elegant residence called Normanstone, where a boarding school for large boys was kept by my Uncle Morris.[51]

1805: a visit to south Wales

Before removing from Craven Hill, however, to Mutford Hall, my cousin William Cobb Hurry, whose father[52] was lying in a very precarious state of health at Clifton Springs near Bristol, invited me to accompany him on a visit to that place and to make an excursion into South Wales. As he had always been my favorite companion, I was well pleased to go with him, for he was far better informed on most subjects and was much attached to me. We travelled in the Mail Coach to Clifton and remaining there a few days found much to interest us, for we did not realize how hopeless a case was that of Mr. Edmund Hurry, who was attended in his sickness by the celebrated Dr. Beddoes, one of the most eminent physicians of that period. His conversation was very agreeable and instructive, and being brother-in-law to Maria Edgeworth, I regarded him with great respect. He was the author of many useful works, and by the aid of his father-in-law, Sir Richard Lovel Edgeworth, founded a Pneumatic Institute in which the wonderful chemist, Sir Humphrey Davy made his first remarkable discoveries.[53]

It was natural, however, for two young lads of fifteen to be glad of an opportunity to change the scene, and having hired two good saddle horses we set out for South Wales. Crossing the Severn with our horses in a ferry boat worked with sails and oars,[54] we were soon on the road to Bridgend, in Glamorganshire, the birth place of my Father and Dr. Price.[55] When we arrived there we were most cordially received by our cousins, the Williams and Coffins, who devoted themselves most earnestly to our comfort and entertainment. A variety of parties of pleasure were immediately devised and the various rides to points of interest and beauty, among the old Welch mountains, were agreeable beyond description, a majority of our companions being very pretty young ladies, who had mounted their ponies and were with us on almost every occasion. Some of the scenery we witnessed surpassed anything I ever remember to have witnessed. In one instance we ascended by a winding road to the top of a little mountain called Margam where we had a view of the Bristol Channel, and the magnificent sea coast for many miles East of Cardiff, studded with elegant villas, and promontories of rocky cliffs almost enveloped by the luxuriant growth of shrubs and timber. This scenery is said to rival the Bay of Naples in many respects.[56] At the foot of this hill is an estate highly improved by cultivation and magnificent green houses, containing every variety of tropical production,[57] the whole of the grounds exhibiting in a striking manner the mildness of the climate, for so high a latitude; produced no doubt by the Westerly winds and remarkable currents which rush during high tides into the Bristol Channel, of this, during our stay at Bridgend, we became conscious by a startling incident. After bathing one day on the beach, which extended from the high cliffs, at low water more than half a mile, we ventured to visit some singular caves at the base of these perpendicular rocks. While exploring them a sudden dashing of water at the mouth of the cave we had entered called us forth by its unexpected proximity, and as we had a long stretch to pass along at the foot of the bluffs before there was any chance for egress, it was a scramble for life part of the distance, being compelled to make our way through the water. We afterwards learned that the spring tides sometimes roll in like a tremendous wave and the tide has with a very strong Westerly wind, been driven up the Severn till at flood it has risen 60 feet.[58] This was the only exciting adventure that we encountered during this exceedingly pleasant little tour.

Nothing could exceed the attention we received from our Welch relations. We went to see the great iron works and the tramway to Cardiff, on which at this early period an attempt had been made to propel locomotives by a continuous line of cogs, in the middle of the track. This was as early as 1805, twenty-five years previous to the opening of the Liverpool and Manchester Railroad.[59] How little did I then foresee the changes which have taken place in the construction of railroads, or the progress of improvement in the nineteenth century up to the present time, but my anticipations were not more imperfect than the ideas I could then form of the occurances of my subsequent life. We returned to Clifton to find my Uncle no better and I had scarcely reached Craven Hill when his death was announced.

At this period our family consisted of two Boddingtons, three Ashburners and six Morgans. My Mother and her sister Elizabeth, a French governess, Madam St. Aubin, and a tutor, John Jones, Esq.,[60] a young Unitarian clergyman made up the complement, and accompanied by two servants, a cook and her husband. The whole crowd soon after took their departure for Mutford Hall, four of the elder boys, tutor and hired man, with the furniture taking passage in a coaster sailing from London to Great Yarmouth, while the ladies and smaller children travelled in Po[s]t chaises, meeting us in the course of a week at our destination, not without perils by sea and many annoyances by land.

Mutford Hall was an old family mansion, built as indicated by the date figured on its walls, in 1605 [1607], and consequently in the architectural style

of that time. There was a large farm attached to it which with the exception
of the garden and orchard was rented separately. There were no houses in
the immediate neighborhood, excepting the farm cottage and the blacksmith's,
but with two or three additional servants we formed a little community of
our own, and our isolation was unquestionably an advantage. I had a workshop and a turning lathe and the farm afforded a wide range for amusement.
Mutford was originally, in all probability called <u>Mud-ford</u>, for a broad marsh
passed through the middle of the farm, which was enlivened by a multitude
of lapwings and herons, as well as an enormous rookery, in the timber of
an adjoining estate, belonging to a certain Lord Rouse, and which swarmed
with rabbits, hares, pheasants and partridges, much to the annoyance of the
peasantry, who had to submit to their depredations, not daring to kill them
owing to the severe penalties of the game laws.

The principle advantages to compensate for living in so remote a situation
was the occupation of a large commodious house at a low rent. We were
six miles from Normanstone, the residence of my Uncle Morris, whose
boarding school was near the road leading to Loestoft, but we had a fine
large black mare and a regular Irish *jaunting car* with seats for a dozen if
required,[61] and as the lanes were smooth and level it was no great task to
meet our Yarmouth cousins at Normanstone where arrangements had been
made for that purpose. During our stay at Mutford Hall I was allowed to
accompany my aunt Betsey and Mr. Boddington's children on a visit to that
gentleman's elegant mansion in London; where we spent a month very
pleasantly. It afforded me many opportunities for pleasure and improvement.

Among the visitors we met there was the great sculptor, Mr. Flaxman,
who although personally deformed was regarded at that time as the most
perfect artist in Europe, and by his engaging manners won universal admiration. It was very gratifying to become acquainted with men of such great
celebrity. The great wealth of Mr. Boddington enabled him to indulge
his taste for the artistic and elegant among which was a fine collection of
engravings as well as books splendidly bound and illustrated. Besides free
access to his library there were many interesting locations in London which
I had the opportunity of visiting. I attended in one instance the Royal
Institute to hear a lecture by Sir Humphrey Davy, and although I understand
but little of the wonderful discoveries he exhibited, the honor of having seen
and heard so extraordinary a man is worthy of record.[62] We had occasionally
at Mr. Boddington's grand dinners and parties of the elite and fashionable,
who sometimes assembled there some to enjoy each others conversation,
some to display their consequence.

This month of aristocratic life had no influence to stir my envy or ambition,
but my brother William, who attracted great notice by his superior intellect,

fine personal appearance and numerous accomplishments, naturally acquired a passion for polished society; which he retained through life. In going to India he determined to make a fortune, and availing himself of all the advantages which London afforded and where he remained during the succeeding year or two, he devoted himself with indefatigable industry to the acquirement of such knowledge as was deemed necessary for the East India service.

Southampton

On our return to Mutford Hall, my brother Luke, in company with our hired man set out for the United States and soon after an event occurred which deprived us of our aunt Betsey, who had been a number of years as much devoted to us all as our own mother. Her hand was solicited in marriage by a rich widower from Gosport a Mr. Goodeve, who had been intimate with my Uncle Edmund Hurry, when in business in that city.[63] The offer was accepted and Mutford Hall soon after abandoned, for my mother could not endure the thought of being so far away from her favorite sister, during the comparatively short period she contemplated remaining in England. Another removal was therefore planned and effected, to a village called Forton,[64] about a mile from Mr. Goodeve's residence in Gosport. This gentleman was erecting a new and elegant dwelling house under the super-intendence of Mr. James Kent, an architect of some note in Southampton. By Mr. Goodeve's advise I was placed with Mr. Kent to study the profession, and accordingly went to live with him.

Southampton was a commodious seaport on an arm of the sea West of the Isle of Wight, about twenty miles from the great naval depot at Ports-mouth, and the country in the vicinity was considered very fine, where many beautiful localities were selected for country residences, several of which were undertaken by Mr. Kent, as architect and builder.[65] I was taken occasionally to view the progress of these villas and become initiated in his peculiar modes of construction, but I preferred working in the joiners shop, learning something of the trade. My mother had paid a large sum for advantages it was supposed I should derive from the prestige of having been instructed by so noted an architect. But Mr. Kent was a visionary speculator and had involved himself in schemes to improve certain lands he owned, by raising levees along the shores of the river I[t]chen near which he had established his residence. He was beset by his creditors nearly the whole period of nearly three years, during which I resided with him. I was con-sequently left to pursue my own fancies and tried my own mechanical skill in building a pleasure boat, about twenty feet long, and according to the mould I obtained from a neighboring ship-wright, by whose assistance I completed and rigged the little craft.

The Kent family consisted of a son and daughter, over twenty-one years of age, a second wife with two little daughters about eight and ten, and a Miss Anne Sutton, governess, and part of the time two young fellows, relatives, about my own age, sent from London to be kept away from bad companions. Fortunately I had no taste for the society of these youths, who soon disclosed their predilection. When not engaged about my boat I was not prone to traverse at night the streets of Southampton. Mr. Kent had some interesting books, and I found much to learn from Chamber's Dictionary, the cyclopaedia of that day. We had too, on the whole, a pleasant little family, although young James who hated his mother-in-law, kept much aloof, while his father was rarely at home, excepting on Sunday evenings, when he used to entertain us over his brandy and water, with various hymn tunes, being a prominent chorister in the Presbyterian church.

The governess was pretty well versed in doctrinal controversy, and spoke French quite fluently, and as I was the only one present having any knowledge of the language, it was not difficult to carry on a little flirtation at the expense of good manners. Anne seemed to be well aware that the French language is very expressive and startled me one evening in a way that caused a blush to the tips of my ears; I managed, however, to parry the attack by affecting to misunderstand her. My sail boat at that time so engrossed my thoughts that I was by no means prepared to engage in the romantic. I invited Anne, however, with her two pupils and their mother to take a sail with me on the beautiful river I[t]chen. The several parties eagerly accepted of the invitation. A convenient time was fixed and a fine breeze prevailing we started in good style on our excursion. Taking the helm with much importance and having engaged a boy to attend to the sails, the pretty craft swept rapidly through the waters much to the delight of my passengers. The shores of the river are very pretty, and as we alternately passed woods, lawns and villas, the beauty of the scenery and balmy mildness of the weather, seemed to leave nothing wanting to render this exhibition of my nautical skill a perfect success, but the glories of this world are often of short duration. We had hitherto sailed with a favorable tide and fair wind. In returning it became necessary to tack, running from shore to shore, with the descending tide. The little vessel answered her helm beautifully, the breeze freshened as we approached the ship yards, and eager to display the good qualities of the new boat to the crowd of ship carpenters, who had full view of our movements, I unfortunately ventured too near to them and before I was aware of it the keel touched the bottom and in spite of all my efforts we found ourselves fast aground on the great Northam mud bank, with a *falling* tide.[66] In ten minutes the mud was bare on every side. Twenty rods of knee-deep mud lay between my boat and the shore.[67] To say I was crestfallen does not express the mortification I experienced. There I was, with my frightened passengers, the laughing stock of the numerous spectators, before whom I was exhibiting my seamanship. Eight hours must pass before the returning tide would set us afloat and night approaching.

While bewailing our misfortune, by good fortune an Irishman, of the tribe called *mud-larks*, made his appearance and with the promise of a reward, came to our relief. He lashed to his feet two pieces of board, with a surface equal to a square foot each called mud pattens, and came off to the boat without difficulty. My Dulcinea threw herself gracefully into his arms and was conveyed safely to the shore, the children were easily carried to her, but the old lady being too heavy for transportation in the same manner took a position faithfully represented in a vignette introduced in Bewicks Natural History,[68] which if my readers have not seen, I will not attempt to describe, but trust to their imagination. The lady, however, too thankful to escape from so disagreeable a predicament, had the wisdom to disregard the uncontrollable laughter which broke forth while the passage to dry land was effected.

After this unfortunate voyage, I did not again attempt to obtain the company of my fair friend on my boating excursions. I frequently steered my course over rougher waters sailing between the Isle of Wight and the Main land, where sometimes, the distance being seven miles, a pretty heavy sea was encountered. In fine weather it was a delightful sail from Southampton to Portsmouth harbor, from whence I could pass through an inlet to a point within half a mile of my mother's house at Forton. Home always has its attractions, and at the period I am describing many circumstances contributed to increase my attachment to mine. I was tired of living at Mr. Kent's, where the embarrassments he labored under so deranged his affairs that I was learning nothing by remaining with him.

During a visit at home I happened while bathing to step on a broken glass bottle, which had been thrown into the river, inflicting a serious wound on the under side of my foot, which prevented me from returning to Southampton for several weeks. Although it was a great annoyance to be lame, the sympathy manifested by Anne Sutton, disturbed me to a much greater extent. She came seventeen miles, with Mrs. Kent, to ascertain the extent of my suffering, and I was obliged to explain to my mother that although she was a very amiable girl, I much preferred that she should place her affections on someone else. I did not, therefore, return to Mr. Kents, and was glad to hear, about a year later, that Anne had found her affinity and was married.

My mother when she removed her family to Forton, intended to remain there till it should be deemed advisable to set out for the United States, but the necessity of incessant removals seemed to be part of her hard lot. We had a large court and garden but with a lane only. Intervening was an immense wooden building used by the British government, in which were confined fifteen hundred prisoners of war.[69] Some additions had been made to it in which were a large quantity of shavings and waste lumber. A spark of fire got amongst them at mid-day and in less than an hour the greater part of the whole fabric was consumed. A large guard, however, arrived from the military barracks in the neighborhood, soon after the fire commenced and the prisoners were conducted to a place of safety. Our house barely escaped, and we might possibly have remained in it in safety, but as Mr. Goodeve's new house was not likely to be completed for some months, a house was hired at Stoke, about a mile distant, near the sea shore, where we could be more pleasantly situated, while Mr. and Mrs. Goodeve could board with us.[70] These arrangements were therefore made to the satisfaction of all parties. I can hardly remember how I spent the next six months. The subject of our emigration to America was often discussed and we were in one sense completely unsettled. We were near the sea and enjoyed bathing and boating to our hearts content. Our rent expired, however, on the first of April, 1808, and the house we occupied could not again be hired excepting for a year. We had now determined on sailing for the United States during the following summer, about the last of June [1808], and although *another* removal seemed terrible the payment of a heavy annual rent for occupying a house three months, was out of the question. In this dilemma, my cousin William Cobb Hurry, generously offered the use of their beautiful country seat at Holly Hill rent free.

It was an elegant mansion with a back ground of young timber upon the summit of an elevated piece of ground, commanding a magnificent view of the sea, at the intersection of the broad inlet to Southampton and the Western Channel, between the Isle of Wight and the main land. The farm surrounding the dwelling house was fenced with Holly, from which the estate derived its name and unique appearance. We spent the last three months of our English life at this pleasant locality, the time passed agreeably enough, but our voyage to the United States engaged all our thoughts. It was considered by far the best plan to cross the country and sail from Bristol. My uncle, Ives Hurry,[71] made the necessary arrangements for my mother, and engaged the cabin of a small American merchant ship bound for Philadelphia, and to sail from Bristol about the middle of July. Our family at that time consisted of only nine individuals, my mother, Mary Ashburner, myself and four brothers, Edmund, John, Septimus and Henry, together with our cook and her child two years old. The Boddington's had remained with their father, and the two Ashburners had also staid in London, under his supervision, William intending to go to India and John to become a surgeon.

The crossing to America 1808

Three days after leaving Holly Hill, by the aid of a huge English wagon with our goods and many things we imagined we should need in the United States, we arrived in Bristol. Mrs. Goodeve and her husband having travelled with my mother, Mary and the younger boys in post chaises. Taking up our quarters near the great basin connected with the splendid docks extending from Bristol to Clifton, in which our ship was lying, we waited a few days till she was ready to sail. There were many objects of great interest around Bristol, but the excitement of our little company hardly suffered us to give them a passing notice. We enjoyed in no small degree the novelty of the scene, and went on board of the *Anne Elizabeth*, in high spirits. It was of course different with my mother, unused to such accommodations as we were forced to put up with in a contracted cabin, surrounded with common berths only, and which served for our dining room, as well as for sleeping. It showed her great strength of mind to notice how cheerfully she encountered the annoyances, inseparable from these arrangements.

At length we parted from our friends and our vessel was lowered some twenty feet, through the lock, into the river Avon, where an ebbing tide soon carried us between the high cliffs on each side to the vicinity of the Bristol Channel, where we came to anchor, a heavy gale from the West having set in. This was a rough commencement for our voyage, particularly as we dragged our anchors till we grounded in shoal waters and after the falling of the tide our ship lay almost on her beam ends, our masts inclining at an angle of forty-five degrees. Many other vessels were in the same predicament and the news of our disaster soon reached Bristol, which brought Mr. and Mrs. Goodeve in their carriage to the nearest point on the shore, off which we were lying and by means of a small boat they came on board. As there was no real danger, the ship merely resting in the soft mud this occurrence was only the source of some delay and the occasion of a second parting between my mother and her sister. In a few hours, however, the gale abated and the ship righted with the rising tide. The second night was, therefore, passed in comfort, every one was tired with the excitement and inconvenience of this delay. Early the following morning we were aroused by the noise of weighing anchor and setting sails. We had scarcely time to finish our hearty breakfast, before our ship with a fine breeze was gliding out of the mouth of the Avon, into the magnificent waters of the Bristol Channel.

Nothing could exceed the grandeur and beauty of the scene which presented itself, as we ascended to the deck. Riding buoyantly over the gigantic swells driven in from the Atlantic by the recent gale, our smart little ship was dashing through the water under a seven knot breeze. We soon found ourselves in the midst of a large outward bound fleet, which had been for several days windbound, and every vessel was crowding sail to keep up with a large armed ship, their convoy to protect them from the depredations of French privateers, but with all their efforts, which were continually urged by the firing of signal guns on board the frigate, she was obliged to shorten sail to avoid running away from them. The sun shone brightly on the crests of the waves, on the numerous crafts rising and falling upon the surface beyond. We had a fine view of the Welch coast where the most remote objects were brightly visible, the white villas, the landings on the projecting promontories and several picturesque villages. This landscape and the lively scene before them awakened no small delight among the little group on the deck. It was indescribably heightened by the rapid movement of our clean built American ship, passing every vessel successively in a few hours distancing the whole squadron, and before night, we could scarcely discern it with a spy glass. Being a neutral vessel we had no apprehensions from the idea of privateers.

At sunset we were abreast of Lundy Island at the mouth of the Bristol Channel. Here our pilot left us, and before dark the last vestige of old England had faded from our view. Soon after, however, we were each ensconced in our several berths, sleeping as soundly as the novelty and peculiarity of our accommodations admitted of. It was a tremendous change for my poor mother accustomed as she ever had been to the luxury of the most comfortable bed that could be devised. But she cheerfully occupied a lower berth in one side of our small cabin, while Mary Ashburner and Rebecca Miles with her little girl disposed of themselves in the adjoining bunks. As for myself and brothers sufficient room was found on the opposite side. Our dining table was screwed to the floor in the center of the cabin, its surface being chequered by cleats to keep the plates and dishes from being thrown to the floor, by the rolling to which the ship was subject in hard weather, during some of which it required the utmost care to avoid being ejected from the upper berths.

It was our lot, however to encounter heavy headwinds and instead of making a quick passage we were driven, in spite of the fine sailing qualities of the *Anne Elizabeth*, very far out of our course. The Atlantic was rough

during the greater part of our voyage and through the first week we experienced much seasickness, several of the sailors, even, suffering from it. Mary
Ashburner was a remarkable exception, not being the least affected, and
enjoyed the fun of plaguing the rest of us to her hearts content.

Our ship was fortunately a very strong built vessel, as well as a fine sailer,
but the avarice of the owners had led them to load her very heavily with
tin and glass bottles in consequence of which we were several times in great
peril, for during a heavy gale she was almost buried in the heavy seas which
rolled over her. When the weather was fine, however, although this was
not often, we found many objects of interest to notice. The little storm
birds, called 'Mother Cary's chickens',[72] which hover perpetually in a ships
wake, the curious fish called the nautilus, or the sailor, which raises its sail
and skims the surface[73] and occasionally a flying fish would encounter our
sails and fall upon deck. Large schools of porpoises would sometimes come
dashing past the *Anne Elizabeth*, swift vessel as she was, with astonishing
rapidity, although under a seven knot breeze. Once a whale of considerable
magnitude made a dive directly under our ship. We had, however, during
the greater part of our voyage to buffet head winds and rough seas. If the
yarns of our sailors were to be credited we escaped many dangers, that we
were not conscious of. We were struck one night by a sudden squall, which
took our sails all aback and with our heavy load, great exertions only saved
us from making stern way filling by the cabin windows and going to Davy's
locker in the least supposable time. At another time during the night, we
shipped so heavy a sea, that the question whether the Morgan family would
ever reach the United States or not seemed likely to be decided in the
negative.

Our captain was a close calculating yankee, part owner of the vessel,
careful not to incur the expense of hiring too many hands, yet very fearful
of any possible misfortune. As several fell sick he was short handed and our
voyage was protracted by the necessity of caution in relation to carrying sail.
He was glad to have assistance from such of the passengers as could be useful.
I was the only one, however, who dare venture in the rigging, and having
had previous opportunities of becoming handy in this way, I was proud to
distinguish my sailor-like qualities. I even assisted to hand the top gallant
sail, when there was considerable sea on, and I once eluded the efforts of
two active sailors who attempted to tie me in the rigging to extort a treat,
when we should arrive in port.

Our captain seemed to have many other anxieties, sometimes a suspicious
looking vessel would come in sight and in spite of the stars and stripes, he
did not know but that some of these Frenchmen might turn pirates. He said
that they might want provisions or water and if such was the case would

not hesitate to plunder us. Our pigs and poultry escaped, however, and we ourselves from being taken to France. His qualities as a seaman were, nevertheless, good, and he was always correct in his prognostics about the weather.

One afternoon the wind died away almost entirely, but as the sun went down the captain's nose seemed redder than common and with a most sour expression of countenance he remarked that the sky looked very dirty and they must be prepared for a blow. Sure enough before midnight we heard an unusual stir upon deck, and soon the first mate and a hand with him came into our cabin to fasten in the dead lights, which were thick planks, well battened and fitted to a recess outside our cabin windows. These were well secured and we were left in utter darkness to listen to the fury of the storm which howled over us. In the morning Edmund and myself were the only two permitted to come on deck. The rest, owing to seasickness and the tremendous lurches of the vessel, were glad to *hold* themselves in their berths. We were ordered to seat ourselves in the lea of the companion. The gale was blowing with tremendous fury, but having plenty of sea room and a strong vessel, we weathered the storm. The ship had only one thick stay sail hoisted, which kept her quartering[74] to the waves, the helm was lashed down while the mate and one man remained on deck to watch, the rest of the hands went below to rest after the fatiguing efforts they had gone through with in making everything strong. It is, however, a grand sight to behold the ocean under the influence of such a gale. The deep blue sea rolling in long swells forty or fifty feet above the level of the deck and crested with white foam. The boyant ship alternately rising as it were, triumphantly over the overwhelming waves and then sinking with alarming velocity, into the deep hollows between them. At the end of twelve hours, however, our lively little ship was again making sail and soon regained the lost distance, over which the storm had driven us. One other risk was incurred from which our escape was apparently Providential. During the night whilst holding our course under a stiff breeze before the watch on deck discovered anything approaching, a large ship under full sail, passed so close to us, that the sides of the two vessels almost came in contact. All our party were sleeping, unconscious of a danger which the sailors in the morning almost shuddered to relate.

The New World

Our tedious voyage of forty-seven days was at length terminated. On the morning of the forty-seventh day we were greeted by a sailor in the foretop, with the joyful cry of "land ho!" In less than two minutes every one was on deck, congratulating each other on this happy event. We were within soundings, the sea smooth and on the arrival of a pilot, who soon came on board, all sail was set to make the Delaware River the same tide. In this we succeeded and before night we were within forty miles of Philadelphia. It would be difficult to describe the impressions felt by a set of raw English boys under the consciousness that they had at last reached the long-looked-for New World, where different pursuits and a new career was about to be entered upon. We were at any rate in high spirits and soon found ourselves admiring greatly the regular streets and well furnished markets of the Quaker City.[75] Mr. Samuel Hurry, a second cousin of my mother, resided there at the time, and having been advised of our departure from England, soon found us and took us to his home, where we were received with much kindness by Mrs. Hurry.[76] Mr. Hurry also treated us with the greatest personal kindness and attention while in Philadelphia, and assisted us to proceed on our journey to Stockbridge.[77]

It was desirable to transport us and our goods with economy. At that period there were few steamers and the fare on them was extremely high.[78] Stage coaches of the most ordinary kind and lumber wagons, constituted the general means of travelling. Leaving our goods, therefore, to be shipped by sea, we embarked on a small sloop, bound for Trenton.[79] She was about the size of a common fishing smack and with accommodations in correspondence. We had hardly any wind to favor our progress, but by the aid of tides and by dint of hard rowing, in which our boys assisted, we nearly reached our point of destination 40 miles, in a day, arriving after dark at a landing a few miles below it. Mr. Hurry was with us and finding a tolerably decent country tavern we took up our quarters there for the night. In the morning we concluded it was useless to ascend the Delaware farther but hiring some Jersey lumber wagons, prepared to proceed towards Brunswick.[80] Cushioning the seats in one of them with bed quilts and pillows, my mother and Mary Ashburner with Becky Miles and her little girl, having also a careful driver, were tolerably well provided for. Mr. Hurry and myself took the front seat of a second wagon, the boys piling in on the straw behind us, while the third wagon took our baggage. This was our first experience in travelling in the United States, being bumped and jolted for forty miles over roots and stones. It must have been rather trying for my mother, who was unused to the rough paths of common life. She was inspired, however, by the desire of placing her family in favorable circumstances, for such was the object of coming to America.

Arrived at Brunswick we spent the night at a pretty good hotel and were called early in the morning to go on board the New York packet. She was a fine vessel with a large cabin, into which we were soon summoned after we had started on our passage down the Raritan river.[81] The breakfast being over every one was soon seated on the quarter deck admiring the scenery on Staten Island to the left and the fine view of Sandy Hook and the ocean on our right. Being English our dress and odd questions soon called general attention. A very good sample of the prosperous New Jersey farmer scraped acquaintance, and with much good nature pointed out everything of interest and gave suitable advice how to proceed on arriving at New York. Mr. Hurry had left us at Brunswick. There was a speck of excitement got up by the captain which added much to the pleasure of the passage. We had a fair wind and strong breeze which caused his vessel to make splendid headway. Coming among the passengers he announced a race with the Brunswick steamer, which had gone inside of Staten Island, all sail was set to get in ahead and after passing the narrows we had a splendid run up New York bay, and as we approached the city the steamer emerged from the Kills as the inside channel was then called. All on board were on the *qui vive* to gain the day, but unfortunately the wind slackened and steam was victorious. Nothing could have been more pleasant or beautiful than this little sail in New York harbor, but the city itself was insignificant, compared to its glories of the present day. Its population was only sixty thousand, the streets were dirty and the hotel we staid at, in a very similar condition.[82]

We were anxious to get to Stockbridge and the next morning again embarked on a packet called *Experiment*, bound for Hudson.[83] She was larger than the Brunswick packet and the table was provided with everything that could be desired, in ample quantities giving us very strong impressions that we had come to a land of abundance as well as of peace and liberty. We were soon passing up the Hudson making progress according to tide and wind, but although our sloop was a fine craft to sail, we had a great deal more time to view the grand scenery of the Highlands than we had any wish for. The winds were light and adverse, so that with all possible diligence in tacking, we were five days in reaching Hudson. Here we met my brother George who had come out to America four or five years previous. He of course was delighted to see us again, while my mother's spirits were much revived by the pleasant event. Becky Miles also met her husband who had come with a team to help us to Stockbridge. He had lived with us as a servant in England for several years but was now an independent citizen of the United States. He had never seen his little girl, having left before she was born, and hence it was a happy time with all of us. Nothing occurred to prevent a pleasant ride to Stockbridge where we arrived the next evening, to another agreeable meeting with my brother Luke who had come out with Miles two years and a half previous, to remain with George till the rest of us should arrive. Luke was delighted to initiate us into American customs and habits, and had the current history of the whole community, ministers, deacons, pretty girls etc.

It was rather difficult, however, for my mother to assimilate herself to the peculiar ways of an American family, for such was that of my brother George, who had married the daughter of deacon Tolman and bought him out, that is the farm he lived on.[84] The old farm house, however, was very different from the dwelling we had been accustomed to in England, while the diet and cooking were totally at variance with my mother's English notions. My brother George, nevertheless, soon succeeded in making her comfortable for no one was so well qualified to make the necessary arrangements. Part of the house was devoted exclusively to her use, and by the aid of Becky Miles, affairs were soon in accordance with English ways. The rest of us cared but little about these things, and we soon learned to devour *Yankee messes* with good satisfaction.[85] We were not slow to enjoy the opportunities which existed for hunting and soon learned to range the woods in pursuit of partridges and squirrels, and during the ensuing winter joined in chopping and hauling up the immense wood pile that was needed at that period for domestic use. My brother George had a large wood-house, and over it was a chamber where I set up my turning lathe and during bad weather found abundant amusement in this workshop.

Mr. Luke Ashburner, my sister's husband, very much admired the independence of the American farmer, thinking it far more desirable for young men to seek its attainment than to take their chances as employees in mercantile houses or in other pursuits especially in England. He had advised my mother to come to the United States promising to join her in a few years with his family. Consequently it was impressed upon our minds that we should all fit ourselves for farmers and my mother in pursuance of this object, purchased sixty acres of land in Stockbridge adjoining my brother George's farm.

The dwelling house, however, being small and dilapidated, she was at the expense of building a more commodious dwelling, and resided with George till it was completed. Full of zeal in the cause my brother Edmund joined me in the studying of English authors on agriculture and soon felt convinced that we should astonish our neighbors with the wonderful crops we felt confident of raising. We learned very soon how to work, drive cattle and manage farm horses, but it required considerable time for us to realize that we knew little or nothing of the world, or how to deal with people whose habits and necessities render them sharp in doing business and to find out the difference between practical and theoretical agriculture. We acquired, however, republican ideas of equality in society and very readily joined the lively parties of farmers sons and pretty country girls who frequently assembled in our neighborhood. The greater freedom of manners prevalent among them naturally captivated our fancy, and our time passed off very agreeably under the influence to which we were subject, but were very far from contributing to our improvement. With a few exceptions, the inhabitants of Stockbridge were punctilious in attending religious services, and there was a general sense of respectability which every family strove hard to maintain. The influence of wealth and education contributed, nevertheless, to establish a degree of aristocracy in this little republican community, which had in some respects a useful effect. The family of Judge Sedgwick[86] and their connections maintained their exclusiveness to a moderate extent, constituting thereby a circle of polished and agreeable people. Miss Catherine Sedgwick, well known as a talented authoress, frequently called on my mother, for whom she had the highest respect. I became acquainted with the family and was cordially invited to visit them. It might have been much to my advantage to have availed myself of this kindness more than I did, but a foolish bashfulness led me to prefer the freedom of manners that prevailed among our plainer neighbors.

Engaged on the farm or in the workshop, the first eighteen months passed smoothly along and but little occurred to make us discontented, so that at the commencement of the second winter, which was enlivened by fine sleighing, we were hopefully looking forward to the ensuing season for the anticipated success of our farming operations. But an event occurred which seriously affected my mother's happiness. Mary Ashburner was at that time fifteen years old and my mother's affection for her could hardly have been exceeded had she been her own daughter. We all regarded her as a sister. Her father had lived unhappily with her mother and had left a will entrusting his children to the care of his brother.[87] This was readily acquiesced in at the period of Mr. Ashburner's death, because the mother, being anxious to marry Sir Charles Forbes, which she did within five months afterwards, and was glad to have them out of the way.[88] But ten years afterwards becoming a second time a widow, and rich, she felt very much outraged because Mary was brought to the United States.[89] Having an indomitable will and the command of any amount of money, she came to Stockbridge bringing the best legal council she could obtain in New York, and claimed her daughter, whom my mother declined to give up to a woman for whom she had no affection and who had never manifested other motives than the revengeful spirit inherent to the Malay race from which she originated.[90] At the entreaties of a child she loved as a second daughter, and a sense of duty, my mother sought protection from the laws, hoping to prove the existence of a will which entitled her to refuse the demands of Mrs. Forbes. A trial ensued at the county court in Lenox[91] where intense interest was excited in the public mind, and had I known that the writ under which the sheriff tore poor

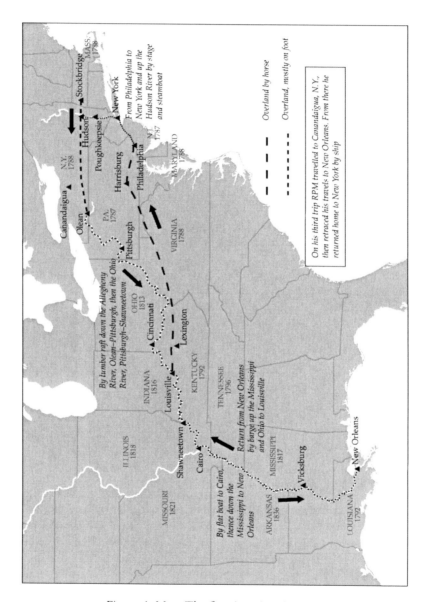

Figure 4. Map: The first American journey

Mary from my mother's arms was fictitious, I could have been sustained by the people in attempting her rescue, but it was supposed to be genuine and we reluctantly submitted. Her mother took her to England, kept her at a fashionable boarding school for a few years, and she was subsequently married to Mr. Mishie Forbes, the brother of her mother's husband, and old enough to be her father, but very rich. She ever retained, however, the deepest affection for my mother and her American brothers, the sincerity of which was manifested in various ways to the latest period of her life.

Her loss was a terrible shock and might be regarded as the first of a succession of afflictions and disappointments attending the ineffectual efforts of our numerous family to make their way in the world, for whom this excellent mother was always ready to encounter any hardships or submit to the severest sacrifices. The admirable letters, however, occasionally received from Bombay contributed in some measure to revive her spirits, by the bright anticipations in which my sister so ardently indulged, looking forward to our reunion under the opportunities of which we might avail ourselves within a few years. Soon after this event my brother William arrived in India and was very successful. He had been appointed solicitor for the East India Company in Bombay and his prospects for lucrative business were very promising.

At the end of another season we began to realize that a small farm of sixty acres with an exhausted soil could produce but a small income, although cultivated wholly by our own labor, and I naturally became desirous of seeing the wonderfully fertile country in the far West. I formed the acquaintance of a young man living near us whose uncle had settled in Ohio. He proposed to me to join him in a tour to visit him and gain some knowledge of the whole of that country. My mother could not afford to spare me a large amount for my expenses and we agreed to start with less than a hundred dollars each, feeling confident that we could accomplish our journey very cheaply.

The first American journey 1812–13

Travelling in 1812 was a great contrast to what is now experienced.[92] Steamboats were just coming into use on the Hudson River, and stages were only to be found on the great thoroughfares, passengers being charged six cents a mile. Our plan was therefore to go to Philadelphia and thence to Lancaster by stage, whence we were to travel on foot across the Alleghany ridges to Pittsburgh. The name of my companion was Benjamin Dreper, brought up in the manner in which most of the New England boys were educated, and though my inferior in some things not to be acquired in common schools, had many qualifications I did not possess, he had always been taught to depend upon himself and was a tolerably efficient millwright, having run his father's saw mill a great portion of the time that it was operated. He knew perfectly every incident of the American Revolution and was far more familiar with the Geography of the United States than I was, he was therefore the leader in our excursions. We were carried twenty-eight miles to Hudson on my brother George's farm wagon free of expense, but it cost us $12.00 each to reach Philadelphia, where we were obliged to pay 12 per cent for gold.[93] Many interesting objects attracted our attention by the way, the stage from New York occupying 15 hours to make the ninety miles between the two cities. We began to feel weary when we stopped for supper and to change horses, but a sudden incident dispersed all thoughts of fatigue on the last sixteen miles of our road. Electric Telegraphs were then unknown and a courier on horse back galloped through the street announcing Perry's victory on Lake Erie.[94] When we arrived in Philadelphia the whole city was illuminated. On our arrival we were too much excited to take much rest, but we were obliged to arouse ourselves at five o'clock the next morning, for the Lancaster stage, from what seemed to be a very short nap. I had never heard of Lancaster before but Ben knew all about it, as the largest inland town in the United States and celebrated for the manufacture of guns.[95] A gun was a luxury that my financial condition did not allow me to indulge in, but he bought a brace of large pistols observing that we might find them of use, which actually proved to be the case, within a few days afterwards.

We now lashed our packs to our backs and set out on the South road, by Little York,[96] to cross the mountains, and fell in company with a little Irishman, emigrating to the West, who carried a kit of tinkers tools besides his pack and paid his traveling expenses by mending kettles and saucepans. He proved to be a jovial fellow and beguiled the tediousness of the way by many entertaining yarns. He kept company with us for several days and was possibly of essential service. We knew nothing of the character of the hotels on the road, and stopped late one evening at one, of which, from its general appearance, we had some reason to be suspicious. After supper we offered to pay our bill and start very early to pursue our journey. Ben who contrary to his usual cautious habits carried his money which was in small gold pieces in the folds of his pocket book, accidently dropped several of them on the floor while selecting the amount of his bill. The result was an attempt to rob us in the night, but the parties retreated on the appearance of the pistols and the exhibition of courage on the part of our friend the Irishman. We hardly waited for daylight to take our departure from lodgings which afforded us so poor an opportunity for sleep. In seven more days with many weary steps we reached Pittsburg over a road which afforded the only means at that time of keeping up the traffic between Philadelphia and the head of the

Ohio River. In many places six stout Pennsylvania horses could scarcely scramble over the steep rocky hills with thirty cwt. of loading. Ben rehearsed the adventures of General Washington when these mountains were infected with tribes of hostile Indians and the Fort Pitt was in possession of the French.[97]

By his suggestion we bought a skiff[98] at Pittsburg and with blankets and provisions determined to descend the Ohio. It would be tedious to recount the numerous little incidents which attended our voyage. The peculiar characteristics of the river created much interest. The water was then at an ordinary stage and we thought the banks very high supposing that the fine bottoms on each side must be out of the reach of the highest freshets.[99] We did not consider the immense extent of country which it drained. We were astonished to learn one day on entering a log cabin, to reach which we had climbed a high bluff, that high water mark was up to the second floor. In a middle stage of water this stream well deserves its name of beautiful river, winding with a gentle current gracefully through hills covered at that time with abundance of the finest timber. So gentle was this stream that we allowed our skiff to drift during the night, watching alternately, a small awning being spread over the stern of the craft under which one of us slept very comfortably. Arriving at Marietta[100] near the mouth of the Muskingum, we found the country much improved and fine looking orchards adjoining the homesteads. This was a matter of astonishment to Ben, for under the impression that our Eastern fruit would be very desirable in the far West, he had brought a little package of apple seeds from Stockbridge, which he decided to throw away after he had tasted the Marietta apples.

We secured our skiff in a safe nook and made our way through the woods, some twenty miles up the Muskingum,[101] where we found his uncle Chamberlain, by whom we were hospitably entertained for several days, and from whom we obtained much valuable information in reference to the country and the habits of the people living on new clearings. Two of his sons were in the army, one of them a commissary stationed at Upper Sandusky.

The rapid growth of Ohio was at that time due to the surplus products of the country [being sent] by way of the Ohio and Mississippi Rivers. An immense number of flat boats were run there at small cost, many farmers near the rivers constructing these rude covered boats at their own expense, running them to New Orleans and selling them for fire wood as soon as unloaded.[102] These men were, however, obliged to return home on foot which was a very arduous undertaking.

We found our skiff safe on returning to Marietta and continued our course down the Ohio. The first object of interest on our way was Blannerhassets

Island.[103] Here Ben was fully posted in relation to events, with which, owing to my previous residence in England, I was wholly unacquainted. Blannerhasset had been the friend of Aaron Burr, and his elegant residence on this fine island was the rendezvous where Burr perfected his arrangements in reference to his ambitious scheme for establishing a monarchy in the South, by which he was to become emperor and Blannerhasset a grand duke. Such at least was the popular belief. Whatever it might have been Burr induced Blannerhasset to involve his whole property, which after their arrest for high treason was siezed by his creditors. The beautiful residence was subsequently burned, and we saw only the ruins and desolation of what must have been one of the most delightful spots in the Western country.[104]

Proceeding on our voyage, which was accelerated by the rising of the river, heavy rains having occurred in the upper country, only one incident worthy of notice took place before we arrived at Cincinnati. A wet evening and probable darkness induced us to enter the mouth of a creek to land and pass the night. Here under the over-hanging trees at the roots of an immense sycamore we built a fire which we kindled by the aid of dry leaves, taken from the hollow of a tree, and by striking light with the lock of one of our pistols. Having eaten our ham, broiled on the coals, and hard biscuit with an excellent relish, we prepared for a nights rest, stretching ourselves under the canvas drawn over our skiff. We were just falling off into a quiet slumber, when we were startled by a tremendous yell in the tree tops near us. If the performance of two young fellows in casting loose and pushing a skiff out of a creek, into the Ohio river, could have been witnessed in broad daylight it would have excited no slight degree of applause for the alertness with which it was conducted. The idea of a panther's claws in the neck is very exciting.

Stopping near the mouth of the Sciota River a few miles below,[105] we took breakfast at the Hotel, and were informed that there had been several of these dangerous animals seen in the neighboring woods. When we arrived at Cincinnati we were astonished at the marks of prosperity everywhere exhibited. Instead of merely a thriving village as we expected, a fine city was springing into existence.[106] Steam had as yet only exercised its influence by running a fine merchant mill for preparing flour for New Orleans market, but the shore was lined with keel boats and barges, which navigated the river, and were propelled by a number of hands using oars and poles, with, the occasional use of sails when a very strong wind was directly in their favor. Ben, who possessed the true Yankee spirit for adventure, found out that the hands employed on these vessels received large wages, and proposed that we should ship as boatmen on board a large barge on the point of starting. We therefore sold our skiff and were soon trying our skill as boatmen. Our shipmates, numbering thirty-four, consisted of the roughest class of men that could be picked up and it required no small degree of resolution to endure the disgust we felt, and the hardships attending our work. Fortunately we had entered into no binding agreement to go beyond the falls of Ohio and when we arrived at Louisville we were perfectly willing to forfeit our wages and leave the barge.[107]

It had now, however, become necessary for us to recruit our financial resources which had become essentially reduced, and finding a house carpenter in want of hands we struck up a bargain with him at a dollar a day and board. To decide which was the roughest, the work or the board, would be rather difficult, but the effect of either did not prevent the action of Ben's Yankee brain. The news-papers were carefully pursued to ascertain what was stirring around us, and we soon discovered some prospects of escape from the horrid drudgery of *matching blue ash floor boards*. A Mr. Scribner from New Jersey had purchased a tract of land on the Indiana side, below the falls, as the rapids of the Ohio at Louisville were called, and was building a steam saw mill; he had advertised for young men accustomed to that kind of business. We did not hesitate to offer our services, which were as eagerly engaged, as was the employment accepted. The place was called New Albany, now a flourishing city and was then a dense forest of heavy timber, with the exception of a few acres partially cleared. Mr. Scribner had built a large log dwelling house and a store, and a few individuals had bought lots on which they had also erected log huts.[108] We were received into the family of Mr. Scribner and treated with great kindness, and worked with much satisfaction under the direction of a Mr. Parker, the millwright. We continued in this situation during the whole winter, having saved about $60.00 a piece.

We had both felt rather homesick particularly as we did not entertain a very high opinion of Mr. Parker and on the 17th of March, 1814, taking our packs on our backs we started to return to Massachusetts, on foot, where no other mode of travelling was available. Our plan was to reach Lake Erie at Sandusky and to proceed to Buffalo by some vessel running down the lake.[109] We found the road muddy, but after becoming accustomed to travelling we sometimes made our thirty miles a day. We admired very much the beauty of the country through Kentucky, particularly around Lexington, passing through Chilicothe and Columbus[110] we at length arrived at Upper Sandusky, where Ben's cousin, the commissary, was located; his duty being to distribute rations to about fifteen hundred Indians, who claimed to have been friendly during the battles at the West end of Lake Erie, and in consequence had been deprived of the opportunity of providing for themselves by hunting or otherwise.[111] We fared well for a few days with our friend Chamberlain who took good care to provide the best of everything for himself. It was a circumstance of considerable interest tinctured with a small degree of apprehensions to find ourselves in the midst of so large a body of these savages with only twelve white men in the fort, but they were dependent on the United States government for food and of course were afraid of committing any overt acts. We were a little surprised, however, at the recklessness of the commissary who did not hesitate to course and abuse them. We had now forty miles of forest to cross, without a single inhabitant, before we could reach the navigable water at Lower Sandusky. We hoped to make it in a day, but going much astray in following the wagon tracks of General Harrison's army, when in that part of the country, night overtook us when nine miles remained to be passed over to complete our journey.[112] Having no overcoats, no blankets or means for making a fire, we had to endure the hardships of lying on the bare ground, which we found covered with white frost in the morning. The moon, however, rising about three o'clock enabled us to trace out the road and we arrived at Fort Crogham soon after sunrise stiff and hungry.[113]

A good breakfast and a few hours rest at the hotel put us in condition to look around and gather interesting particulars in relation to Col. Crogham's defen[c]e of the Fort, where he had been stationed with only one hundred men. The fort was an enclosure about 200 feet square with two projecting block houses commanding a view of the outside of the palisades on all sides of the enclosure. The palisades were twelve feet high, a double set pinned together and standing upright, with a small ditch of about three feet in depth around the whole fort and the earth from these ditches thrown against and banking up the palisades. Col. Crogham had four small cannon concealed in the block houses and with their nuzzles pointing along the ditches. Ignorant of the fact, the British forces twelve hundred strong made a charge on two sides of the fort intending to make a breach by cutting down the palisades. A hundred rifles were firing on them from between [and] over the palisades with unerring aim and when the ditches on two sides of the fort were filled with troops the concealed port holes were opened, and a shower of musket balls, old nails and pieces of iron was poured forth from the jaws of the cannon. The slaughter was terrible, two hundred British soldiers having been killed in a few moments, and the retreating forces assailed by rifle bullets while their own shots were ineffectual. A panic ensued and it being reported that General Harrison was approaching with a large force the whole batallion took to their boats and descended the Sandusky river in confusion. The event had occurred only a year previous and on going over the ground [we saw] two hundred fresh graves and the palisades filled with the balls and grape shot fired from the brass pieces brought along by the British troops, which they left behind in their hasty retreat.[114]

There were no vessels, however, at the West end of Lake Erie when we arrived at that place and we had to trust to our own resources to get to Buffalo. Ben took the lead again and purchased a large canoe, which I ought to have objected to, but concluded that he might as well buy a little experience. Ben had never been on a larger piece of water than the Hudson or Ohio Rivers and formed no adequate idea of the impossibility of navigating a canoe along the shores of Lake Erie, but before we had paddled over half the way to the mouth of Sandusky Bay we were swamped and driven ashore in a squall barely saving our packs. There was now no alternative but to shoulder them and try to reach some settlement. The first we reached was a ship yard seven miles from the mouth of the Huron River where we arrived just after the daylight had left us.[115] We found a country hotel and ferry at this point, from whence there was a travelled road to Buffalo, about two hundred and fifty miles distant where we arrived in nine days in spite of the muddy roads.

The whole city had been burned by the British army, on the Niagara frontier, who had crossed early in the spring and soon after retreated.[116] We found General Scott, however, encamped there and many new dwellings under construction.[117] After witnessing the drill of the celebrated flying artillery which distinguished itself in the great battles which afterwards occurred in Canada, finding we had money enough left to pay our fare in the stage to Stockbridge, we immediately secured our places and although gaining two or three days in point of time, endured as much fatigue on the journey as if we had walked the whole distance, for the roads had been so much cut up by the teams supplying the army that they were scarcely passable. On my return to Stockbridge I learned that my mother had been offered a liberal price for her little farm and dwelling house by a company desirous of establishing a cotton manufactory upon the mill site belonging to it. Having lost all taste for farming we were all willing that the sale should be made. Edmund, John and myself were anxious to attempt some new enterprize and as our indulgent mother was willing to place one half the proceeds of the farm in our hands to enable us to carry out our plans, we resolved on a trading expedition down the Ohio River. It was based, of course on the information I had obtained on my previous tour. My brother Luke was at this time settled on a farm at Oak Orchard, in the Western part of the State of New York, where he had gone with Anthony Miles our cook's husband. Septimus and Henry, the two youngest, remained with their mother in Clavarach near Hudson, where she had rented a house.[118]

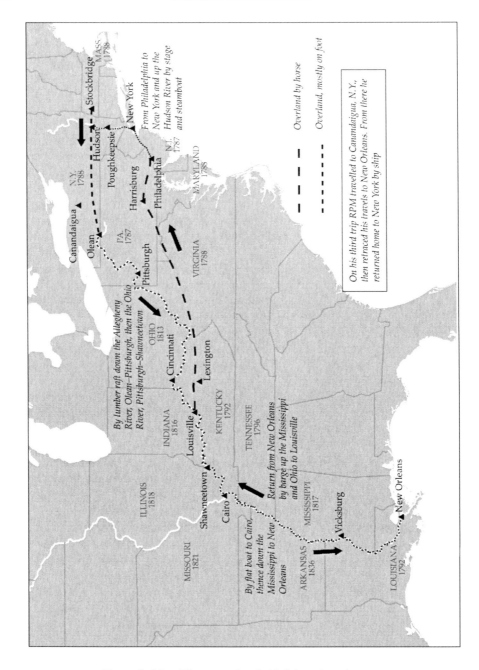

Figure 5. Map: The second and third American journeys

The second journey 1815–16

Our scheme was to make our way to Olean[119] at the head of the Allegheny River, and run rafts of pine lumber from that locality down the Ohio River to supply the numerous settlements near it, exchanging it for flour to be transported to New Orleans. Loading a one-horse wagon with various articles which we supposed would be necessary and carrying as much weight as our little animal could draw over the long hills we had to travel over, we started from Hudson about the 1st of March, 1815. It necessarily followed that we had to walk nearly all the way, a distance of nearly three hundred miles, and also hire an extra horse on the last fifteen miles, the road being otherwise impassable. Instead, however, of being able to purchase our lumber very cheaply as we had expected we found that it had nearly all been bought up by a large crowd of emigrants, who had spent the winter near the saw mills and aimed to defray the expenses of moving by the sale of their boards and singles. One lot only of 200,000 feet could be had at prices twenty per cent higher than any that had been sold. This took $2,000.00 of our $2,500.00 but as the lumber was superior in quality we hoped to make it pay. Good pilots and smart hands were essential to security in descending the Allegheny River and we could only obtain these at pretty high prices, which on the whole we had no reason to complain of as it enabled us to escape the losses sustained by the owners of several other rafts.

Our boards were floated in platforms sixteen courses deep; connected together in the usual manner, the whole lot comprising two double rafts, one commanded by Edmund the other by myself.[120] The water being considered sufficiently high we embarked with a supply of provisions to last us as far as Pittsburg. The current was running nearly five miles per hour, and great care and labor were often required in passing islands and sudden bends in the river. Edmund had the owner of one of the saw mills, well acquainted with the business, to aid in conducting his raft, and passed all the dangerous points without any serious difficulty. My pilot was a half-breed Indian, but although considered reliable had the misfortune to ground in on a bar. Two other rafts were a mile or two ahead of us. Edmund with his man had landed in safety, the other party had *stove* his raft on the head of an island, part of it scattered with the current, part adhering in square platforms, and lodged on the bushes on gravel banks where it struck. The pilot and hands amounting to eight or ten men having lost all their provisions came back to assist us, under a pledge that we were to do as much for them. They first devoured a great part of our supply which was designed for only one meal a day, to be replenished whenever we stopped over night. Every man was then compelled to enter the ice cold water waist deep to pry off our raft which we effected in about an hour and landed it safely below opposite the wreck of the other raft on *Sun Fish* Island. The hardships we had so far gone through were light, however, compared with what we subsequently encountered. We worked from one o'clock till nearly sunset, not only up to our waists but frequently to our necks in water before we got the remnant of the raft together in which the unfortunate owner had probably invested all his little property. Fortunately there was an abundance of dry wood on the shore and with the embers of our cooking fire on my raft which had not been reached by the water we soon kindled an enormous log heap by which we passed the night, but almost exhausted with cold and hunger which we had no means of satisfying, till the following night, at the landing fifty miles below.

We encountered, however, no farther hardships in the Allegheny River and the descent of the Ohio was easily effected without pilots. But there seemed to have been an unusual supply of lumber offered for sale at every village along the river, and from the mouth of the Little Miami[121] to Cincinnati, a distance of nine miles, the shore was lined with large rafts of pine lumber, which could hardly be sold at first cost. This was rather discouraging but we ventured to run down to Louisville in Kentucky at the head of the rapids. There were no lumber dealers at this point who would purchase a whole raft and we had no choice but to sell out in small quantities. Louisville was reputed to be very sickly in the latter part of summer for the unaclimated, which made us averse to the slow but sure method of making profits, by the retail system, and the river rising suddenly, high enough to cover deeply all the rocks in the rapids, we took the advice of the captain of a keel boat which he was running up the river and started with our rafts for Shawnee Town in Illinois, a new settlement much in need of lumber.[122] The falls were crossed in safety and we arrived in a few days at our destination. The houses in this place had been hitherto built of hewn logs, and as pine lumber was much preferred for joiners work and many new dwellings were in contemplation we made a rapid sale of the whole of our lumber at good prices. Selling much of it, however, on credit, which ultimately, from the difficulty of collections, took off our entire profits.

In pursuance of our original plan of operation, we returned to Louisville to purchase flour for shipment to New Orleans but met with considerable delay in consequence of the deficiency of water at the mills where we expected to obtain it. While waiting on this account, however, Edmund and John were both taken seriously sick, requiring for some time the attendance of a physician. As soon as they were convalescent, which was in the course of two or three weeks, Edmund, being anxious to aid in pushing forward our business, started for Cincinnati, taking his passage on board a boat ascending the river.

His object was to buy a flat boat,[123] that would carry three hundred barrels of flour down the river. Such boats were often to be purchased very cheaply at that city. I waited a long time in expectation of hearing from him, but got no intelligence whatever. As John was much better I determined to go and find out the cause of his detention, but as no boats were at hand I started to cross the country, through Frankfort and Lexington on foot. Having proceeded about half the distance my journey was brought to a close by a circumstance involving a very remarkable coincidence. The country at that period was covered to a great extent by a dense forest, and being absorbed in travelling by various reflections as to carrying on our business, I lost the main track and in trying to recover it became so uncertain as to the true direction that I resolved to take a course due North to the Ohio River which I was convinced was not many miles from me.[124] The weather being clear the position of the sun enabled me to determine the points of the compass, and travelling rapidly, for there was no under brush, I arrived on the river bank just before it became dark, and near a house where I was readily accommodated with a good supper. I had scarcely finished, however, when a voice I was well acquainted with from a skiff in the river hailed a man on the shore. It was that of one of the hands we had employed to bring our raft down the river. On my answering he immediately landed, and between two buffalo robes, lying in the bottom of the skiff, I found my brother Edmund shaking with the fever and ague. It appeared that he had experienced a relapse of his first attack and had been for a week on a sick bed, when fortunately meeting with Delano, our old fellow raftsman, arrangements had been made to bring him back to Louisville, in a skiff. Edmund had been unable to find a flat boat in Cincinnati and there was apparently no alternative but to build one.

With both my brothers as invalids, I had now to depend wholly on my own exertions. My own remarkable good health, I might almost say, was providentially continued to me. Making active enquiry as to the best mode of proceeding, I heard of a second-hand boat that could be refitted, and finding the timber sound I hired a colored carpenter whom I had previously known, and we went resolutely to work to repair the boat thoroughly. It seemed to others I was running great risk from the exposure I endured, working on my back in the water, to caulk the bottom of our craft; but I had a very good fellow to help me and the boat was made ready for its loading by the time the flour was made ready for shipment.

By the last of October [1815] I had to take the boat up the Ohio River several miles against the current to receive that part of our load which consisted of one hundred and sixty barrels of flour. In effecting this object an incident occurred which I put on record to indicate the degree of physical power I then possessed to resist exposure. When a number of rods from the shore I fell overboard and being unable to regain the boat, had to make land by swimming with a heavy pair of boots on. The water was exceedingly cold, cakes of ice having been running and it required no small degree of energy to save myself. Edmund was now fast recovering his strength, but John, as we afterwards learned, and who had preceded us on a keel boat going to Shaw[nee] town, had met with a terrible relapse and when we arrived there with our boat, was barely able to crawl about. At Shaw[nee] town we completed our load by buying pork, venison, hams and Pecan nuts. It cost us a hundred and ten dollars to hire a pilot to New Orleans and by the tenth of December 1815, we reached the mouth of the Ohio, landing near the spot where the docks of Cairo are now located.[125]

The weather had been extremely cold and immense cakes of ice were floating down the Ohio, by which we were in great danger of being crushed. We succeeded at length in forming a barrier by falling in timber above the boats, for there were several others which made the same landing whose owners were glad to aid in screening them. The ice was also running thickly in the Mississippi. In about a week, however, it stopped, apparently, and we ventured to proceed on our voyage in company with those who had landed with us and several others from landings on the river above us. It required much care in descending the Mississippi to avoid being carried precipitously by a four mile an hour current against various dangerous obstacles, that are continually presenting themselves. Numerous islands, where by entering wrong channels boats are greatly endangered and some-times entirely lost. Huge trees with their roots lodged in the bottom sinking by the force of the current and springing up again with great force. In other instances forming immovable snags equally dangerous. The boatman has also to guard carefully against being thrown by the force of the current too close to the heavy timber in the numerous sharp turns of the river. We were compelled to land every night near some willow point or in eddies that occur in many places. On the second or third day all the boats in company (not less than ten or twelve) started very early but to our great dismay on floating into the main channel we discovered that the ice was running, and had overtaken us just as we were approaching two of the most dangerous localities on the river, *Plum Point*[126] and *Hour Island*. We immediately com-menced working for life, as it were, to avoid Plum Point was impossible and therefore all our force was directed to land before we should be drifted upon the island. We propelled our boat by large sweeps balanced over the eves of our flat roof or deck,[127] but with a square front twelve feet in width and the ice constantly gathering before us all the energy we could use produced but little headway. Edmund, although quite well in other respects, had been laid up with scalded legs from an accident which had upset a kettle of boiling hog's lard upon him.[128] Our dangerous situation however brought him to our rescue, disregarding all pain he mounted the deck and added all his strength, which was not considerable, to working the sweeps. By this means after many narrow escapes in avoiding snags, on the channel by Plum Point, we made the gravel beach just above the island. Securing our boat by driving stakes and attaching ropes to them we looked round to witness the disasters befalling other crafts to which, however, we could lend no help. Much property went to the bottom but no lives were lost. On this desolate spot we remained nearly another week before the ice ceased running. A large barge from Cincinnati had been sunk by striking a snag. They saved some of their sails and provisions and encamped near us but I believe returned home instead of proceeding down the river in their jolly boat.[129]

After this adventure no particular incident occurred till we arrived in New Orleans, landing at the levee just above the shipping. As the market for flour was low and the Kentucky miller had cheated us shamefully in the quality of what we had bought of him, the result of our voyage down the Mississippi was the loss of several hundred dollars, which together with bad debts in Shaw[nee] Town, created in selling our lumber, together with sickness and general expenses reduced our finances to a very low ebb. Dividing with Edmund and John, who were naturally very homesick, I made up my mind to return up the river and make one more effort to redeem our losses. They engaged a passage on the first ship that sailed for New York, while I remained in New Orleans to ascertain what I could do to the best advantage. I found a barge of something over a hundred tons bound for Cincinnati with a load of sugar, coffee and other freight. This vessel was schooner rigged,[130] carrying considerable sail, in order to stem the current when possible by very direct winds, but it was necessary to man her with thirty-six boatmen commanded by a captain and pilot. The expense of transporting freight in this way for 1500 miles was enormous and I had to pay four cents a pound for a few barrels of coffee that I shipped on board. It was a question, however, whether in ascending the river I should pay $100.00 for a cabin passage or receive $112.00 for working as a hand. I hesitated in reference to placing myself among so rough a crew as I met on board, but finding one decent man who was in the same predicament as myself and considering that a passenger would have a very tedious time of it, I determined, as my new friend expressed it, to 'face the music'. His name was Ingraham and he had purchased eight or ten barrels of sugar to take to Louisville.

The mode of working barges and kee[l] boats on the Mississippi which at that time afforded the only means of transporting freight, consisted of five different operations, rowing, poling, cordelling, warping and sailing. Each man used a barge oar, which by means of a pin driven into the gunwale of the boat, projecting about six inches above it, was held to its place having a raw hide throng [= thong] around it and slipped over the pin, the boatman was enabled rapidly to ship and unship his oar in cases of emergency, laying it across the boat when not in use.[131] By this arrangement each man could quickly seize his pole, which was laid upon the upper deck, which protected the cargo. The sides supporting it were set in about fifteen inches, leaving a space along the gunwale for the convenience of poling. The effect of poling depended on the position of the boatman's body, which in extreme cases was brought in a direct line with the pole, the head of which being placed on the shoulder behind the collar bone, and in deep water I have seen the head of the boatman close to the surface, with his elbow underneath it.

The power of thirty-six men exercised in this way was sufficient at times to overcome the resistence of a very heavy current. Cordelling was simply towing the vessel by a long rope as on a canal, the men taking the place of horses. But the Mississippi River is extremely crooked and consequently there is a succession of sand bars, on all the points and heavy timber along the opposite bends, where the current washed out a very deep channel frequently undermining the trees; which were carried down and lodged below or sometimes driven out to sea. From these facts it may be readily understood that it was an arduous task to ascent with heavily laden boats. An experienced navigator works around the sandy bars, which afford a good bottom, by means of poles, but as soon as his vessel meets the full force of the current, where the water is too deep for poles he lands and sends forward a skiff, containing a long rope or wa[r]p, as it is termed, and which, being generally half a mile in length, and coiled near the stern is as much as four good oarsmen can stem the current with. With this ascending far enough according to the helmsman's judgment, the wa[r]p is tied to a tree and passed out from the skiff as it floats back to the barge, where all hands walk the deck with it. It is passed around pulleys in such a manner that they constantly utilize their strength. To avoid following around the long bends in this manner which would be to increase greatly the time and labor of getting up the river, a crossing is made, as soon as practicable, requiring immense exertions with the oars, to prevent falling far below the opposite point. In fact it was the practice to stimulate the crew by a gill of whiskey for each man previous to the effort.[132] This neither Ingraham nor myself would take and yet we held out full as well as the best of them. To judge of this difficulty of the operation it is only necessary to know that we got the praises of the captain if we did not lose more than half a mile in crossing.

In this way working from daylight till dark, we averaged scarcely nine miles a day exclusively of the distance made by sails on two or three occasions.

It might have been more had our movements been entirely free from accidents, but sometimes our wa[r]p would get tangled with logs in the bottom of the river, and sometimes by its breaking, we were liable to fall back a long distance.

We were a hard looking set, our dress consisting simply of a red cap, a red woolen shirt and a pair of tow cloth pantaloons.[133] Our fare was hard biscuit, *soft* pickled pork or salt beef, and a tin cup full of coffee. Nights and mornings clouds of mosquitoes poured forth from the willows, compelling us to eat with a bush in one hand to fight them off. Every man, however, was provided with a mosquito bar under which we slept upon a blanket or bear skin laid upon the deck. The most serious occurrence, however, was during a strong gale of wind from the South, of which we were endeavoring to take the utmost advantage by spreading out all our canvas, making six or seven miles an hour against the stream. The barge suddenly run upon a log which fortunately lay inclining up the stream and slid along it till a huge snag was encountered which broke a hole about eight inches square through her bottom, near the bow, however, which had risen two feet by riding upon the log. The water, of course, rushed into the hold at a frightful rate. The captain was panic stricken and utter confusion prevailed. Ingraham stepped up to me with the question, "What will become of our sugar and coffee?" I answered, "We must save it," and we instantly engaged in the task.

About ten bars of iron were lying with their ends directly over the shattered plank, and a hogshead of sugar on the opposite ends. By no small effort we bent back this iron, the water spouting in up to our knees, while the rest of the crew walked the deck, endeavoring to press back the broken plank. I called upon the ship's carpenter who, at my request prepared a piece of plank of the right dimensions, covered with tarred canvas, which by means of upright shores we pressed firmly over the breach and succeeded in stopping the leak, *completely*, so that before night the hold was freed from water. We were detained, however, for a whole day and lost the benefit of a fine wind.

A few days later another serious incident occurred with the same result. Our captain had only one skiff, and as it was evident we could make much better progress with two, not having saved any money out of his gambling operations in New Orleans, he connived at the conduct of one of his men, in stealing a beautiful little craft which he had noticed as we passed a fine plantation below. Thinking he had passed all danger of detection, the captain was so unscrupulous as to receive him on board just below Walnut Hills, afterwards called Vicksburg. Unknown to the captain one of the hands with whom he quarrelled deserted in the night and informed against him and before morning the shore on the opposite side was lined with an armed force to aid in the intended arrest. He saw how easily he could escape if he could get around the point and avail himself of the strong South East wind that was blowing. We crossed and the excitement on board was intense, the men ready for a [f]ight if necessary and our sailors actually mounted a small gun, belonging to the vessel, loaded with old nails and pieces of iron.

We sent out a wa[r]p by which we meant to reach the locality for setting our sails, but the men in the skiff were made prisoners which was followed by a proposal to make a charge with our pike poles to liberate them and it was with some difficulty that Ingraham supported by all I could do prevented blood shed, representing to the men that they would be regarded as outlaws and pirates. Our captain, consequently was given over to the sheriff and was glad to settle the affair with six barrels of coffee for it seems he had no money. In this disgraceful way, therefore, we were delayed all day and lost another fine wind that might have carried us forty miles up the river.

It may be easily imagined how anxious we were getting to be freed from the slavish life and the company of our rough associates. In 112 days we arrived at Louisville and as the owners of the barge wished to reduce the number of the crew above the falls where the navigation did not require half the original complement of men, we gladly withdrew, our coffee and sugar being safely landed. I accompanied Ingraham to an auction store where our goods were soon sold at a very fair profit. When I left New Orleans I weighed 175 pounds; on my arrival at Louisville, although I had been in perfect health during the interval, I had shrunk to 158 pounds.

My financial condition, however, was improved between two and three hundred dollars since leaving New Orleans, but as I could see no strong inducements at that time for remaining in the West, I bought a horse, therefore, and in company with several merchants travelling to Philadelphia determined to go home by that route.

After the fatigue of getting accustomed to riding, my journey proved very pleasant till on reaching Harrisburg[134] I discovered that the saddle had been galling my horse's back.[135] I had concluded to cross the country through [New] Jersey and Newburg, [New York] but soon after crossing the Delaware River, the idea of the cruelty in riding an animal evidently suffering more and more every day we went forward, so annoyed me that I sold a very excellent beast at a great sacrifice, and reached Hudson by stage and steamboat.

The third journey [?1816]

My mother was still living in Clavarach three miles East of Hudson, with Edmund, John, Septimus and Henry, my four youngest brothers, who had all become disgusted with American life, and were looking forward for some opportunity to return to England; but as no immediate prospect for such purpose presented itself, Henry proposed to go with me if I would undertake another trip Westward. To this I consented more readily as I was unfit for any business that I could enter into in Hudson or the vicinity.

Taking the stage to Canandaiqua[136] and thence to a different point on the head waters of the Allegheny River, from the location whence we procured our lumber on my trip with Edmund and John and where lumber was much cheaper, we soon got up a small raft of 50,000 feet and without encountering any serious difficulties descended the River to Louisville. The profits on the sale of our lumber, however, barely paid our expenses, and as we intended going home by way of N[ew] Orleans instead of buying valuables to speculate upon, I availed myself of my knowledge of the river and purchased a second-hand flat boat as the surest way of making money, for the purpose of carrying freight to New Orleans, and agreed to freight fifty hogsheads of tobacco to that city at $10.00 each. A gentleman named Irvin, a fellow boarder owning a good flat boat on which he had brought freight to Louisville, also loaded it with tobacco and instead of hiring a pilot offered to pay all my expenses to be allowed to lash his boat along side of mine. By this means I made my $500.00 clear of all expenses, in less than a month, having arrived in New Orleans safely within that time. We staid in that city only a few days when we sailed for New York on a brig,[137] which arrived there about five weeks later in the season.

Working life in America: the farmer

During our absence my brother Septimus had gone to England to finish his studies in medicine, but died in London within the following year.[138] This was a severe blow to my mother, but other trials were at hand of the same character. My sister,[139] with her family of five children had returned to England in a very precarious state of health, intending to proceed to the United States to meet her husband as soon as she grew strong enough, should the change of climate improve her health. Unhappily the reverse was the case, and her condition became so critical that my mother in company with John went to England to meet her in 1817. I returned, therefore, with Henry and Edmund to Stockbridge where we awaited the arrival of Mr. Ashburner, who had been for some time expected. When he joined us accounts of his family were rather more favorable and he remained with us for several weeks, discussing plans for improved agriculture in which he was quite an enthusiast. My brother George wished to quit his farm and open a hotel on the road from Stockbridge to Hudson. It was proposed, therefore, that I should take his farm and try my hand again in *improved* agriculture. With my natural impulsiveness I agreed to undertake it and the necessary arrangements were made. These were scarcely perfected, however, before advices were received from England that the recovery of my sister was hopeless, and Mr. Ashburner took his departure immediately, to remain with her while she survived. In the meantime, Edmund having received letters from which he supposed he might do well to join his brother William in India, took passage on board an American ship bound to Bombay. Henry, too, with similar views sailed for England.

I commenced the management of my farm with the aid of a hired man and that of my brother Luke, who lived with me during a few months before going to the Western part of the State of New York to clear and improve a tract of new land. I had engaged a Mrs. Waters, a widow lady, to keep house for us and she conducted affairs very satisfactorily for the first year. During this period, however, I became acquainted with Eunice Mary Sexton, the daughter of Mr. Timothy Sexton, a respectable farmer in my neighborhood, who although less than eighteen years of age consented to become my wife,[140] and engage in what appeared to her the formidable undertaking of superintending my household affairs. She had been educated by her excellent mother to habits of industry and usefulness, and having easy access to her former home for advice in the art of housekeeping she gradually acquired confidence in her new position.

Possessed of more than a common share of personal beauty, accompanied by remarkable ease and simplicity of manners with a fine intellect and energetic temperament always controlled by her affectionate disposition, she gained the love of all who knew her. For sixteen years, the brief period during which she was spared to me, it seems to me admissible to say that we enjoyed as much happiness as ever falls to the lot of humanity, due in a great measure to the patient sympathy she exercised under adverse circumstances as well as the influence of her presence during more promising periods.

As to my farming, I pursued a system for several years which I imagined must be eventually successful. By manuring my land highly I succeeded in raising several remarkable crops, which gained me premiums for agricultural societies. Although no immediate profits were thus realized the productive powers of the soil were greatly increased but without capital to carry out this mode of improvement the greatest efforts were ineffectual. I continued, however, to pursue this course till after the arrival of Mr. [Luke] Ashburner, who returned from England with his son George in 1820. He had attended the funeral of his wife a few weeks previously. His design was now to settle on a farm of his own. When he arrived in the first instance from India in 1817, he was much pleased with the society of Stockbridge and with the beauty of the country and, therefore, on his return he purchased a small farm in the neighborhood of the village and built on it a commodious dwelling-house. He had met with many intelligent and highly educated people in this place, who showed him much attention, for he was regarded as a man of high attainments, who had mixed with all the best societies in Europe and India. On Stockbridge Plain where the village is located, were the residences of several families of note.

The old mansion house of Judge Sedgwick was then occupied by his eldest son, Theodore Sedgwick,[141] a lawyer of considerable eminence who had retired from business. His wife Mrs. Susan Sedgwick,[142] was justly esteemed as a very superior woman, and as Miss Catherine Sedgwick resided with her, her home was both attractive and improving to all that were intimate with the family. Under these circumstances it is probable that Mr. Ashburner could not have located himself and family more advantageously. He was able to indulge his passion for experiments on a small scale, in improved agriculture, while his children enjoyed the benefit of pleasant associates. His original plan, however, in relation to the emigration of my mother's family and the establishment of his own in the United States was entirely dissipated. The remainder of his family came to him from England in 1823.[143]

In 1825 he married Miss Whitney of Stockbridge,[144] under the idea probably that an American lady would be better qualified to carry out the peculiar ideas he had entertained of becoming an independent farmer, than his daughter who had been brought up under the refined habits of English society. He had regarded my effort as the pioneer movements of a new system of improved agriculture, but eventually discovered that he must content himself to remain a gentleman farmer, while the views of every individual, whose interests he had sought to promote, according to his Utopian ideas, were leading them in an opposite direction.

My eldest brother, George C. Morgan, was keeping a hotel on the road from Stockbridge to Hudson. Luke had gone West to clear up new land. Three of my brothers had returned to England and one was living in Bombay, while I had arrived at the conviction that it was impossible for me to maintain my family by farming. George Ashburner, whom his father had vainly endeavored to inspire with a taste for agriculture, determined to go to India and Samuel to study engineering.

The engineer

In 1826 the Erie Canal had gone into operation, and its effect upon the internal commerce of the country began to be fully appreciated.[145] A survey from Boston to Albany had demonstrated the practicability of a canal, and the merchants of Boston began to realize that their trade was declining. About that time, 1826, I published an article in the Berkshire Star suggesting the substitution of a railroad, which was immediately quoted in the Boston newspapers, and the subject soon became the topic of general interest. A small subscription was raised in Stockbridge and the adjoining towns, which proved sufficient to meet the expenses of a survey, that I agreed to make, to determine the practicability of a route through them. My report proving favorable I was subsequently employed in surveys to the Hudson inaugurated by the state, under the direction of Mr. James Baldwin[146] and commissioners appointed for the purpose. A Northern route, however, by Pittsfield was finally recommended and although a railroad as far as Worcester was undertaken it was not till 1836 that the location between Connecticut River and Albany was decided upon.[147]

In the meantime my interest in agricultural pursuits entirely ceased. My attention was directed exclusively to railroads and the profitable improvements in their construction. I made several futile attempts to introduce what I imagined at that time was a great invention and went to Boston to seek patronage for the purpose, and subsequently to Baltimore, incurring much expense to find out the difficulties of introducing innovation of any kind.

I was in Baltimore in 1828 when the first reports were received of the opening of the Liverpool and Manchester Railroad for public use, which at once placed all previous efforts to construct railroads, in the shade.[148] I therefore immediately returned home to Stockbridge, devizing new plans to avail myself of the great change which must inevitably take place in reference to the construction of railroads. Messrs. Robert and Edwin Stevens,[149] who had distinguished themselves in building steamboats on the Hudson River, undertook the construction of the Camden and Amboy Railroad between New York and Philadelphia, and being full of the spirit of improvement, were ready to test any plans suggested to them that took their fancy.[150] I called on them and recommended the adoption of granite rails with flat iron bars secured to them in the manner practiced at the Quincy stone quarries in Massachusetts.[151] I was in hopes in this way to advance my interests as an *expert* in the construction of railroads. Unfortunately, however, I did not understand my position. I took the laboring oar and the risk of success, as far as it might be a precedent in the construction of other railroads; I was then over forty years of age, a mere pioneer of new undertakings, instead of assuming the standing of a civil engineer to which I should have been entitled, but which at that time was principally monopolized by students from West Point, who commanded large salaries without difficulties.

I became, however, assistant engineer on the Harlem Railroad with a salary of $1500.00 a year, on which I managed to support my family in a low rented dwelling in New York.[152] A quarrel among the directors made it expedient for me to resign and to take a contract for the removal of a large amount of earth on the line of that road for which purpose I incurred heavy indebtedness in the construction of dumping cars for which I was only enabled to pay by the assignment of part of my claims on the reversion of my grandfather Hurry's legacy to my mother. This was a serious error and eventually resulted in great pecuniary loss. As I made no profit on the contract, I found myself without the means of support and with nothing in the form of property, but a lot of unsaleable dumping cars and some plain furniture. It was, therefore, a natural consequence that I should not await the tedious and uncertain process of seeking for a suitable position as engineer. A letting for grading the Stonington and Providence Railroad was about taking place and I ventured to bid for a section,[153] although I could hardly raise sufficient money to convey my family to the necessary locality in Rhode Island and to pay the freight charges on my goods. My bid was accepted and as no securities were required, excepting a fair recommendation, I was enabled to commence my work on the credit of my prospective earning. The company, however, retained fifteen per cent of the estimates. It was a time when the currency of the country was greatly inflated. President Jackson had withdrawn the National deposits from the United States Bank and placed them in the hands of local institutions, the management of which was so reckless that I was able to borrow *$100.00 on my own note* without endorsement, provided the notes of a New Jersey bank should be given a wide circulation by paying the small bills, in small sums to my workmen. The inevitable crash that was impending soon followed and the company with whom I had made my contract stopped payment being $1500.00 in my debt, the greater part of which I owed to my men and other parties. I paid about one half of their claims, giving my note for the remainder, which were generously accepted.[154] My family then consisted of seven children, two girls and five boys, who together with their excellent patient mother I placed on board a sloop, bound for New York, and returned to that city leaving my cars and other tools on the half finished work.

On our arrival I immediately sought General Swift, with whom I had been associated on the Harlem Railroad (who had also resigned his position as chief engineer of that road).[155] By his kind influence I was employed on the Brooklyn and Jamaica Railroad, which I was extremely glad of, although at a very low salary.[156] Moving into a house in Brooklyn, in the vicinity of my work, we managed to live in tolerable comfort till the following spring. We were cheerful because hopeful, having promise of farther aid from the

noble old General. In 1834 the Stonington Company[157] resumed their work
and my contract was renewed with a handsome increase in the prices. We
immediately prepared to return to Rhode Island, but were most fortunately,
if not Providentially detained a day longer than we intended. The boiler
of the steamer on which we had in the first instance proposed to sail exploded
on her way to Stonington, killing and injuring a large number of her passengers. Our passage the next day was safely and pleasantly effected.[158]

It was not my good fortune, however, to realize any profits from my
Rhode Island contract. During the progress of my work, after the birth of
my youngest daughter in October 1834, the health of my wife failed rapidly,
and early in the spring of 1836, the only hope of her recovery was her
removal from the effect of the sea air.

I therefore left the management of my contract in the hands of my brother-
in-law, Henry Sexton, and moved to Simsbury[159] with all the children
bringing my wife to the residence of her mother and father to spend her
few remaining days where she could at least receive the most affectionate
attention. She survived the time of our arrival only ten or twelve days. Our
little son, Edmund, had been also suffering for some time from a fatal disease
(enlargement of the heart) and dying almost simultaneously with his mother,
was consigned to the same grave.

This calamity fell upon me with crushing force, but from a strong sense of
the necessity for immediate efforts to provide for my family, and having the
offer of employment in surveying a route for the Boston and Albany Railroad
from Stockbridge to Springfield, I at once took my bereaved children to
the old homestead occupied by my brother George with whom my mother
and brother John were then living. Taking my two eldest boys into my
surveying party, I left the rest of my family temporarily in Stockbridge. My
youngest daughter, however, only eighteen months old, became the especial
care of my mother, and without doubt the interest and affection she
entertained for the child contributed much to alleviate the sorrows and sad
experiences of the previous twenty years, during which her family had been
separated in pursuits entirely in contrast with the results which had been
anticipated when emigration to the United States was first projected.

At the time when I undertook farming in Stockbridge, in 1818 news was
received that my sister, Mrs. Luke Ashburner, instead of coming to the
United States, as had been at first proposed, was compelled to defer it from
extreme debility. The fatal climate of India had done its work and the
recovery of her health seemed hopeless. My mother still suffering from the
grief occasioned by the death of Septimus (who had gone to London to
follow his studies as a physician) hastened with John across the ocean to
be with her daughter again, after the cruel separation she had endured for

fourteen years. She found her a melancholy wreck of herself, with her little family of five children under the motherly care of Abbie Ayton in Stoke Newington near my Uncle Morgan's residence at Stamford Hill.[160] Miss Ayton had been lady's maid and nurse to my mother from the time of her marriage till after my father's death. The English physicians expressed the opinion that Mrs. [Luke] Ashburner, must, as the only chance of recovery, remain quietly in England for several years.

Soon after my mother's arrival in England, Edmund returned from Bombay having ascertained that he must study law for five years in England before he could be allowed to practice in the courts of India. He was therefore installed in an office in London with Henry who subsequently came from the United States. John, by the influence of good friends, was employed as a clerk in a large mercantile house. Edmund expected to take his brother William's place in Bombay, within six or eight years. Henry being also promised a good position, as soon as he made himself competent.

Mr. [Luke] Ashburner came soon afterwards to England, but with no idea of abandoning his original plan of settling in the United States, and returned with his eldest son George a few months after the death of his wife which occurred in 1820. William at this period was doing a lucrative business in Bombay as solicitor to the East India Company. He married a Miss Ibbotson, whom he had met with on board the India ship in which he took his passage out. She brought him two daughters, with whom, however, she also, had been obliged to return to England on account of the failure of her health.

At the time of my mother's visit to England, she had hired a cottage in Landaff in Glamorganshire,[161] and after their father had gone to America, Sarah's children, Anne, Sarah, Grace and Samuel remained in her care till 1823 when they all came to Stockbridge. The loss of their mother was for a long time deeply felt by the eldest children. It was a loss of no common magnitude, fully appreciated by a large circle of friends, whose sympathy was afterwards made manifest by various acts of kindness to our whole family. It is by no means surprising that the residents of Bombay regarded Mrs Luke Ashburner as a very superior woman. Noted for her personal loveliness and amiable manners, with a powerful intellect highly cultivated, and with unsurpassed affection for her family and friends, she was a treasure in society. The deep interest she took in the welfare of her brothers and her devotion to her mother is beautifully illustrated in the voluminous correspondence which she kept up for their instruction and encouragement. A few of these letters still remain which readily excite the admiration and love of her descendents.

After Mr. Ashburner's family left England in 1823 my mother kept house for her three sons, Edmund, John and Henry till Henry took his passage for

India, Edmund having married his cousin Anne Williams, and left England a year or more previous. Henry was accompanied, on his voyage, by George Ashburner, who had prevailed with his father to allow him to seek his fortune in Bombay instead of attempting farming in the United States. My brother John had been living part of the time, during which his mother remained in England, with his cousin Charles Tolme in Hamburgh, but not being successful in what he undertook he returned with my mother to Stockbridge and remained with her in my family till 1827, when William returned from Bombay intending to settle permanently in England.

On learning this fact my mother again crossed the Atlantic to meet him. He had been very prosperous and had realized considerable money, but having lived in all the extravagant style and luxury indulged in by residents in India, he was induced to keep it up in London, by the influence of his family who refused to listen to his expostulations in relation to the necessity of retrenchment. He had flattered himself that having many wealthy friends in India, he might derive a large income on his return to England from their patronage as an attorney. But although he had been the India Company's solicitor for a number of years, he was excluded from the English courts by the rigid observance of established rules. Being disappointed, therefore, in what he had anticipated, he resolved to return to India, and set out for Bombay in 1829. His health, however, had been previously undermined by remaining so long in a tropical climate and probably his mind having been acted on by great anxiety, his trouble occasioned a severe attack of sickness on the voyage out, which terminated his life.

In the meantime my mother had returned to the United States to rejoin her surviving children and grandchildren. My brother Luke had died during her absence.

It was seven years after this period when I brought my children again to Stockbridge.

Of the Boston and Albany Railroad, the survey, however, opened no opportunity for me to acquire a prominent position as a civil engineer. The line I had partially located, was not adopted, and in 1837 my services were not required by the company owing to the financial panic then prevailing.[162] I therefore went again to New York, taking all my family excepting the two youngest, who remained with their grandmother.[163]

With no resources and depending on the possibility of finding employment as an engineer, I hired a house in 13th street. Sending the children to school to the care of an old friend of my mother's, Mrs. Errington, I occupied myself in visiting several gentlemen of influence with whom I was acquainted, in search of business. Succeeding in obtaining only one small opportunity to earn anything, the ensuing winter would have been terribly gloomy, but for my constitutional hopefulness and readiness to lay down the dignity of a civil engineer, to provide against the wolf at the door. My eldest daughter, my sole dependence at that time, although only sixteen years old had a severe attack of scarlet fever, and it was only by the sale of some valuable books, which had been sent me by Mr. Boddington, and an annuity of ten pounds sterling he had left me that I was enabled to obtain the necessaries of life. Early in the following spring, however, I succeeded in getting an appointment at a low salary, for superintending masonry on the Croton aqueduct at Sing Sing,[164] to which place we removed as soon as it was practicable. Difficulties, however, continued to beset us. Sarah, my house-keeper, was again attacked with sickness, pleurisy in its worst form set in, and but for the remarkable strength of her constitution would never have survived the severity of the disease and the excessive bleedings administered by her physician. As it was, our situation would have been truly deplorable but for the kindness of Miss Margaret Hurry who came to our relief, by superintending the household and careful nursing till my daughter was restored to her usual strength.

From this time forward my prospects seemed to grow somewhat brighter. Having occasion to go to New York, I met on the steamer, an agent of parties anxious to survey a line for the extension of the Harlem Railroad through Putnam and Dutchess Counties to Albany, by an interior route, and before my return I agreed to undertake it.[165] Mr. Henry A. Gardner,[166] who had assisted in my surveys for the Boston and Albany Railroad had completed an engagement in a party locating the Northern route, and at my solicitation took the lead in a party I had formed for the proposed survey. It was composed, otherwise, of trustworthy hands furnished by subscribers, and my two eldest boys to carry the chain, under my own immediate direction with the transit.

My second daughter, Mary, at the time referred to, was living with her mother's sister, Mrs. Stocking, while Sarah boarded in Sing Sing, awaiting our return. After the survey was completed it was deemed advisable to hire an office in Wall St., where our drawings, estimates and reports were to be made. While engaged in the surveys we had become acquainted with Mr. Ebenezer Cole, a very superior draughtsman, who aided us essentially in exhibiting our work, to advantage. By these movements I was induced to rent a house in 17th St. where Sarah again kept house for me until the ensuing spring when we all repaired to Pauling in Dutchess County, in anticipation of the future progress of the road. Owing to a continuance, however, of the financial difficulties of 1837, there was a great backwardness evinced on the part of the directors of the company, particularly of those residing in New York in relation to progressive measures. The Dutchess

County men, on the contrary were very sanguine, and expressed themselves as very confident that the road must be carried through.

Under these circumstances, although by no means a prudent act, we went to work and located the road with sufficient accuracy for grading, at least through Putnam and Dutchess Counties, but it was at our own expense, and no provision was made for reimbursement. In the mean time, a gentleman by the name of Edwin H. Johnson,[167] was appointed chief engineer, who introduced a company of responsible contractors, who were to invest considerable capital and take largely of the stock. I opposed it because I thought the work could be done cheaper which produced a division among the directors, and for a time stopped the progress of the enterprize. I was consequently separated from it and turned my attention elsewhere for business. The idea occurred to me that there might be another route to Albany discovered nearer to the Hudson River and in exploring the country, with a view to shun the Highlands near the Hudson River, it became clear to me that the popular belief as to the impracticability of constructing a railroad through them near the shores of the Hudson River, was decidedly an error.

I took passage in a steamer from Poughkeepsie to New York and made a careful reconnoisance from the deck, in passing near the precipitous rocks, regarded as insuperable obstacles. My impression did not discourage me, and inviting Mr. Gardner to go with me, we traversed the whole perilous line on foot. His opinion was coincident with mine and at the instance of Governeur Kemble of Cold Spring,[168] a convention was called in Pough-keepsie to raise funds for defraying the expenses of a survey. A small sum was realized, very inadequate for the purpose, but as Mr. Gardner and Mr. Coe did not hesitate to unite with me in the enterprize, I removed my family to Poughkeepsie and the survey was undertaken and completed. A storm of opposition was the consequence, which was not only poured forth in the New York papers, but carried to Albany, the whole affair being represented as fictitious and got up by parties in the river villages to defeat the railroad, projected in the interior. Many of the citizens of New York were led to receive these malicious representations as true, and all the members in the Legislature representing New York were instructed to prevent that body from granting a charter to the Hudson River interest.[169]

Instead, therefore, of improving my financial condition this survey was a loss, attended with many collateral expenses in subsequent efforts to turn it to account. I removed my family to Albany and made a joint report with Mr. Gardner, to a committee of inquiry, showing clearly the superiority of the Hudson River Railroad; but two years elapsed before a charter was obtained although some of the most prominent men in New York made the application for it. Up to the time I moved to Albany I had been the pioneer of three great lines of railroads, had carried through several large contracts for grading and had in several instances aided in the construction of their superstructure, yet after constant efforts of the kind, had at last been forced to the conclusion that I had made no progress towards gaining a desirable position in life. Mr. Gardner obtained an appointment as resident engineer in improving the terminus of the Mohawk and Hudson Railroad,[170] by so changing the location as to dispense with stationary power. Having determined on taking my family to Illinois, he married my daughter Sarah, having agreed to follow us as soon as his immediate engagements were fulfilled.[171]

I could not have effected this purpose, however, if my brother Edmund had not very opportunely made us a visit. He had left his home near the cape of Good Hope, to make us a short visit, but it was necessary for him to return soon, and therefore remained with us for a limited time only, but he kindly enabled me to anticipate the remainder of the reversion to which I was entitled at my mother's death, a share of the property left by my grandfather Hurry, on which security he advanced me about $1500.00. $1200.00 of this I invested in land and farming stock etc. in Kendall County, Illinois,[172] the whole purchase of land being 480 acres. We commenced farming with much ardor and succeeded in raising some good crops, but the market prices were extremely low and the cost of transportation, over muddy roads to Chicago, very heavy; consequently our position was far from being encouraging.

We had been in Illinois about fourteen months when we received the melancholy intelligence that the residence of my brother George in Stockbridge had been burned to the ground, that he had perished in the flames, while my mother and my little daughter Anne had been rescued with great difficulty, by the courage and extraordinary efforts of my niece Nancy Morgan. Anne and her grandmother were taken to Hudson, where they remained under the affectionate care of Mrs. William B. Skinner, my brother George Morgan's youngest daughter, till in 1847, when the death of my mother occurred.[173]

Subsequently wishing to have Anne with me, she was brought to Illinois by a gentleman moving his family from Hudson to Plainfield, within eight miles of my farm in Kendall County. Anne's career in life was, however, full of vicissitudes and very severe trials. The necessity of changing my residence often, after engaging in the duties of a civil engineer, induced me to send her back to the Eastern States, to the care of her elder sister, Mrs. Gardner, who resided in Poughkeepsie, where she remained till 1850, when I took charge of the Peoria and Oquawka Railroad, providing a home for her in Peoria. She returned, however, to Poughkeepsie in 1854 and was married in 1859 to Mr. James Patterson of New York, he was employed as an accountant, with a good salary, but his wife being threatened with consumption he obtained a consulate to Marenham[174] and took her to Brazil as the only chance for recovery.

The voyage proved very beneficial to her but they had scarcely reached the place of destination, when her husband was attacked with yellow fever, which proved fatal within a few days. Under the pressure of this dreadful event, although among entire strangers she gained the sympathy of all the foreign residents, who showed her every possible attention, offering her a home free of expense as long as she chose to remain. It is *possible* that if she had accepted of their friendly and pressing invitations, she might have recovered, but to use her own words, she preferred to, "Come back to us and die". This sad event occurred in March, 1863.

I had then been living in Illinois nineteen years, during which I had made several ineffectual attempts to gain the standing as a civil engineer to which I should have been entitled. In 1846 the Hudson River R.R. Co., obtained a charter and prepared to construct their road. My friends, residing along the Hudson River, advocated my appointment as chief engineer, but a majority of the directors elected Mr. John B. Jervis.[175] As I would not accept of a subordinate position, I recommended Mr. Gardner, who took charge of a division near Tarrytown.[176] In the following year a company was formed at Chicago to construct a railroad to Galena.[177] They employed me to make a preliminary survey, which I accomplished at a very small cost by the aid of my two eldest boys and only one extra hand.[178] My services were appreciated by the expense rather than by the ability and industry with which the work was done, for after exerting myself faithfully for a year at a very moderate salary I was superseded by a particular friend of one of the directors, the plea being made that I was merely a *pioneer*.[179] My next effort was at Milwaukee where I located and surveyed fifty miles of railroad, with a similar result.[180]

In 1848 I located a line from Rock Island to Peru, on the Illinois River and was appointed chief engineer.[181] When preparing for construction, however, a proposition was made to the company by Messrs. [Henry] Farnham and [Joseph E.] Sheffield, who were reputed as having considerable capital at command, to construct and put the road in operation, provided provision should be made for its extension to Chicago.[182] I remonstrated against the measure, believing that the company could save a great deal of money by keeping the work under their own control. I was sustained by a majority of the directors then in office but the plan for extending to Chicago was adhered to, for which purpose Legislative enactments were necessary, and consequently the whole affair was so manipulated that by increasing the number of directors, I was superseded.

In 1850, therefore, I went to Peoria and took charge of the Peoria and Oquawka Railroad with a salary of $2500.00 per annual.[183] I remained as chief engineer for three years. There was, however, in the prosecution of this enterprize a strong diversity of interests, and as had begun to be common in railroading, an unscrupulous course was pursued by the faction in power. I withdrew from my place as chief engineer under the promise of a contract for grading and furnishing with ties, fifty miles of what was termed the Eastern Extension. As the prices agreed upon were remunerative, I hoped and expected to realize fair profits, and devoted myself assidiouly to it. I was first to expend $50,000.00 the subscription of Iroquois County, and then to receive the bonds of the company for the balance that might be due to me. Before I was ready to claim these bonds, a new board of directors was elected and who repudiated their payment, forcing me into a lawsuit by which I obtained judgment against them for nearly $50,000. On the strength of this success I raised a considerable sum of money and sold the remainder of my interest to parties who gave me their notes for the amount, secured on the judgment.[184]

In the mean time my two eldest daughters being married, and believing that I was sure of a competence, I solicited the hand of a widow lady, who I had known from childhood and who professed qualities, which under more favorable circumstances, would have seemed to me a desirable and permanent home. My proposal was accepted and we lived together for several years in Chicago, contentedly enough, till we began to realize the uncertainty of collecting the amount of my notes, and the income I had anticipated.[185] In four or five years a change became absolutely necessary and accepting the offer made by her mother to leave to my wife the little property she possessed in Stockbridge, if she would go and take care of herself and father. I did not object to the plan, believing that I could engage in some good enterprize, by which I might offer her inducements to return to me. Although I have repeatedly failed in my efforts to accomplish this object, I have been able occasionally to render her pecuniary assistance and by the additional contributions of her eldest son, to make her home comfortable.

The direct evils arising from being engaged in a lawsuits, are in themselves of a serious nature, but the valuable time I lost in connection with the one referred to was still more injurious to my interests. This lawsuit was a great misfortune to me for it occurred at a period when otherwise I might have obtained a desirable situation as a civil engineer. I was, in consequence, induced to turn my attention to the introduction of improvements in railroad machinery. I spent much time and what money I could raise, in several inventions which I imagined could not fail to gain the necessary patronage.

I had yet an important lesson to learn, in relation to the selfishness and ignorance of railroad corporations, and as it is with all inventions, it took considerable time to establish the fact in my mind, that there could be no greater mistake they could fall into than to expect the least support from the directors or employees of a railroad company, when any outlay of money was required to test its value, however important the improvements.

I was at length convinced that nothing could be done in this way, except by having a controlling influence in the management of a railroad. My attention was directed therefore, to gain such an influence, but not being able to command the amount of capital deemed necessary I too hastily resorted to a visionary scheme suggested by a fellow boarder. There was a general railroad law in Iowa admitting the formation of railroad companies, simply by filing a notice with the secretary of State, of the name and location of the road and the names of the parties concerned. This person with whom I associated myself made a very plausible statement in relation to a railroad that had been projected and some ten miles of it graded near McGregor, which had been abandoned by the company and sold by the sheriff to a man who would sell it to new parties on a long credit. This grading was through a long ravine where the right of way was, for the most part, donated. We took the necessary means to avail ourselves of this opportunity. I made surveys at my own expense and had my partner succeeded in bringing in the capital he pretended he had the power of controlling we could have made money and I could have gained the object I was aiming at, of introducing a new system in the construction of railroads. Other parties, however, having capital supplanted us and built the McGregor Western, which has now become a prominent and extensive line of railroad.[186]

Although after wasting nearly a year in this adventure, during which time I made extensive explorations of the country, I went to a village about forty miles from McGregor called Waukon,[187] the center of a very productive country, but unprovided with any facilities for transportation. A railroad had been projected and a line surveyed from the Mississippi River through the place extending Westward. About $40,000 had been subscribed, but as the construction involved great expenses in tunnels and heavy rock cuttings, the people were afraid to engage in the undertaking. I suggested to them that by cars rightly constructed which would pass around sharp curves the tunnels could be avoided, and that they could use a wooden track that would temporarily answer all their purposes.[188]

About this time my cousin William Coffin died and left me a legacy payable on the death of his brother. As this might not take place for several years, I sold the reversion, which I ought not to have done, at a great sacrifice, in order to carry out my plans at Waukon. I built a car which cost me

$500.00 and laid a short temporary track of wood, but it required more extensive illustrations of its practicability to satisfy all the parties that were interested, and two of the principle men, the only warm advocates of the scheme, sold out their property in Waukon, and left me to make my way alone. I was in consequence compelled to abandon it and the opportunity of perfecting my invention. I returned to Chicago having uselessly thrown away a great deal of money, and feeling convinced that if I ever engaged in similar undertakings, I must avoid placing implicit confidence in other people.

An excellent resolution; but I was subsequently interested in three other railroad projects, in which the cause of failure might be justly attributed to the same cause. The Chicago and Plainfield,[189] the Pekin and Southwestern,[190] and the Hamilton, Lacon and Eastern[191] railroads were all originated and brought into a tangible form by a great deal of labor on my part, by surveys at my own expense, holding railroad meetings and getting up reports, setting forth the resources of these several lines, not only in the country, but by spending much time and money in New York.

To enter into a detailed account of the proceedings of each of these companies would be tedious and uninteresting and although illustrating the disposition of railroad corporations, to take advantage of their position and the unscrupulous methods by which it could be done, it would only show the consequences repeatedly occurring from having made bad selections in the choice of my partners.[192] In the case of the Pekin and Southwestern, however, I received a note as a bonus, for yielding up my claims, from which I realized about $2500.00. Of this I gave my wife, who was then much in debt, about $700.00, and drew the rest in installments from a friend who took the note off my hands. Part of these instalments were used in subsequent operations during the next two years, in attempts to construct the Hamilton, Lacon and Eastern Railroad, an enterprize that would have been highly remunerative if it could have been carried through, but they were entirely frustrated under the panic of 1874 and 1875.[193]

In connection with the various events referred to in the journal, occurring at intervals during so long a period, a great many incidents might have been introduced, which although illustrating the difficulties contended with, would tend to exhaust the patience of the reader, without affording either entertainment or instruction.

Some individuals by their abilities and discretion, in connection with well directed efforts, have effected much for their fellow creatures; others, much for themselves at the expense of the community, but a large number appear to have done neither one nor the other. Indirectly, however, a man may have been of some use in the world, although his efforts may have produced no visible good to himself or family and apparently this has been my own case, under the numerous reverses and disappointments I have experienced. Trials and afflictions invariably accompany a long life, and the loss of friends by death is common to the whole human race – whatever may be the circumstances affecting their position in society.

There seems, however, to be a compensating principle in our own nature by which we become reconciled to the inevitable and our sympathies with the succeeding generation, to a considerable extent, absorb the sense of privation by the loss of our dearest friends. On the day I had attained my eightieth year not a single member of my mother's or father's family had survived; but six of my own children with their husbands and wives assembled to celebrate my birthday, July 29, 1870. This reunion has been repeated annually, till 1875, when the unexpected death of my son-in-law, Henry A. Gardner, which occurred July 26th, naturally caused its omission. His loss was deeply felt. I had known him for forty years during which period I had experienced numerous and repeated proofs of his friendship.[194]

In early life he was always spoken of as a promising young man earnestly striving to avail himself of every possible opportunity for education, within his reach. He stood well as a scholar in the Stockbridge academy, particularly in the study of mathematics and surveying. In the spring of 1837 he took the leveling rod[195] in my party organized under Captain Swift, to make an approximate location of a railroad line from West Stockbridge to Springfield, and soon became familiar with the use of the level. In the following autumn he was entrusted with the use of it in a location made by Mr. Chesborough, of part of the Northern line of the Boston and Albany Railroad by Pitts-field. His assistance was subsequently highly valuable to me in my surveys of the Harlem and Hudson River railroads, in relation to which I was sustained by his advice and ability. He also made a valuable report to the committee appointed by the Legislature of New York, to investigate the relative merits of these two lines. The reputation this acquired enabled him to obtain an appointment at Albany to locate the terminal changes proposed in the line of the Mohawk and Hudson Railroad, in order to dispense with stationary power.

At this time he married, and after occupying his position as assistant engineer for about a year he removed to Illinois to take charge of the con-struction of part of the Michigan and Illinois Canal.[196] Having fulfilled this engagement he was called back to the state of New York to superintend the construction of a division of the Hudson River Railroad, under Mr. John B. Jervis, who had been appointed chief engineer. He at first resided in Tarrytown, but eventually removed to Poughkeepsie to aid in the location of the line, between that city and Albany, in relation to which Mr. Jervis found some difficulties, which were not very readily to be overcome. Mr. Gardner, however, boldly and successfully devised a plan which shortened the line and saved an immense amount in the cost of construction. It was therefore not surprising that on the retirement of Mr. Jervis, he became chief engineer of the Hudson River Railroad.

He retained this place for about a year, when Mr. Oliver H. Lee,[197] prevailed on him to become chief engineer of the Chicago, Alton and St. Louis R.R., of which he was subsequently Vice President, his residence being in Joliet till 1857,[198] when in consequence of the unsatisfactory condition of the Company, he retired with his family to his farm near Dwight,[199] where he remained for nearly two years, when the affairs of the Hudson River R.R. Company needing his services, induced him to reassume his position as chief engineer for a short period.

With a remarkable strong mind and qualities which rendered his services as a civil engineer highly valuable, he always gained the respect of his employers, and all that became acquainted with him. His devotion to his family was only equaled by the perseverance and self denial he exercised for their benefit. He possessed considerable landed property, but in its accumulation he did not neglect to provide his sons with the best attainable opportunities for acquiring a good education. With these recollections of my excellent friend and son-in-law, which bring me nearly to the present time, I may as well close my journal.

The long period in which the events recorded are embraced is acknowledged to have been one of the most remarkable in history, and although the writer may have indirectly contributed to the progress of improvement, he can only look back with deep regret to many opportunities lost, and efforts misapplied, which might, under more favorable circumstances have been beneficial to his family and to the interests of society.

A plain statement of facts gives little more than the dark side of the picture, but it should be remembered that these occurrences include long intervals of comparative happiness. The social relations of the various families referred to were often the source of much enjoyment. Even in relation to my excellent mother, whose life was subject to a succession of the deepest afflictions and disappointments, realized from the affection of her children and all who knew her many days of pure contentment, while her perfect resignation to the decrees of an all wise and benevolent Creator, sustained her under the most trying ordeals to which she was subjected.

Epilogue: a brief conclusion by Richard Price Morgan, junior[200]
October 6th, 1898

Richard Price Morgan, my father, after whom I was named, died at Dwight, Ill[inois]. on the 19th day of January 1882, in the 92nd year of his age. His home for several years of his declining life had been with his second daughter Mary, Mrs. Francis Berkman, at Chicago, and the last few years until his death, it was with his eldest daughter, Sarah, Mrs. Henry A. Gardner, at Dwight, Illinois. The tender care which he received at this time from his daughters, and the devotion to him of his children, grandchildren and great grandchildren caused him to say, two or three years before his death, "I feel that I am one of the wealthiest men in America. I have only to hold up my finger, to call around me scores of my direct descendants, all filled with affectionate zeal to care for my wants." Although entirely blind during the last year of his life, he maintained to the end the cheerfulness which character- ized him under the most trying conditions in his eventful life, and he said, but a short time before his death, "I have not been weary and heavy laden". He was a Unitarian and when religious discussions occurred in his presence he would say in respect to the divinity of Christ, "If Christ was not divine he was nearer divinity than any one who has ever lived on earth, therefore is the best example to follow." He lost his eyesight by too close application attempting to solve the problem how to save the power to steam engines wasted by the crank motion, and also an improvement in cars to reduce the friction of trains moving around curves.

In his 86th year he was invited to deliver the principal address at the meeting of the National American Board of Trade. This great assembly of distinguished men interested in the question of transportation, occurred at the Grand Pacific Hotel in Chicago, on the 14th of December, 1875. Father's address drew out strong and satisfactory marks of approval and the news papers of the country commented upon it in a highly complimentary manner.

His wonderful serenity of spirit was manifested after his blindness, when a neighbor having called on him, at leaving said, "I hope Mr. Morgan we shall soon see each other again," to which he replied with a smile, "Nothing would give me greater pleasure." The warm interest he manifested at all times for young children who gathered around him to hear his stories, practically said, "Suffer them and forbid them not to come unto me, for of such is the Kingdom of Heaven." His probity of character gave cast to everything he did, his wisdom being in the rectitude of his heart, and although generally deceived in the temporal affairs of life by designing and selfish men, his was the victory at last, and he gave as his only legacy to his children, the instruction and example of a pure life carried through to the end upon the advice of his revered mother. His physical and intellectual strength and energy were of the highest order, the bent of his mind being to invention.

He lived to be the oldest Civil Engineer in the United States and in many respects one of the most eminent members of the profession. For more than fifty years he was actively engaged, mainly upon the promotion and construction of railways, commencing practically with their inception in this country. One of his early engagements was on the surveys and location of the Boston and Albany Railroad. He surveyed and located the Harlem Railroad, after which he originated the Hudson River Railroad, at a time in the age of railway construction, 1842–3, when such a great work was deemed by the public to be next to an impossibility and that "A railroad was not needed on the bank of the finest navigable stream in the world."

He was a bold and fearless advocate of the development of this country by the means of great railway enterprises and throughout his life a large share of his vitality was expended *Pro bono publico*.[201] He came with his family to Illinois in 1843, settling in Kendall County, where for two years he led his boys in the art of farming. Upon the revival of public interest in railroad construction he became chief engineer of the Galena and Chicago Union railway now the Northwestern. He was the pioneer of the Chicago, Rock Island and Pacific, and chief engineer of several other roads.

In connection with his loss of sight the occasion of which I have mentioned, I quote the following paragraph from his address:

The expression that railroads are yet in their infancy is hardly too strong. The time will come when the locomotive of the present day will be looked back upon as a clumsy wasteful machine, constructed in violation of the fundamental principles of mechanics. Machines will be substituted by which instead of wasting half the heating power of the fuel, combustion shall be far more perfect, and the full action of the steam utilized. And it may be safely predicted that this great propelling machine shall glide smoothly along, passing with facility and safety around the sharpest curves. The same principles will attend all other rolling stock. Instead of constantly deranging the track by its impulsive vibrations, crushing and abrading the rails, colliding at the joints, and receiving corresponding damages by reaction, trains will rival the steamboat in the smoothness of their motion. These striking advantages will be attainable only by adhering to scientific principles.

His last active service for which he received compensation was in his 88th year when by request of the New York Cheap Transportation Association, composed of 1600 prominent merchants of the city of New York, he personally examined the properties of the New York Central and Hudson

River railroads and made an estimate and report upon the cost of repro-
ducing them in the construction of parallel lines of railways. His report
was used before the noted Hepburn Committee of the New York Legislature
in connection with its consideration of transportation rates,[202] and it is no
exaggeration to say that its great influence was a material factor in promoting
the construction of the West Shore[203] and Nickle Plate[204] railroads as competitive lines to the Hudson River, New York Central and Lake Shore
railroads.[205]

At a meeting of the Association on the 12th of December 1876, after
suitable remarks the following was adopted:

> WHEREAS, Richard P. Morgan, the oldest living American Civil Engineer,
> and whose name is honorably associated with the pioneer rail-roads of this country,
> has, through consultation and correspondence, rendered this Association valuable
> aid, and co-operation in its aims and objects, and who has through a long life,
> marked by singleness of heart and purpose, and self-sacrifice, contributed largely
> in numerous ways to the enlightenment of the public on the general subject of
> transportation,
>
> Resolved, That as a token of our appreciation of the life and services of Richard
> P. Morgan, his name be enrolled on the records as an honorary member of this
> Association, and that a certificate be issued to him accordingly.

He continued his earnest interest in his profession and also in current events,
until the day of his death. His manner was especially free from ostentation,
and all of his habits were strictly temperate. His literary talent and cultivation
was of the highest order. At home and in the social circle he manifested his
genial nature, large heart, constant charity and love for his fellow beings.
All of his associates were men of prominence in the affairs of this country.
He died without an enemy, loved by his descendants and highly respected
by all who enjoyed his acquaintance.

Notes

1   Glamorgan, Welsh Morgannwg, means 'territory of Morgan'. It is believed to
    take its name either from the eighth-century Morgan ab Athrwys or the tenth-
    century Morgan Hen. See Hywel Wyn Owen and Richard Morgan, *Dictionary
    of the Place-Names of Wales* (Llandysul, 2007), p. 166.
2   The grandfather of Richard Price Morgan (hereafter RPM) was William Morgan
    (1708–72), a doctor who practised in Bridgend and married Sarah Price (1726–
    1803), sister of the philosopher and political reformer Dr Richard Price (1723–91).

For the Morgan/ Price family history, see Sir William P. Elderton, 'Some Family Connections of William Morgan (1750–1833), F.R.S.', *The Genealogists Magazine*, 12, no. 10 (June 1957), 329–39, and Maurice Edward Ogborn, *Equitable Assurances* (London, 1962). See also the Morgan and Price family tree in the present volume, Fig. 3.

[3] William and Sarah Morgan actually had four sons and four daughters. Of the sons, William Morgan, junior (1750–1833) and George Cadogan Morgan (1754–98) had relatively long lives but John Morgan (1756–71) and Richard Morgan (1759–60) died young. Of the four daughters, Catherine Morgan (1746–?1823) married Jenkin Williams (1732–1816) of Bridgend, Anne Morgan (1752–1823) married Walter Coffin (1731–1812), Elizabeth Morgan (1748–71) married Thomas Williams and Sarah Morgan (1761–1831) married David Huddy. Sources as for note 2, with additional material courtesy of David Perry, John Morgan and Nicola Bennetts, pers. comm.

[4] George Cadogan Morgan actually went to Oxford (see pp. 4–5).

[5] For details of the Hurry family, see Hurry-Houghton, *Memorials of the Family of Hurry*.

[6] Ives Hurry (1772–1830), with his brother Edmund Cobb Hurry and others, ran the London-based firm of Ives Hurry & Company which was part of a wider network of merchants, mariners and shipbuilders with strong family connections. See Robert Craig and Rupert Jarvis, *Liverpool Registry of Merchant Ships* (Manchester 1967), p. xxxvii. He is noted amongst the founders of the 'Society of Ship-Owners' in *Cobbett's Political Register*, 1 (1802), p. 1130. He was George Cadogan Morgan's brother-in-law, and is the Ives Hurry who appears in the letters of Amelia Opie, and twice in William Godwin's diary, both times in September 1794. See Brightwell, *Memorials of the Life of Amelia Opie*, pp. 42–3; Guest, 'Amelia Alderson Opie'; Myers, O'Shaughnessy and Philp (eds.), *The Diary of William Godwin*. For his capture and imprisonment by the French, see p. 126.

[7] Priscilla Hurry actually married Michael *Maurice*. Born in 1766 and educated at Hoxton and New College, Hackney, he became afternoon preacher at Richard Price's last meeting house – Old Gravel Pit, Hackney – in 1792. See Thomas, 'George Cadogan Morgan', pp. 57, 69.

[8] John Frederick Denison Maurice (1805–72). Though his father was a Unitarian minister Frederick became an Anglican. He was also a writer, magazine editor and important educationalist. He helped found Queens College for the education of governesses in 1848, the Working Men's College in 1854 and in 1874 helped create the Working Women's College. He was not always appreciated by those around him. For Thomas Carlyle his company felt like being attacked 'with a sort of paroxysm of mental cramp'. See H. G. Wood, *Frederick Denison Maurice* (Cambridge, 2008).

[9] Margaret Mitchell, who published after her marriage as Mrs Hurry, was the author of several books for children, such as *The Faithful Contrast; or Virtue and Vice Accurately Delineated in a Series of Moral and Improving Tales* (London, 1804).

[10] William Morgan (1750–1833) was born in Bridgend, Wales. He later moved to London and lived for a time at Newington Green with his uncle Richard Price,

whose biography he later wrote. Having given up a medical career, William became actuary to the Equitable Life Assurance Society in 1775 at the instigation of Richard Price, who acted as an unpaid advisor to the society for fifteen years. William held the post for fifty-five years during which time the society became one of the largest financial institutions in the world. On his retirement in 1830 his son Arthur Morgan took over as actuary for a further forty years (see Ogborn, *Equitable Assurances*, p. 261). William also experimented in scientific matters and is credited with being the first to produce what are now known to have been X-rays (see J. G. Anderson, 'William Morgan and X-rays', *Transactions of the Faculty of Actuaries*, 17, (1945), 219–21). He published widely on financial and scientific matters and in 1789 received the Copley Medal of the Royal Society, one of its highest honours, for his actuarial studies. He became a fellow of the society in 1790.

[11] Southgate actually lies to the north of London between Wood Green and Enfield.

[12] GCM had been Richard Price's choice to succeed him as pastor to the congregation at Old Gravel Pit, Hackney, but this proposal failed. See p. 5.

[13] For discussion of Price, see pp. 124–5 and 140–1.

[14] Benjamin Franklin (1706–90), American founding father, revolutionary and polymath was one of Price's closest friends; John Adams (1735–1826) was Vice President to Washington and America's second president. When Adams served as American Ambassador in London (1785–88) Richard Price became one of his few close friends: 'There are few portions of my life,' he later wrote, 'that I recollect with more entire satisfaction than the hours I spent at Hackney, under your ministry; and in private society, and conversation, with you at other places.' See Peach and Thomas (eds.), *The Correspondence of Richard Price*, III, p. 225. Dr Benjamin Rush (1746–1813) was a radical medical practitioner who advocated the abolition of slavery and capital punishment. Seen as the 'Father of American Psychiatry' he corresponded extensively with Price during the American Revolution.

[15] Price actually died in 1791.

[16] This paragraph is a good example of how history is transmitted and altered within families; as we know from the letters, GCM did not climb Mont Blanc itself, and visited Switzerland *after* having experienced the Revolution in Paris. Nor was he actually 'present at the taking of the Bastille'.

[17] The 'Marseilles Hymn' or 'Marseillaise' was composed by Joseph Rouget de Lisle in 1792, and adopted by the Marseilles *fédérés* on their march into Paris; 'Ça Ira' had appeared in May 1790; the notorious version sung by the sans-culottes later in the Revolution included lines denouncing the clergy and aristocrats and suggested the latter be hung from lamp-posts. See Laura Mason, *Singing the French Revolution: Popular Culture and Politics 1787–1799* (Ithaca, 1996); Marion Löffler, 'The "Marseillaise" in Wales', in Constantine and Johnston (eds.), *Footsteps of Liberty and Revolt*.

[18] GCM's library also contained books inherited from Richard Price. See Richard Brinkley, 'The Library of Richard Price', *The Price-Priestley Newsletter*, 4 (1980), 4–15.

[19] The Dollond family (John Dollond, 1706–61, and his son Peter, 1731–1821) were famous for the invention and manufacture of high-quality optical instruments.

This telescope was probably that presented to Richard Price by the Equitable Life Assurance Society in appreciation of his otherwise unpaid services to them.

20 Unusually for the time this included both his sons *and* daughters, since GCM and his brother William had 'very liberal notions as to female education'. See Williams, *A Welsh Family*, p. 131.

21 Goddard was 'a noted fencing master' who challenged the famous duellist Chevalier de Saint George to fence with him at the Pantheon. His unexpected victory was thought to be the result of a large bribe. See *Reminiscences of Michael Kelly, of the King's Theatre and Theatre Royal Drury Lane* (2 vols., London, 1826), I, p. 344; Philip H. Highfill, junior, Kalman A. Burnim and Edward A. Langhams, *A Biographical Dictionary of Actors, Actresses, Musicians, Dancers, Managers and other Stage Personnel in London 1660–1800: Volume 6, Garrick to Gyngell* (Carbondale, 1978), p. 244. We are grateful to Bethan Jenkins for this reference. After GCM's death in 1798 these political meetings transferred to the home of his brother William Morgan at Stamford Hill.

22 In March 1796 Napoleon had been appointed Commander in Italy and he invaded the country in April 1796.

23 Thomas Hardy (1752–1832), founder and secretary of the London Corresponding Society, was one of a number of radicals arrested in 1794 for 'treasonable practices'. The arrest marked the beginning of Pitt's clamp-down on reformist and radical societies in Britain. While Hardy languished in prison, first in the Tower of London and then Newgate, his pregnant wife died as a result, it was said, of their home being attacked by a loyalist mob. Eventually tried over nine days in November 1794 and found not guilty, Hardy was released but his ordeal had been a warning of the seriousness with which the government viewed the radical reform movement. His defence lawyer Thomas Erskine (1750–1823), first Baron Erskine, defended a number of notable radicals including Tom Paine. See John Barrell and Jon Mee (eds.), *Trials for Treason and Sedition 1792–1794* (8 vols., London, 2006–2007).

24 In May 1804 the French Senate proposed that Napoleon be made Hereditary Emperor of the French. He was duly proclaimed as such on 19 May.

25 Sir William Petty (1737–1805), second earl of Shelburne and first marquis of Lansdowne served in the army during the Seven Years' War and, from 1766 to 1768, in the government of Pitt the Elder. As prime minister from 1782 to 1783 Lansdowne oversaw early British moves towards peace with the American Revolutionaries. *ODNB*.

26 Prof. Porson is probably Richard Porson (1759–1808). Born in Norfolk, and in his early years largely self-taught, he had an exceptional memory and mathematical ability. In 1782 he became a Fellow of Trinity College Cambridge and in 1792 Regius Professor of Greek. *ODNB*.

27 Sarah Morgan Ashburner, Luke's daughter, tells us that William and Luke Ashburner, whose family lived in India, were received by the Morgans in Yarmouth as pupils and paying guests in the 1780s. They were treated 'with loving care', and both boys 'became affectionately attached to my grandfather [GCM] and always spoke of him as their best friend, their model of goodness and high character'. William and Luke returned to India and both married there. Following his first wife's

death, and shortly after GCM's death in 1798, Luke visited England, where he
met and married Sarah Price Morgan, returning with her to Bombay. See SMA,
'Memoir'; see also *http://www.findagrave.com/cgi-bin/fg.cgi?page=grdGRid=64731348.*

[28] Sir George Cayley (1773–1857) is today known as the father of aeronautics. In
1799 he created the concept of fixed wing aircraft with separate mechanisms for
lift and propulsion and in 1809–10 published a paper detailing the basic principles
of aircraft flight. Like GCM he was also interested in agricultural improvements
and political reform. *ODNB.*

[29] Grace Ashburner (1774–1812), sister of William and Luke, was presumably also
living at Southgate with the Morgans at the time of her marriage to Samuel
Boddington (1766–1843) in 1792. After her divorce, the two Boddington children
(also called Grace and Samuel) joined the Morgan household. For Samuel
Boddington see p. 9.

[30] The case became a *cause célèbre* resulting in a sensational court battle and a settlement
of over ten thousand pounds against Benjamin: anon., *The Trial of Mr. Benjamin
Boddington for Adultery with his Cousin, the Wife of Mr. Samuel Boddington, before
Joseph Burchell Esq. and a Special Jury, at the Sessions House, Clerkenwell, on Friday,
September 8, 1797: with the Speech of the Hon. T. Erskine accurately taken in Shorthand*
(London, 1797).

[31] Probably *The Stranger* (1798) by Benjamin Thompson, although since this was a
translation of an original German play about adultery by August von Kotzebue
(1761–1819), whose works were a household name in Britain, the link to the
Boddingtons may be coincidental rather than inspirational. This play has been
suggested as a source for William Godwin's novel *St. Leon* of 1799 (see David
O'Shaughnessy, 'Kotzebue and Thompson's *The Stranger*: A New Source for
Godwin's *St. Leon*', *Notes & Queries*, 52 (2005), 452–6). Since Godwin certainly
knew GCM and his circle quite well his inspiration for the subject may have
perhaps been more direct.

[32] Elizabeth Vassall Fox (Lady Holland; 1771?–1845), was a political and literary
hostess who disdained religion and led a fairly unconventional life. The 'Hon.
Mr. Webster' is presumably one of her sons (Godfrey or Henry) from her first
marriage to Sir Godfrey Webster. After meeting Henry Richard Fox (nephew of
politician Charles James Fox) in Naples in 1794 she refused to return home with
her husband. Though he divorced her in 1797 she kept her West Indies estates
and fortune. *ODNB.*

[33] William died in India in 1798; the children who joined the family William, John
and Mary (see note 87 below).

[34] The name is unclear; possible spellings include Bule, Buel, Buee and Bull. Though
GCM was sometimes vigorously anti-Catholic in sentiment this employment of
an emigré priest suggests that religious toleration was practised in the Dissenting
Morgan family. Richard Price was a notable advocate of religious toleration; his
own wife, Sarah, continued as an Anglican throughout her marriage despite her
husband's prominence as a Dissenting clergyman.

[35] The neighbours at Stamford Hill included 'the original Rothschild' with whom
William Morgan is said to have exchanged caustic comments through the garden

hedge, though both men managed to remain good friends (see Williams, *A Welsh Family*, pp. 88–9). This is probably Nathan Meyer Rothschild (1777–1836) who was sent to London by his father in 1798.

[36] During these evenings at Stamford Hill, with shutters drawn 'against the intrusion of an enemy', Amelia Alderson would sing, to music by John Taylor of Norwich, 'The trumpet of Liberty sounds through the world / And the Universe starts at the sound' with the chorus: 'Fall, Tyrants, fall, fall, fall! / These are the days of Liberty / Fall, Tyrants, fall!' (Williams, *A Welsh Family*, p. 140; see also Brightwell, *Memorials of the Life of Amelia Opie*, p. 46). John Taylor (1750–1826) was a Unitarian hymn-writer, poet, businessman and political radical. Although RPM's comments here seem to imply that William Morgan was less radical than his brother, he had worried, in 1794, that his name was on a list of those scheduled for arrest on treason charges (Williams, *A Welsh Family*, p. 139). We do not know if he is the William Morgan noted as secretary of 'Division 34' of the radical London Corresponding Society in 1798. See Mary Thale (ed.), *Selections from the Papers of the London Corresponding Society 1792–1799* (Cambridge, 1983), p. 420.

[37] Benjamin West (1738–1820), an American painter in London and a favourite of George III, became second president of the Royal Academy of which he was a founder member. He painted the portrait of Richard Price that today hangs in the National Library of Wales, Aberystwyth.

[38] Cornishman John Opie (1761–1807) had a studio in Norwich from 1799 and is said to have painted a portrait (now lost) of George Cadogan Morgan (see Williams, *A Welsh Family*, pp. 81–2). He married Amelia Alderson in 1798. *ODNB*.

[39] John Flaxman (1755–1826), was a neoclassical sculptor and book illustrator of European reputation; he became a member of the Royal Academy in 1800. *ODNB*.

[40] Lansdowne House in Berkeley Square was built 1762–8 by Robert Adam for Lord Bute but it was sold to the earl of Shelburne in 1766. At one time, thanks to Richard Price's help, Joseph Priestley was the librarian there. On the earl's death in 1805 most of the paintings and contents of the library were sold; the sale of the books and manuscripts alone ran for thirty days. Though the surviving house has been substantially remodelled, two of its original rooms survive. The principal drawing room is in the Museum of Arts in Philadelphia and the dining room in the Metropolitan Museum, New York. See Ben Weinreb and Christopher Hibbert (eds.), *The London Encyclopedia* (London, 1990), p. 446.

[41] The 'Lansdowne Portrait' depicting Washington is today back in America where it was originally commissioned from the American artist Gilbert Stuart (1755–1828) by Senator William Bingham of Pennsylvania as a gift for Lord Shelburne (later marquis of Lansdowne). Shelburne had been a sympathiser with the American cause and, ultimately, a supporter of their independence. The portrait was completed in 1796. See *http://www.npg.si.edu/collect/lansdowne2.htm*.

[42] It may be on this trip that Luke Ashburner returned overland to England from India, where his first wife had died. His journey took him along the Euphrates and Tigris valleys, through Asia Minor to Constantinople, Hungary and Germany. He then travelled through Austria where he saw preparations for the coming battles with Napoleon (Williams, *A Welsh Family*, p. 124).

[43] Sarah Morgan Ashburner relates that most other members of the family, Hurrys and Morgans, reacted very badly to her father's 'folly' and opposed 'this desparate step of emigration to America', SMA, 'Memoir', p. 9.

[44] This is most likely the current site of Holly Hill Woodland Park, Fareham, and the historic estate that stretches down to the river Hamble. The river, which is navigable in its lower reaches, enters Southampton Water where the India fleet no doubt gathered.

[45] Joseph Masclet (1760–1833), following his proscription in France, spent a number of years in Britain at a country residence near London. Called the 'Liberal Journalist' he wrote under the pseudonym *Eleutheros* (freeman) defending the actions of Lafayette during the French Revolution and, later, challenging Napoleon to secure the release of Lafayette from imprisonment by the Austrians in Olmutz. He contributed to a number of British, Dutch and German publications. He was given the Freedom of Edinburgh and after the revolution of 1830 in France became French Consul at Nice where he died. See M. Jules Cloquet, *Recollections of the Private Life of General Lafayette* (London, 1835).

[46] The Treaty of Amien, signed in March 1802, established a brief peace in the French Revolutionary Wars between Britain and France. During it many British people visited France, among them William Morgan. By May 1803 the situation between the two countries had deteriorated badly and on 22 May Napoleon, as First Consul, ordered the imprisonment of all adult British males, so trapping many visitors. They were not allowed to return home until 1814.

[47] The British East India Company provided general and vocational training for sixteen- to eighteen-year-olds destined to work in the overseas civil service; in 1806 it founded a college at Hertford Heath some nineteen miles from London, which William Morgan may have attended.

[48] First settled in 1734 as a mission to the Mahican (or Mohican) Indians, the town was set aside for the Indians in gratitude for their help in the French-Indian wars (the Seven Years' War). The town officially became Stockbridge in June 1739. Despite their further help in the war of independence the Indian land was later sold and the tribes moved elsewhere. The town was then taken over by mainly English settlers.

[49] Lowestoft, Suffolk, with its view of what is now called the North Sea.

[50] Mutford Hall is a Tudor/Jacobean house built in 1607. It still stands today.

[51] Michael Maurice (see note 7). Normanstone is near Lowestoft, Suffolk.

[52] Edmund Cobb Hurry, brother of Anne Morgan.

[53] Dr Thomas Beddoes (1760–1808) lived in Rodney Place, Clifton and was another man of radical sympathies. Despite a well-earned reputation as a physician he was forced to leave his University of Oxford lecturing post because of his republican and atheist views. Richard Lovell Edgeworth (1744–1817) later helped Beddoes establish his Pneumatic Institution in Hotwells, Bristol for the treating of disease by the inhalation of different gases. Beddoes had been writing about the application of gas and airs to the treatment of disease as early as 1794; it is just possible that it was in emulation of Beddoes's work that GCM undertook his last and fatal experiment, which, according to some sources, involved symptoms of fever and the

inhalation of a gas. See Richard Holmes, *The Age of Wonder: How the Romantic Generation Discovered the Beauty and Terror of Science* (paperback edn., London, 2009).

[54] This is either the Aust Ferry, which in various forms operated from antiquity until the building of the first Severn Bridge in 1966, or its eighteenth-century rival the Redwick-Sudbrook ferry. Details of the crossing and tides can be found in Damian Walford Davies's exploration of Wordsworth's 1798 crossing of the Severn Estuary: 'Romantic Hydrography: Tide and Transit in "Tintern Abbey"', in Nicholas Roe (ed.), *English Romantic Writers and the West Country* (Basingstoke, 2010), pp. 218–36.

[55] RPM's father GCM had been born in Bridgend but although some of Richard Price's immediate family eventually went to live there, Price was actually born in the village of Llangeinor, situated a few miles north of Bridgend, and in a house called Tynton, which still stands.

[56] Mynydd Margam (Margam Mountain, 1129 feet) is on the coast of south Wales to the west of Cardiff, and not the east as RPM says. The area likened to the Bay of Naples is Swansea Bay, which is clearly visible from Margam Mountain.

[57] The original mansion of Sir Rice Mansel at Margam was demolished by Thomas Mansel Talbot in 1768 after he moved to the family's other estate at Penrice in Gower, west of Swansea. The Margam grounds were then turned into a private pleasure garden dominated by the still-extant orangery built 1787–90. This garden is the highly improved estate seen by RPM. In 1830 a new mansion was built at Margam the shell of which remains today in what is now Margam Country Park. See John Newman with Stephen Hughes and Anthony Ward, *The Buildings of Wales: Glamorgan* (London, 1995), pp. 421–2.

[58] The Bristol Channel has the second highest tidal range in the world (*circa* fifteen metres or forty-nine feet).

[59] The visit is likely to have been to the iron works at Penydarren or one of the other works that stretched as far as Merthyr Tydfil. Rack and pinion working, of the sort described by RPM, was used on part of the Penydarren-Cardiff railway but not until 1832, much later than Morgan suggests. See G. Rattenbury and M. J. T. Lewis, *Merthyr Tydfil Tramroads and their Locomotives* (Oxford, 2004).

[60] Although not 'young' in 1805, one possible candidate is John Jones (1766?–1827) a Unitarian divine and classical scholar (see *DWB*). He may have known the Morgan family as he had been a divinity student at Hackney Academy where GCM briefly taught. We have not identified Mme St Aubin.

[61] An Irish jaunting car was a small, two-wheeled, one-horse carriage intended for two or four passengers seated back to back with their feet on footboards over the wheels. A longer version is implied by RPM's intimation that theirs carried up to twelve.

[62] The Royal Institution in Albermarle Street London was founded in 1799 and in March 1801 Davy took up the post of assistant lecturer in Chemistry and director of the Chemical Laboratory. He was elected to the Royal Society in 1803.

[63] John Goodeve was a banker who married Elizabeth Hurry in July 1806; she died on 13 October 1814 (*The Universal Magazine*, 6 (1806), 79; *The European Magazine and London Review*, 66 (1814), 312).

[64] Forton is on the east side of the road from Fareham to Gosport and overlooks Portsmouth Harbour. It expanded rapidly in the nineteenth century with the building of Forton Barracks as a home for the Royal Marines.

[65] This is probably the Southampton architect John (not James) Kent. For examples of his work, see the history of Leigh Park House in Hampshire, which was substantially rebuilt by Kent in 1802, and Ryde Pier, the first of the pleasure piers to be built. See *http://www.leighpark.stauntoninfo.co.uk/27501.html*.

[66] The area of Northam includes the shores of the Northam peninsula and adjacent areas of the river Itchen with its significant mud banks. It became an area of shipbuilding over 250 years ago.

[67] One rod is five and a half feet, so RPM was about 110 feet from the shore.

[68] Thomas Bewick's illustrated *A General History of Quadrupeds* (Newcastle-upon-Tyne, 1790) was intended to encourage interest in natural history.

[69] Prisoners from the French Revolutionary Wars were held at the Forton military prison. Some 100,000 such prisoners were held around Britain in the Napoleonic Wars and despite the development of purpose-built camps, such as Norman Cross near Peterborough, they were often held in ships' hulks and other buildings. No details of the prison fire reported by RPM have been found. A plaque on the remaining wall of the prison also indicates that over 1,500 American Revolutionary War prisoners were held there between 1777 and 1783 (see *http://www.geograph. org.uk/photo/388466*). Richard Price had involved himself in trying to alleviate the suffering of American prisoners in Britain.

[70] 'Stoke' refers to Stokes Bay and Alverstoke in south Gosport, overlooking the Solent.

[71] This suggests that Ives Hurry (see p. 199 n. 6) had returned from France by June 1808.

[72] Storm petrels.

[73] Nautilus is Greek for 'sailor'; RPM is probably referring to the very large ocean sunfish (*Mola mola*) which often swims near the surface and can appear as tall as long when its dorsal fin is raised.

[74] Quartering is the upper part of the ship's side.

[75] Philadelphia had been founded in 1682 by William Penn as a Quaker settlement.

[76] Crossed out lines in the original text at this point (top of page 49) suggest a loss of money through a poor investment: '. . . condition. He risked everything, including the money my mother had authority to secure in Philadelphia, in a foreign speculation which failing, he failed with it and our last money was lost.' The bottom of the preceding page (p. 48) is, however, incomplete and the name of the person responsible lost.

[77] Stockbridge, Massachusetts (see p. 204 n. 48).

[78] John Fitch of Connecticut built a steamboat that successfully traversed the Delaware River in 1787. By 1806 Robert Fulton, an Irish-born American, backed by Robert Livingston, tried out a steamboat on the Hudson River to Albany and, in 1807, a regular service was available at $7. This was more than twice the cost of the traditional sailing sloops that RPM used for his journey to Stockbridge. See Edwin G. Burrows and Mike Wallace, *Gotham: A History of New York City to 1898* (New York, 1999), pp. 341–42.

[79] First settled by Quakers in 1679 and named after an early settler William Trent, Trenton became the New Jersey state capital in 1790.

[80] New Brunswick, New Jersey, which was first settled in 1681.

[81] The Raritan River is a major New Jersey river and has long been used for transportation. It flows into Raritan Bay just south of Staten Island.

[82] Rubbish and disease were rife in New York at this time. Night soil was still discharged or thrown into the street, harbour and rivers and in the late eighteenth century there had been major outbreaks of yellow fever and cholera.

[83] Hudson, New York State was founded in 1785 and is on the east bank of the river Hudson, north of New York City.

[84] George C. Morgan married Eunice Tolman in Stockbridge on 30 June 1808. She is likely to have been the daughter of Ebenezer Tolman (1748–1826) and Dorcas Tolman (née Ayres, b. 1750?). Eunice died in 1832. See *http://thomas.tolmanfamily. org/gedcom-tree/gtp1605.htm*.

[85] Though RPM appears to be using it as a descriptive term for American food, 'Yankee messes' generally denotes a division of men on board ship or in the army, as in this example from the American Civil War: 'In the field, Yankee messes consisted of four to eight men, each of whom took his turn as "dogrobber" or cook': Marilyn W. Seguin, *Dogs of War: And Stories of Other Beasts of Battle in the Civil War* (Boston, 1998), p. 134.

[86] For the Sedgwicks, see p. 136 n. 22.

[87] William Ashburner (who had originally lodged with the Morgans back in the 1780s in Great Yarmouth, see note 27 above) found work in India, where he married Elizabeth Cotgrave, the daughter of Major John Cotgrave of the Madras army. On William's death in 1798 three of his children (John, William and Mary) were entrusted to his brother Luke Ashburner, and came to live with Anne Morgan; Mary was the only one to go with them to America.

[88] Sir Charles Forbes (1773–1849) was a politician and businessman resident in India. Returning to England he became a politician and advocated the franchise for women and Catholic emancipation. He married Elizabeth Ashburner in 1800. *ODNB*.

[89] RPM is mistaken here. Mary Ashburner's mother did not became a widow in 1810 because Sir Charles Forbes did not die until 1849. However the incident must have taken place around 1810; in her 'Memoir' Sarah Morgan Ashburner also indicates that Mary was returned to her mother during Anne Morgan's lifetime. Surviving Forbes family papers claim that Mary Ashburner had been 'kidnapped' to America in 1809 (see *ODNB*, s.n. Sir Charles Forbes).

[90] This is a rare racial slur from RPM who appears to have been on good terms with the various other races he met and worked with on his American journeys. That Elizabeth Ashburner was of mixed Malay and English parentage is perhaps not surprising given her father's position in the Madras army. There was much trade and movement of people between East India Company holdings in Madras and those in Malaysia and Aceh in north Sumatra.

[91] The town of Lenox is less than five miles north of Stockbridge.

92   The year is significant as it marked the outbreak of the 1812–14 war between the
     United States and Britain. This conflict forms a backdrop to parts of RPM's first
     American journey.
93   The federal government first issued the American dollar bill, the greenback,
     during the American Civil War. Prior to that, banks in the various states printed
     and issued their own notes and these were 'often of . . . dubious value'; hence,
     presumably, the desire to carry gold as a sure means of exchange. See Bill Bryson,
     Made in America (1994; paperback edn., London, 1998), p. 81.
94   At the outbreak of the 1812–14 conflict between the United States and Britain,
     control of Lake Erie passed to the British. At the battle of Lake Erie (or Put-in-
     Bay) in September 1813 the Americans under Oliver Hazard Perry (1785–1819)
     won a significant victory, capturing six British ships.
95   Lancaster, Pennsylvania was particularly famous for producing the Conestoga
     Wagon used throughout the frontier west, and the Pennsylvania Long Rifle. For
     one day in 1777 Lancaster became the capital of the United States when Congress
     fled to the city from Philadelphia during the Revolutionary War with Britain.
     The next day they moved to York, Pennsylvania (see below).
96   Little York was commonly used in reference to the city of York, which lies west
     of Lancaster and on the opposite side of the Susquehanna River.
97   During the French and Indian wars (Seven Years' War 1754–63) Washington led
     expeditions against the French in this region, so gaining his early military experi-
     ence. Fort Pitt, named after William Pitt the Elder, was built between 1759 and
     1761 at Pittsburgh where the Allegheny and Monongahela rivers join to form the
     Ohio River.
98   A skiff is a small fishing boat powered by oar or sail.
99   A freshet, in the sense used here, is a river flood resulting from heavy rain or a spring
     thaw.
100 Marietta, Ohio was an important town at this time. It was founded in 1788 as the
     first permanent settlement in the North-west Territory, i.e. the area between the
     Ohio and Mississippi rivers and the great lakes, set aside by the British as Indian
     reservation prior to the American War of Independence. The area was assigned
     to the US in 1783 in the Treaty of Paris which ended that war.
101 The Muskingum River enters the Ohio River at Marietta. From 1812 until 1861,
     during the time RPM visited, the river formed a major part of the 'Underground
     Railroad', the route by which escaped southern slaves moved north.
102 A modern replica of an American river flat-boat from the early 1800s can be seen
     at *http://en.wikipedia.org/wiki/Flatboat*.
103 Blennerhassett Island is a short distance downstream from Marietta, near the city
     of Parkersburg, West Virginia.
104 Harman Blennerhassett was an Irish American lawyer who settled on the island
     in 1798, building a palladian style mansion there. His entanglement with Aaron
     Burr occurred in 1806 during the presidency of Thomas Jefferson. The president
     came to believe that Burr and Blennerhassett were seeking to set up an empire in
     the south-west – probably, it is now believed, in Texas or what was then northern
     Mexico. The mansion burned down in 1811 but the foundations were rediscovered

in 1973 and it has since been rebuilt. The island is now a West Virginia state park (see *http://www.blennerhassettislandstatepark.com/history.html*).

[105] The Scioto River enters the Ohio River at Portsmouth in southern Ohio.

[106] Cincinnati was founded in 1788 and became a city in 1819, shortly after RPM's visit.

[107] Situated at Clarksville, Indiana, just opposite Louisville, Kentucky, the Falls of the Ohio were the only major rock hazard to navigation in the river's 981 miles. Here the river fell some twenty-six feet in two and a half miles; the falls were later drowned by the building of the McAlpine Dam.

[108] Joel Scribner and his brothers Abner and Nathaniel came to the Ohio Falls in 1813. Having bought land on the Indiana side of the river they established the settlement that became New Albany, named after the capital of their home state New York, a place RPM would certainly have known quite well. The house built by Scribner still stands (see *http://www.countyhistory.com/scribnerhouse*).

[109] Sandusky in northern Ohio lies on the shores of Lake Erie. Established as Portland in 1816 the name became Sandusky in 1818. Buffalo, New York, also on the shores of Lake Erie, began in around 1789 as a trading settlement.

[110] Named after the Massachusetts site of the battle of Lexington in the Revolutionary War, the town of Lexington, Kentucky, was founded in 1775 and established permanently in 1782. Chillicothe, Ohio was originally a settlement of the Shawnee people and was capital of Ohio between 1803–10 and 1812–16. It also formed part of the 'Underground Railroad' for escaped southern slaves moving north.

[111] Upper Sandusky dates back to the 1780s and lies on the upper reaches of the Sandusky River, which flows into Lake Erie fifty miles away. The Wyandot or Wendat Indians lived in the area.

[112] General William Henry Harrison (1773–1841) had command of the army of the Northwest from September 1812. In October 1813, and after Perry's September victory at the battle of Lake Erie, Harrison had defeated the British and their Indian allies at the battle of the Thames, which effectively ended the war in the Lake Erie region. Harrison went on to become America's ninth and shortest term president in 1841. Having given a very long inaugural speech in terrible weather he later developed pneumonia and pleurisy and died after just one month in office.

[113] RPM is actually referring to Fort Stephenson on the Lower Sandusky, the command of which General W. H. Harrison gave to Captain George Croghan (1791–1849) and 160 regular American troops in summer 1813.

[114] Ordered to evacuate and burn Fort Stephenson, but fearing an ambush from British-employed Indians gathering outside, Croghan decided to hold it instead. Following Croghan's refusal to surrender, the British general Henry Proctor attacked the fort with a substantial army but was beaten back by Croghan, his regulars and a single (not four as RPM suggests) artillery piece called 'Old Betsy'. For his action Croghan was promoted to Colonel. Meanwhile Harrison had not moved from Fort Seneca just ten miles away. See Stephen Heidler and Jeanne T. Heidler (eds.), *Encyclopedia of the War of 1812* (Annapollis, 2004), pp. 138–9.

[115] The Huron River rises in the Huron Swamp and flows into Lake Erie a distance of 136 miles.

116   Buffalo had been burnt by the British on 30 December 1813 during the 1812–14
      war with the US.
117   Brigadier General Winfield Scott (1786–1866) had a major army-training estab-
      lishment in Buffalo in 1814 and adopted the 1791 instruction manual of the
      French Revolutionary Army (previously the American army used a variety of
      manuals, which caused problems in battle manoeuvres). In July the battle of
      Chippawa on the banks of the Niagara River – and some weeks later, the battle
      of Lundy's Lane – showed that the newly disciplined Americans could hold their
      own against British regulars. Scott was badly wounded in the latter battle.
118   Now Claverack in New York State, a town formed in 1778.
119   Olean, in the south-west of New York State and on the Allegheny River became
      an important timber town *circa* 1830–50, some years after RPM's trip.
120   Rafts could be of many types and varied in design on the different major rivers.
      On the Allegheny timber, spar, log and lumber rafts are noted. On the Mississippi
      a lumber raft comprised planks fitted into crate or crib frames sixteen feet wide,
      sixteen to thirty-two feet long and ten to twenty inches deep. A cook's shanty
      and 'dog-houses' (crew sleeping cabins) would often be built on larger types of
      raft. See *http://steamboattimes.com/rafts.html*.
121   Just to the east of Cincinnati and named after the Native American Miami people.
122   Now Old Shawneetown, Illinois on the banks of the Ohio River; it was visited
      by Lafayette in 1825. New Shawneetown was founded inland in 1937 after severe
      river flooding of the old town left one million people homeless. 'In pre-steamboat
      days the town had been overrun periodically by bargers and keelboatmen, a rough
      and lawless crowd': R. Carlyle Buley, *The Old Northwest: Pioneer Period 1815–1840*
      (2 vols., Bloomington, 1950), I, pp. 40–1.
123   Literally a flat-bottomed wooden boat similar to a modern landing craft, but with
      deck and superstructure above the hold.
124   From Frankfort due north the river could have been anywhere between thirty
      and fifty miles.
125   Cairo, Illinois lies on a spit of land between the Ohio and Mississippi rivers and
      was only founded in 1837.
126   Plum Point Reach is opposite the town of Osceola, Arkansas. It was the site of a
      Civil War naval battle in 1862 (the battle of Plum Point Bend).
127   Sweeps are long heavy oars used for steerage and propulsion. In some instances
      they could be as long as thirty to fifty feet.
128   Pig fat is boiled at high temperature so that the insoluble lard can be skimmed
      from the surface. Lard is then used for cooking, as a spread similar to butter, or
      in the making of soap.
129   A small boat stowed on board the main vessel or towed behind and of general
      purpose use.
130   A schooner is a small sailing vessel rigged fore and aft on two masts. The schooner
      was an original American design. RPM appears to imply that this form of schooner
      rigging had been added to a barge rather than a typical sailing vessel.
131   Barge oars could comprise a main stem thirty feet long and one foot in diameter
      at the river end and three inches at the other. Into the river end was inserted a

blade made of a plank of wood three inches thick and sixteen to eighteen feet long, making the complete oar forty-five to fifty feet. See *http://steamboattimes. com/rafts.html.*

[132] One gill = a quarter pint.

[133] Tow cloth is a cloth made of coarse hemp.

[134] Founded by John Harris (1673–1748); after receiving a trader's licence in 1705 he later developed a trading post on the Susquehanna River at what eventually became Harrisburg, Pennsylvania and the State Capital in 1812.

[135] Galling causes a painful swelling or sore as a result of chafing.

[136] Canandaigua in Ontario County, New York State, founded in about 1789.

[137] A brig is a two-masted square-rigged (yards and sails across the mast) vessel.

[138] Septimus was the seventh son of George Cadogan Morgan. He died aged nineteen in December 1816 (*The Gentleman's Magazine*, LXXXVI (July–December 1816), 626).

[139] Sarah Price Ashburner (née Morgan), who had gone to India with her husband Luke.

[140] RPM would be about twenty-six at the time of his marriage

[141] Theodore Sedgwick II (1780–1839). For an early photograph of the Sedgwick house, see *http://www.berkshireweb.com.*

[142] Susan Anne Livingston Ridley Sedgwick (1788–1867) was a children's novelist; her books include *The Morals of Pleasure* (1829) and *Allen Prescott, or the Fortunes of a New England Boy* (1834).

[143] Among the family to come over in 1823 was Luke Ashburner's daughter Sarah Morgan Ashburner, the author of the unpublished 'Memoir'. She would later marry Theodore Sedgwick III. Their own daughter, Sarah Price Ashburner Sedgwick, went on to marry William Erasmus Darwin, the son of Charles Darwin.

[144] Luke Ashburner (1772–1884) married Cornelia Whitney (d. 1 April 1884) in Stockbridge on 2 February 1825.

[145] The Erie Canal was built between 1817 and 1825 largely by 'Irish and Welsh' labourers. It was 363 miles long, forty feet wide and four feet deep with over eighty locks and eighteen aqueducts. When it opened shipping costs plummeted from $100 a ton to about $9 and many goods once destined for transport further south, along the Ohio River for example, now travelled via the canal to Manhattan for onward shipping. See Ronald E. Shaw, *Canals for a Nation: The Canal Era in the United States, 1790–1860* (Kentucky, 1990), p. 38.

[146] James Fowle Baldwin (1782–1862) an early civil engineer in America who worked on many canal, railroad and water supply projects.

[147] At the time RPM worked on the line, this section was called the Western Railroad (later part of the Boston & Albany). In November 1840 the Western R.R. opened from Worcester to Springfield in Massachusetts. In 1842 the line extended west to Greenbush, New York, opposite Albany on the Hudson River. The Boston and Albany was chartered in 1867. See George P. Baker, *Formation of the New England Railroad Systems: A Study of Railroad Combination in the Nineteenth Century*, (Cambridge, 1937), pp. 7, 13.

[148] The Liverpool and Manchester Railway was founded in 1823 and opened in 1830. RPM's presence in Baltimore in 1828 means he probably knew of the Maryland

legislature's 1827 decision to charter the Baltimore and Ohio Railroad using horse power. The first sod was broken on 4 July 1828 by Charles Carroll, the last surviving signatory to America's Declaration of Independence. By 1830 the steam powered *Tom Thumb* was running on the railroad at eighteen miles per hour. See Burrows and Wallace, *Gotham*, pp. 563–4.

[149] Robert Livingston Stevens (1787–1856) with his father John Stevens (1749–1838) built steamships, including the first ocean-going steam ship which travelled from Hoboken to Philadelphia via the Delaware River. Both men were also heavily involved in inventions for, and the building of, the early railroads in America. Edwin Augustus Stevens (1795–1868) engineer and inventor founded the Stevens Institute of Technology in Hoboken, New Jersey.

[150] The Camden and Amboy Railroad was chartered in February 1830. Part of the route opened under horse power in October 1832. Camden, New Jersey, is across the Delaware River from Philadelphia and Amboy, New Jersey, is at the south end of Long Island Sound. Robert Stevens was president of the Camden and Amboy Railroad in the 1830s and 1840s.

[151] The Quincy Quarries were near Boston. The last quarry closed in 1963. The Granite Railway was completed October 1826. It originated to carry stone for construction of the Bunker Hill Monument in Boston. Resting on deep stone foundations, 'the ties or sleepers were made of stone placed 8 feet apart, upon which were laid longitudinal pine timbers 6 inches wide & 12 inches high. On top of the rails was an oak strip 2" × 4" faced with an iron plate 3 inches wide and ¼ inch thick, which was fastened with spikes . . . The wood rails were subsequently replaced with stone rails': William C. Edwards, *Historic Quincy, Massachusetts* (3rd edn., Quincy, 1957), pp. 121–9.

[152] Construction of the Harlem Railroad began in February 1832 and it was originally horse-drawn. Part of the system used rails bolted to foot square granite blocks rather than the more usual wooden ties or sleepers. These granite blocks rose several inches above the street and since the Harlem Railroad ran through the streets of New York it must have made cross-town travel particularly difficult (see Burrows and Wallace, *Gotham*, p. 565).

[153] The Stonington and Providence Railroad, which at first ran from Stonington in Connecticut to South Providence, Rhode Island, was chartered in 1832 and opened in 1837.

[154] In September 1833 President Andrew Jackson removed government funds from the privately owned Second Bank of the United States. He opposed renewing the bank's charter which was due in 1836 and, after an investigation, accused the bank of using its funds to influence the election of public officers. At this time there was no uniform currency, banking regulation (a state responsibility) was lax and there was a combination of state-chartered and private banks which issued their own banknotes. RPM's 'local institutions' appear to be the state-chartered banks. The lax control meant he could borrow $100 with no collateral. He appears to have been given banknotes from a New Jersey bank to pay his workers. This bank may then have collapsed, the notes became worthless, and he was also stuck

with being owed $1,500 by the (railroad?) company who employed him. (Thanks to Peggy Tuck Sinko for this information.)

[155] Joseph Gardner Swift (1783–1865) was in the first graduating class of West Point in 1802. He undertook the development of New York's defences in the war of 1812 and later helped in the rebuilding of the Capitol building in Washington after its destruction by the British in that war. Following resignation from the army he became surveyor of the port of New York and carried out a number of civil engineering projects in the city. He became chief engineer of the New York and Harlem Railroad in 1832 but later resigned after a disagreement with the directors.

[156] The Brooklyn and Jamaica Railroad was incorporated in 1832 to run from South Ferry on the East River in Brooklyn to Jamaica on Long Island. As such it became the first Long Island Railroad. It opened in 1836.

[157] The Stonington and Providence Railroad.

[158] Between 1816 and 1848 it is estimated there were 233 steamboat explosions (see John G. Burke, 'Bursting Boilers and the Federal Power', *Technology and Culture*, 7 (1966), 1–23). No reference to an explosion on a steamboat in 1834 has been found but the steamer Lexington is recorded as having suffered 'a conflagration' on 13 January 1840 on route from New York to Stonington. Over one hundred and fifty people died. See S. A. Howland, *Steamboat Disasters and Railroad Accidents in the United States* (2nd edn., Worcester, 1840), III, p. 167.

[159] Simsbury, Connecticut.

[160] William Morgan (1750–1833). Stoke Newington and nearby Newington Green had also been the long time home of Richard Price.

[161] Llandaff (Welsh Llandaf) today lies within the city of Cardiff, but was formerly an important ecclesiastical centre in its own right; it boasts a cathedral in the churchyard of which Sarah Price Morgan was buried in 1820.

[162] The 1837 financial panic was akin to that which affected the USA and other countries in 2008–9. It arose from a combination of feverish speculation in property for profit but coupled with rampant inflation caused by the economic and financial policies of the government. The consequences included very high unemployment and a collapse of the stock market in New York with railroad shares being particularly badly hit. Many proposed new lines were abandoned, some never to be resurrected. In March 1837 thirty thousand people attended a mass meeting in New York urging the cashing-in of banknotes in order to make 'soulless corporate extortioners pay their debts to the people as promptly as they compel payment from the people'. The result of the panic was a five-year depression. See Burrows and Wallace, *Gotham*, p. 613.

[163] An account of this period from the children's point of view can be found in an unpublished memoir written by RPM's son George Cadogan Morgan (b. 1833); we are grateful to Newberry Library, Chicago, for giving us access to this document.

[164] The Croton Aqueduct, built between 1837 and 1842, formed a major infrastructure project which aimed to supply New York with fresh water from the dammed Croton River some forty miles north of the city. The aqueduct's course ran

through New York City and the length of Manhattan Island and across the Harlem River onto the mainland. From there it ran north through the area of Sing Sing to the Croton River. Sing Sing was the original name for an area now known as Ossining in the Hudson Valley north of New York City; it was the home of the infamous Sing Sing Correctional Facility.

[165] The railroad was officially called the New York and Harlem R.R. It reached Albany in 1852. The line was never profitable and was acquired by Cornelius Vanderbilt in 1857. Putnam and Dutchess counties lie north of New York and on the east side of the Hudson River.

[166] Henry Alanson Gardner, senior was born 20 April 1816 in Berkshire County, Massachusetts. He went on to hold the post of engineer and chief engineer on various railroads. His descendants deposited with the Newberry Library, Chicago, the GCM and RPM works that comprise this volume.

[167] Edwin Ferry Johnson (1803–72), a major civil engineer who became chief engineer on a number of lines including the New York to Albany line, although sources differ as to the precise date of his appointment. See the obituary in the *New York Times*, 20 April 1972, and *Memoir of Edwin Ferry Johnson* (Philadelphia, 1880).

[168] Governeur Kemble (1786–1875) was born in New York and died at Cold Spring, which lies opposite West Point on the Hudson River. Kemble established a cannon foundry at Cold Spring in company with General Joseph Gardner Swift and others. He was a two-term US Congressman as well as an industrialist who in later years promoted the Hudson River Railroad.

[169] RPM appears to have found himself embroiled in one of the many scams that plagued the development of railroads in America at this time, as 'investors' attempted to make quick profits by fair means or foul. In 1835 New York State senators John C. Kemble and Isaac W. Bishop were charged that, in March 1836, while a bill was in progress through the New York Senate for extending the time to complete the New York Harlem Railroad, they resolved to delay passage of the bill until they could buy substantial volumes of stock at the reduced price that resulted from the delay. They then let the bill pass and made a profit as the share value rose again. A senate enquiry found them guilty with Bishop expelled from the senate. Kemble appears to have voluntarily withdrawn and is said to have died two years later in a mental institution. We have not been able to ascertain whether John Kemble was related to the Governeur Kemble with whom RPM became acquainted. See *Niles' National Register* (March–September 1836), 230–2.

[170] The Mohawk and Hudson Railroad was chartered in 1826 with a sixteen-mile section between Albany and Schenectady opened in 1831.

[171] Henry A. Gardner married Sarah Morgan in Stockbridge, Massachusetts on 27 September 1842. They had five sons: Richard, Henry, George, William and James. See O. F. Pearre, W. H. Perrin, H. H. Hill and A. A. Graham, *The History of Livingston County, Illinois* (Chicago, 1878), p. 670.

[172] Kendall County is about forty miles south-west of Chicago.

[173] Anne Morgan (née Hurry) died at Hudson, New York on 16 March 1846 (see *The Gentleman's Magazine*, n.s. XXV (1846), 670). Sarah Morgan Ashburner notes

in her 'Memoir' that this fire resulted in the loss of all of Anne Morgan's family papers and this may be one explanation for the lack of any substantial archive relating to her husband George Cadogan Morgan.

174 Maranham or Maranhão is an administrative region in north-eastern Brazil with its state capital and port at Sao Luís, the likely base of Patterson and his wife. Historically the area's principal exports were sugar cane, the cocoa bean and tobacco, although at the 1861 outbreak of the American Civil War it also began to export cotton to Britain.

175 John Bloomfield Jervis (1795–1885) was a major American civil engineer working on railroads, canals and water supply projects. He also developed plans for some of the earliest steam locomotives in the US. In 1836 he had been made chief engineer of the Croton Aqueduct scheme in New York on which RPM had worked. He was chief engineer of the Hudson River Railroad from 1847 to 1849. See Robert L. Frey (ed.), *Railroads in the Nineteenth Century* (New York, 1988), pp. 202–7, and William D. Middleton, George M. Smerk and Roberta L. Diehl (eds.), *Encyclopedia of North American Railroads* (Bloomington, Indiana, 2007), p. 568.

176 Tarrytown is located in the Hudson Valley between Poughkeepsie and New York City.

177 Galena, founded in 1826, is situated in the north-west corner of Illinois and was important for lead mining and its position on the Galena River, which runs into the Mississippi. The Galena and Chicago Union Railroad was chartered in 1836 to connect Galena with Chicago and was the first railroad in or out of Chicago.

178 RPM is recorded as surveying the first section from Kinzie Street in Chicago to the Des Plaines River in September 1847. See *http://www.cnwhs.org/articles/ 1166734167.pdf* and *http://encyclopedia.chicagohistory.org/pages/1039.html*.

179 The first locomotive on the railway, the *Pioneer*, is in the Chicago History Museum.

180 Originally the Milwaukee and Waukesha Railroad, chartered in 1847, the name changed in 1850 to the Milwaukee and Mississippi Railroad to reflect the extension of the line from Lake Michigan (Milwaukee) to the Mississippi River. See Daniel L. Lanz, *Railroads of Southern and Southwestern Wisconsin: Development to Decline* (2nd edn., Monroe, 1986), pp. 4–7.

181 According to Alfred T. Andreas, *History of Cook County From the Earliest Period to the Present Time* (Chicago, 1884), p. 181, this survey took place from December 1850 and by April 1851 was nearly complete. This is slightly later than indicated by RPM.

182 The Rock Island and Peru (or more properly La Salle) Railroad was chartered in 1847. With money difficult to raise because of a lack of interest in simply connecting the Mississippi (at Rock Island) and Illinois rivers (at Peru / La Salle) it was decided to encourage investment by extending the railroad to Chicago and Lake Michigan. An amended charter came about in February 1851 when the railway became the Chicago and Rock Island Railroad (see *http://www.rits. org*). John B. Jervis, with whom RPM had dealings earlier, became the first president of the railroad. William E. Hayes in *Iron Road to Empire: The History of 100 Years of the Progress and Achievements of the Rock Island Lines* (New York, 1953), p. 11, notes that 'Richard Morgan, acting as engineer, had made a survey of the line and it was down on the map of Illinois. On paper, that was all.'

[183] The Peoria and Oquawka Railroad was supposed to link the Mississippi (at Oquawka) and Illinois (at Peoria) rivers but the line did not reach Oquawka. It was organized in 1849.

[184] On its foundation Peoria and Oquawka stock sold at $100 dollars. RPM's mention of the sum of $50,000 dollars is significant as in May 1851 this was precisely the amount of a proposed investment in the railroad that voters in Henderson County, which contained Oquawka, overwhelmingly refused to approve. The line's route was then changed toward Monmouth (to the north-east of Oquawka in Warren County) which had subscribed $100,000. See Robert P. Sutton, *Rivers, Railroads, and Roads: A History of Henderson County, Illinois* (Raritan, 1988), p. 39.

[185] RPM's second marriage was to Eliza S. Teall in Chicago on 6 October 1856. See Sam Fink, *Index to Chicago and Cook County Marriages and Deaths Reported in Chicago Newspapers, 1834–1889* (microfilm of typescript at Newberry Library, Chicago, n.d.). RPM is also recorded in 1859–60 advertising himself in D. B. Cooke & Company's *Chicago City Directory* as a civil engineer based at 415 West Madison.

[186] McGregor was founded as McGregor's Landing by Alexander McGregor, a descendant of Rob Roy McGregor, in 1847 in Clayton County, Iowa on the west side of the Mississippi. RPM appears to be referring to the fact that in 1854 a railroad to run west from McGregor was proposed. Limited work was carried out but then: 'Times grew hard, money was far from easy and the work was turned over to other parties. These failed, and it was turned to a third company, which was also unable to push it forward. By some legal process the franchise reverted to Judge Brown, one of the most active of the original promoters. Brown sold the interest of the old company to the McGregor Western Rail Road Company.' Work recommenced on the railroad in 1863. See Realto E. Price (ed.), *History of Clayton County, Iowa From the Earliest Historical Times Down to the Present* (2 vols., Chicago, 1916), I, p. 176.

[187] Situated north-west of McGregor it is said to be named after a member of the Ho Chunk (or Winnebago) tribe native to Wisconsin and Illinois. Waukon is the administrative centre for Allamakee County in the far north-eastern corner of Iowa. It was settled in 1849.

[188] Attempts to finance a railroad from Waukon to the Mississippi had been ongoing for some time. RPM's involvement was probably in the late 1850s or early 1860s. In October 1857 the Prairie du Chien & Mankato Railroad was organized in Waukon. Despite initial surveys for parts of the line this too failed. There were several further attempts to revive the line across northern Iowa but there was little development until a narrow gauge railway was partially executed in the 1870s. See W. E. Alexander, *History of Winneshiek and Allamakee Counties, Iowa* (Sioux City, 1882), pp. 690–1.

[189] The Chicago and Plainfield Railroad was chartered in February 1859 with the aim of running south-west from Chicago through Plainfield towards Ottawa on the Illinois River.

[190] In March 1869 the Chicago and Plainfield Railroad charter was amended in order to build a route to Pekin on the Illinois River just south of Peoria. The name also

changed to the Chicago, Plainfield and Pekin Railroad. In April the name changed again to the Chicago, Pekin and Southwestern Railroad. See Anon., *History of Tazewell County, Illinois* (Chicago, 1879), p. 741.

[191] The Hamilton, Lacon and Eastern Railroad was incorporated in March 1867. The line was to run from Hamilton on the Mississippi River through Lacon on the Illinois River and on to Monee just south of Chicago but 'nothing was ever done to start construction'. See Gene V. Glendinning, *Chicago and Alton Railroad: The Only Way* (DeKalb, 2002), p. 83.

[192] The *History of Tazewell County*, p. 742, notes that 'The first contract for building the road [Chicago and Plainfield R.R.] was made between the Chicago & Plainfield Company and Richard P. Morgan, who was afterwards joined by E. T. Pierce. This contract was declared forefeited by the first Board of the Chicago, Pekin & Southwestern Railroad Co., and another contract entered into by said Board & Messers. Roderick Clark of LaSalle Co., Cragie Sharp of Woodford Co., and Edgar T. Pierce of LaSalle Co.' They did not finish the work. The railroad was finally opened in 1873.

[193] The panics of 1874 and 1875 were a continuation of the panic of 1873 which saw an almost world-wide depression result from a fall in the price of silver after Germany abandoned the silver standard. In America, where most silver was then mined, the situation was exacerbated by the after-effects of the American Civil War and a railway construction boom based on massive over-investment and subsidy often with little chance of a substantial return. Of 364 railroads in the country, 89 went bankrupt and in 1877 a major railroad strike took place. Chicago became one of the centres of strike action. Vigilantes, the National Guard and federal troops were needed to restore order following massive demonstrations and riots in the city on 25 July 1877 when some twenty people were killed and there was major destruction of property.

[194] Henry A. Gardner died at Bloomington, Illinois.

[195] The graduated wooden or metal rod used to determine differences of elevation along the course of the railroad track being surveyed.

[196] Begun in 1836 and finished in 1848 the Illinois and Michigan Canal connected the Chicago River at Bridgeport in Chicago to the Illinois River at La Salle, a distance of 155 km or 96 miles.

[197] In 1850 Oliver H. Lee is noted as superintendent of the Hudson River Railroad Company. See *Documents of the Senate of the State of New York* (Albany, 1851), I, part 12, p. 61. In June 1852, Oliver Lee and three assistants – James Spencer, Henry Gardner and Richard Price Morgan, junior – arrived at Bloomington, Illinois, to open an office there and in Springfield, Illinois. See Glendinning, *Chicago and Alton Railroad*, p. 29.

[198] Joliet is the county seat of Will County, Illinois and is forty miles south-west of Chicago. It was settled in 1833.

[199] RPM's son Richard Price Morgan, junior was one of the three founding fathers of Dwight, Illinois.

[200] Richard Price Morgan, junior was born in Stockbridge, Massachusetts on 17 September 1828. As Colonel R. P. Morgan he fought in the American Civil

War and, like his father, was a railway engineer. In 1853, while in Bloomington, Illinois, helping build the Chicago and Alton Railway, he met and became friends with Abraham Lincoln after they shared a room together in an otherwise full boarding house. RPM, junior became chief engineer of the United States Pacific Railway Commission and in 1896 President Cleveland appointed him to help locate and plan a deep water port in California. He was also heavily involved in projected designs for elevated railways in New York. He died on 20 May 1910 at Dwight, Illinois, which – as one of the towns three founding fathers – he had helped to lay out. See Owen T. Reeves, James S. Ewing, Richard P. Morgan, Franklin Blades and John W. Bunn, *Abraham Lincoln By Some Men Who Knew Him* (Bloomington, 1910), pp. 83–104.

[201] 'For the public good'.

[202] A committee under the chairmanship of Alonzo Barton Hepburn (1846–1922) was appointed to investigate alleged abuses in railroad management in New York State and the often secretive relations between the railroads and other industries. One company under scrutiny was Standard Oil, owned by John D. Rockefeller, senior. The Hepburn report of 1879 described the railroads' bias toward Standard Oil as 'the most shameless perversion of the duties of a common carrier to private ends . . . in the history of the world'. The report heavily influenced the Federal Interstate Commerce Act adopted eight years later. See Ron Chernow, *Titan: The Life of John D. Rockefeller, Sr.* (London, 1998), pp. 213–14 and the entry on Alonzo B. Hepburn in *DAB*, VIII, p. 566.

[203] The West Shore Railroad ran from Weehawken, New Jersey to Albany and Buffalo. It was incorporated in 1867 and operated between 1872 and 1885, after which it became part of the New York Central System. See Middleton, Smerk and Diehl (eds.), *Encyclopedia of North American Railroads*, p. 746, and Frey (ed.), *Railroads in the Nineteenth Century*, pp. 275, 414.

[204] Otherwise known as the New York, Chicago and St Louis Railroad, it operated 1881–1964.

[205] The Lake Shore Railroad was controlled by William Henry Vanderbilt (the son of Cornelius Vanderbilt) and had high freight charges, hence the desire for competition, but Vanderbilt eventually gained control of both the West Shore and Nickel Plate railroads. They were then incorporated into his New York Central System.

Select Bibliography

Adams, John, *A Defence of the Constitutions of Government of the United States of America* (London, 1787).

Adams, William Howard, *The Paris Years of Thomas Jefferson* (New Haven, 1997).

Addison, Joseph, *Remarks on Several Parts of Italy &c. in the Years 1701, 1702, 1703* (London, 1705).

Alexander, W. E., *History of Winneshiek and Allamakee Counties, Iowa* (Sioux City, 1882).

Ambrose, Tom, *Godfather of the Revolution: The Life of Philippe Egalité Duc d'Orléans* (London, 2008).

Anderson, J. G., 'William Morgan and X-rays', *Transactions of the Faculty of Actuaries*, 17 (1945), 219–21.

Andreas, Alfred T., *History of Cook County From the Earliest Period to the Present Time* (Chicago, 1884).

Andress, David, *The French Revolution and the People* (London, 2004).

Anon., *A Hand-Book for Travellers in Switzerland and the Alps of Savoy and Piedmont*, John Murray editions (London, 1838).

Anon., *History of Tazewell County, Illinois* (Chicago, 1879).

Anon., *The Trial of Mr. Benjamin Boddington for Adultery with his Cousin, the Wife of Mr. Samuel Boddington, before Joseph Burchell Esq. and a Special Jury, at the Sessions House, Clerkenwell, on Friday, September 8, 1797: with the Speech of the Hon. T. Erskine accurately taken in Shorthand* (London, 1797).

Anon., 'Account of the late Mr George Cadogan Morgan', *The Monthly Magazine*, VI (1798), 475–80.

Anon., 'Tour in France in 1818', *The Gentleman's Magazine*, XC (January–June 1820), 25–7.

Baker, George P., *Formation of the New England Railroad Systems: A Study of Railroad Combination in the Nineteenth Century* (Cambridge, 1937).

Baker, Lee, 'The French Revolution as Local Experience: The Terror in Dijon', *The Historian,* 67 (2005), 694–711.

Barrell, John, and Jon Mee (eds.), *Trials for Treason and Sedition 1792–1794* (8 vols., London, 2006–2007).

Barrell, John, review of Pamela Clemit (ed.), *The Letters of William Godwin, Vol I: 1778–97* (Oxford, 2011), *London Review of Books*, 33, no. 17 (8 September 2011), 21–3.

de Beer, G. R., *Alps and Men: Pages from Forgotten Diaries of Travellers and Tourists in Switzerland* (London, 1932).

—— *Early Travellers in the Alps* (London, 1930).

Bevis, Richard, *The Road to Egdon Heath: The Aesthetics of the Great in Nature* (Montreal, 1999).

Bewick, Thomas, *A General History of Quadrupeds* (Newcastle-upon-Tyne, 1790).

Bindman, David, *The Shadow of the Guillotine: Britain and the French Revolution* (London, 1989).

Black, Jeremy, *The British Abroad: The Grand Tour in the Eighteenth Century* (Stroud, 2003).

—— 'On the Grand Tour in a Year of Revolution', *Francia*, 13 (1985), 333–53.

Boulloche, Paul, *Un avocat du XVIIIè siècle* (Paris, 1893).

Boyer, Marjorie Nice, *Medieval French Bridges: A History,* Publications of the Medieval Academy of America, 84 (Cambridge, 1976).

Bransby-Williams, George, 'Letters from Revolutionary France', *The New English Review Magazine*, II, no. 2 (February 1949), 114–21.

Brightwell, C. L., *Memorials of the Life of Amelia Opie* (Norwich, 1854).

Brinkley, Richard, 'The Library of Richard Price', *The Price-Priestley Newsletter*, 4 (1980), 4–15.

Bryson, Bill, *Made in America* (1994; paperback edn., London, 1998).

Buley, R. Carlyle, *The Old Northwest: Pioneer Period 1815–1840* (2 vols., Bloomington, 1950).

Burke, John G., 'Bursting Boilers and the Federal Power', *Technology and Culture*, 7 (1966), 1–23.

Burley, Stephen, *New College, Hackney (1786–96): A Selection of Printed and Archival Sources* (2nd edn., 2011), at *http://www.english.qmul.ac.uk/drwilliams/pubs/nc%20hackney.html*.

—— 'Hazlitt the Dissenter: Religion, Philosophy and Politics 1766–1816' (unpublished University of Oxford DPhil thesis, 2011).

Burrows, Edwin G., and Mike Wallace, *Gotham: A History of New York City to 1898* (New York, 1999).

Carra, J. L., *Le Comte de Lorges, prisonnier à la Bastille pendant trente-deux ans, enfermé en 1757, du temps de Damiens, et mis en liberté le 14 Juillet 1789* (Paris, 1789).

Chagniot, Jean, *Paris et l'armée au XVIIIè siècle: Étude politique et sociale* (Paris, 1985).

Chernow, Ron, *Titan: The Life of John D. Rockefeller, Sr.* (London, 1998).

Clifford, Dale Lothrop, 'The National Guard and the Parisian Community 1789–1790', *French Historical Studies*, 16, no. 4 (1990), 849–78.

Cloquet, M. Jules, *Recollections of the Private Life of General Lafayette* (London, 1835).

Conant, Kenneth John, *Carolingian and Romanesque Architecture 800–1200* (3rd edn., Harmondsworth, 1973).

Cone, Carl B., *The English Jacobins: Reformers in Late 18th Century England* (1968; paperback edn., New York, 2010).

Constantine, Mary-Ann, and Dafydd Johnston (eds.), *Footsteps of Liberty and Revolt: Essays on Wales and the French Revolution* (Cardiff, forthcoming).

Conway, Moncure D., *The Life of Thomas Paine* (2 vols., New York, 1892).

Crook, Malcolm, *Toulon in War and Revolution: From the Ancien Regime to the Restoration, 1750–1820* (Manchester, 1991).

Davies, Damian Walford, 'Romantic Hydrography: Tide and Transit in "Tintern Abbey"', in Nicholas Roe (ed.), *English Romantic Writers and the West Country* (Basingstoke, 2010), pp. 218–36.

Doyle, William, *The Oxford History of the French Revolution* (2nd edn., Oxford, 2002).

Druce, Robert, 'From *A Tale of Two Cities* to *Mam'zelle Guillotine*: The French Revolution seen through Popular Fiction', in C. C. Barfoot and Theo D'haen (eds.), *Tropes of Revolution: Writers' Reactions to Real and Imagined Revolutions 1789–1989* (Amsterdam, 1991), pp. 324–50.

Dumouriez, Charles-François, *The Life of General Dumouriez* (3 vols., London, 1796).

Eastlake, Lady [Elizabeth] (ed.), *Dr Rigby's Letters from France &c. in 1789* (London, 1880).

Edmonds, W. D., *Jacobinism and the Revolt of Lyon 1789–1793* (Oxford, 1990).

Edwards, Gavin, *Narrative Order 1789–1819: Life and Story in an Age of Revolution* (Basingstoke, 2006).

Edwards, William C., *Historic Quincy, Massachusetts* (3rd edn., Quincy, 1957).

Elderton, Sir William P., 'Some Family Connections of William Morgan (1750–1833), F.R.S.', *The Genealogists Magazine*, 12, no. 10 (June 1957), 329–39.

Farge, René, *Un épisode de la journée du 12 juillet 1789: Camille Desmoulins au jardin du Palais-Royal* (Paris, 1914).

Frame, Paul, *Liberty's Apostle: The Life and Times of Richard Price 1723–91* (Cardiff, forthcoming).

—— and Geoffrey W. Powell, '"Our First Concern as Lovers of Our Country Must Be to Enlighten It": Richard Price's Response to 1789', in Constantine and Johnston (eds.), '*Footsteps of Liberty and Revolt*'.

Frey, Robert L. (ed.), *Railroads in the Nineteenth Century* (New York, 1988).

Garrett, Martin, *Provence: A Cultural History* (Oxford, 2006).

Glendinning, Gene V., *Chicago and Alton Railroad: The Only Way* (DeKalb, 2002).

Godechot, Jacques, *The Taking of the Bastille, July 14th, 1789*, trans. Jean Stewart (London, 1970).

Graham, Jenny, *The Nation, The Law and The King, Reform Politics in England, 1789–1799* (2 vols., Lanham, 2000).

Guest, Harriet, 'Amelia Alderson Opie: Sociability and Politics', *Bodleian Library Record*, 24, no. 1 (2011), 44–50.

Hafter, Daryl, 'Women in the Underground Business of Eighteenth Century Lyon', *Enterprise and Society*, 2 (March 2001), 11–40.

Haig, Robert L., *The Gazetteer 1735–1797: A Study in the Eighteenth-Century English Newspaper* (Carbondale, 1960).

Harris, Robert D., *Necker and the Revolution of 1789* (New York, 1986).

Hayes, William E., *Iron Road to Empire: The History of 100 Years of the Progress and Achievements of the Rock Island Lines* (New York, 1953).

Heidler, Stephen, and Jeanne T. Heidler (eds.), *Encyclopedia of the War of 1812* (Annapollis, 2004).

Hill, David, *Turner in the Alps* (London, 1992).

Hobsbawm, E. J., *The Age of Capital 1848–1875* (London, 1975).

—— *The Age of Revolution 1789–1848* (London, 1962).

Holmes, Richard, *The Age of Wonder: How the Romantic Generation Discovered the Beauty and Terror of Science* (2008; paperback edn., London, 2009).

Homer, *The Iliad*, trans. E. V. Rieu (London, 1963).

Howland, S. A., *Steamboat Disasters and Railroad Accidents in the United States* (2nd edn., Worcester, 1840).

Hurry-Houghton, Thomas, *Memorials of the Family of Hurry of Great Yarmouth, Norfolk, and of America, Australia, and South Africa* (Liverpool, 1926).

Isherwood, Robert M., *Farce and Fantasy: Popular Entertainment in Eighteenth-Century Paris* (New York, 1986).

Jewson, C.B., *The Jacobin City: A Portrait of Norwich in its Reaction to the French Revolution 1788–1802* (Glasgow, 1975).

Johnston, Kenneth R., 'Whose History? My Place or Yours? Republican Assumptions and Romantic Traditions', in Damian Walford Davies (ed.), *Romanticism, History, Historicism: Essays on an Orthodoxy* (London, 2009), pp. 79–102.

Langhorne, John, and William Langhorne (ed. and trans.), *Plutarch's Lives* (revised edn., Baltimore, 1836).

Lanz, Daniel L., *Railroads of Southern and Southwestern Wisconsin: Development to Decline* (2nd edn., Monroe, 1986).

Lefebvre, Georges, *La Grande Peur de 1789* (Paris, 1932).

Löffler, Marion, 'The "Marseillaise" in Wales', in Constantine and Johnston (eds.), *'Footsteps of Liberty and Revolt'*.

Longfellow, D., 'Silk Weavers and the Social Struggle in Lyon during the French Revolution 1789–1794', *French Historical Studies*, 12 (1981), 1–40.

Lough, John, *France on the Eve of Revolution: British Travellers' Observations 1763–1788* (Chicago, 1987).

Lüsebrink, Hans-Jürgen, and Rolf Reichardt, *The Bastille: A History of a Symbol of Despotism and Freedom*, trans. Norbert Schürer (Durham, 1997).

McCallum, David, 'The Volcano: From Enlightenment to Revolution', *Nottingham French Studies*, 45, no. 1 (Spring 2006), 52–68.

McCartney, Eugene S., 'Spontaneous Generation and Kindred Notions in Antiquity', *Transactions of the American Philological Association*, 51 (1920), 101–15.

Mansfield, Paul, 'The Repression of Lyon, 1793–4: Origins, Responsibility and Significance', *French History*, 2, no. 1 (1988), 74–101.

Maréchal, Sylvain, *Le Jugement dernier des Rois, Prophétie en un Acte, en prose . . . jouée sur le Théâtre de la République, au mois Vendemiaire et jours suivant l'an second de la République Francaise* (Paris, 1793).

Mason, Laura, *Singing the French Revolution: Popular Culture and Politics 1787–1799* (Ithaca, 1996).

Maza, Sarah, *Private Lives and Public Affairs: The Causes Célèbres of Prerevolutionary France* (Berkeley, 1993).

Mercier, Louis-Sébastien, *Tableau de Paris* (12 vols., Paris, 1781–8).

Middleton, William D., George M. Smerk and Roberta L. Diehl (eds.), *Encyclopedia of North American Railroads* (Bloomington, 2007).

Morgan, George Cadogan, *An Appeal to the Public, in Answer to a Letter from the Rev. Mr. Brand to* ★★★★★ ★★★★★★★ (Norwich, 1782).

—— *Lectures on Electricity* (2 vols., Norwich, 1794).

—— 'Observations on the Light of Bodies in a State of Combustion', *Philosophical Transactions*, 75 (1785), 190–212.

Morgan, William, *Memoirs of the Life of the Rev. Richard Price* (London, 1815).

Morris, Celia, *Fanny Wright: Rebel in America* (Chicago, 1992).

Myers, Victoria, David O'Shaughnessy and Mark Philp (eds.), *The Diary of William Godwin* (Oxford, 2010) at *http://godwindiary.bodleian.ox.ac.uk*.

Necker, Jacques, *An Essay on the True Principles of Executive Power in Great States, Translated from the French of M. Necker* (London, 1792).

Newman, John, with Stephen Hughes and Anthony Ward, *The Buildings of Wales: Glamorgan* (London, 1995).

Nugent, Thomas, *The Grand Tour* (4 vols., London, 1749).

Ogborn, Maurice Edward, *Equitable Assurances* (London, 1962).

Opie, Amelia, *Lays for the Dead* (London, 1834).

O'Shaughnessy, David, 'Kotzebue and Thompson's *The Stranger*: A New Source for Godwin's *St. Leon*', *Notes & Queries*, 52 (2005), 452–6.

Owen, Hywel Wyn, and Richard Morgan, *Dictionary of the Place-Names of Wales* (Llandysul, 2007).

Paine, Thomas, *Rights of Man,* ed. by Gregory Claeys (Indianapolis, 1992).

Peach, W. Bernard, and D. O. Thomas (eds.), *The Correspondence of Richard Price* (3 vols., Durham, 1983–1994).

Pearre, O. F., W. H. Perrin, H. H. Hill and A. A. Graham, *The History of Livingston County, Illinois* (Chicago, 1878).

Postle, Martin, 'Thomas Gainsborough's "Lost" Portrait of Auguste Vestris', *The British Art Journal*, IV, no. 1 (Spring 2003), 64–8.

Price, Realto E. (ed.), *History of Clayton County, Iowa From the Earliest Historical Times Down to the Present* (2 vols., Chicago, 1916).

Price, Richard, *A Discourse on the Love of Our Country* (London, 1789).

—— *A Review of the Principal Questions and Difficulties in Morals* (London, 1758).

—— *Observations on Reversionary Payments* (London, 1771).

—— *Observations on the Importance of the American Revolution* (London, 1784).

—— *Observations on the Nature of Civil Liberty, the Principles of Government, and the Justice and Policy of the War with America* (London, 1776).

Rattenbury, Gordon, and M. J. T. Lewis, *Merthyr Tydfil Tramroads and their Locomotives* (Oxford, 2004).

Rees, D. A., 'George Cadogan Morgan at Oxford', *Enlightenment and Dissent*, 1 (1982), 89–90.

Reeves, Owen T., James S. Ewing, Richard P. Morgan, Franklin Blades and John W. Bunn, *Abraham Lincoln By Some Men Who Knew Him* (Bloomington, 1910).

Ribeiro, Aileen, *Dress in Eighteenth-Century Europe 1715–1789* (London, 1984).

Rodger, N. A. M., *The Command of the Ocean: A Naval History of Britain 1649–1815* (2004; paperback edn., London, 2005).

Rougé, Jean, and Robert Turcan (eds.), *Les Martyrs de Lyon, 177: Colloque, Lyon, 20–23 septembre 1977* (Paris, 1978).

Rousseau, Jean-Jacques, *The Confessions and Correspondence, including the Letters to Malesherbes*, trans. Christopher Kelly, ed. by Christopher Kelly, Roger D. Masters and Peter G. Stillman (1995; paperback edn., Hanover, 1998).

Rudé, George, *The Crowd in the French Revolution* (Oxford, 1959).

Schama, Simon, *Citizens: A Chronicle of the French Revolution* (paperback edn., London, 1989).

Scott, Samuel F., *The Response of the Royal Army to the French Revolution: The Role and Development of the Line Army* (Oxford, 1978).

Seguin, Marilyn W., *Dogs of War: And Stories of Other Beasts of Battle in the Civil War* (Boston, 1998).

Shaw, Ronald E., *Canals for a Nation: The Canal Era in the United States, 1790–1860* (Kentucky, 1990).

Spagnoli, Paul G., 'The Revolution Begins: Lambesc's Charge 12 July 1789', *French Historical Studies*, 17, no. 2 (Autumn 1991), 466–97.

Strabo, *The Geography*, trans. H. C. Hamilton and W. Falconer (London, 1854).

Sutton, Robert P., *Rivers, Railroads, and Roads: A History of Henderson County, Illinois* (Raritan, 1988).

Tackett, Timothy, *Becoming a Revolutionary: The Deputies of the French National Assembly and the Emergence of a Revolutionary Culture (1789–1790)* (1996; paperback edn., Pennsylvania, 2006).

—— 'La Grande Peur et le complot aristocratique sous la Révolution française', *Annales historiques de la Révolution française*, 335 (Janvier–Mars 2004), 1–17.

Thale, Mary (ed.), *Selections from the Papers of the London Corresponding Society 1792–1799* (Cambridge, 1983).

Thomas, D. O., *The Honest Mind: The Thought and Work of Richard Price* (Oxford, 1977).

—— 'Edmund Burke and the Reverend Dissenting Gentlemen', *Notes & Queries*, 29 (1982), 202–4.

—— 'George Cadogan Morgan', *The Price-Priestley Newsletter*, 3 (1979), 53–70.

—— (ed.), 'Richard Price's Journal for the Period 25 March 1787 to 6 February 1791', *National Library of Wales Journal*, 21 (1979–80), 366–413.

——, John Stephens and P. A. L. Jones, *A Bibliography of the Works of Richard Price* (Aldershot, 1993).

Thompson, Victoria, 'Foreign Bodies: British Travel to Paris and the Troubled National Self, 1789–1830', *Studies in Travel Writing*, 15, no. 3 (September 2011), 243–65.

Turner, J. M. W., 'France, Savoy, Piedmont Sketchbook', at *http://www. tate. org.uk*.

Tyndall, John, *The Glaciers of the Alps, being a Narrative of Excursions and Ascents, an Account of the Origin and Phenomena of Glaciers, and an Exposition of the Physical Principles to which they are related* (London, 1860).

Vallentin, Antonina, *Mirabeau: A Man of the French Revolution* (Clifton, 1948).

Verhoeven, W. M., 'Land-jobbing in the Western Territories: Radicalism, Transatlantic Emigration and the 1790s American Travel Narrative', in Amanda Gilroy (ed.), *Romantic Geographies: Discourses of Travel 1775–1844* (Manchester, 2000), pp. 185–203.

Weinreb, Ben, and Christopher Hibbert (eds.), *The London Encyclopedia* (London, 1990).

Whiteman, Jeremy J., *Reform, Revolution and French Global Policy 1787–1791* (Aldershot, 2003).

Williams, Caroline E., *A Welsh Family from the Beginning of the 18th Century* (2nd edn., London, 1893).

Wood, H. G., *Frederick Denison Maurice* (Cambridge, 2008).

Yearsley, Ann, *Poems, on Several Occasions* (London, 1785).

Young, Arthur, *Travels, during the Years 1787, 1788 and 1789, undertaken more particularly with a View of ascertaining the Cultivation, Wealth, Resources, and National Prosperity of the Kingdom of France* (Bury St Edmunds, 1792).

Index

The original spellings of George Cadogan Morgan and Richard Price Morgan are given in square brackets.

Index to the main families
Ashburner, Boddington, Hurry and Morgan

RPM and Eunice had eight children
in all, three girls and five boys. Six are
mentioned:

SAINT

ANTOINE DE PADOUE

ET

LE PAIN DES PAUVRES

SERMON PRÊCHÉ A BIARRITZ

PAR LE PÈRE EXUPÈRE

Capucin

BAYONNE

IMPRIMERIE-LIBRAIRIE DE L. LASSERRE

rue Gambetta, 20

1894

que ...
... pour l'obt...
... pour obtenir
... le, promet ...
... une aumô...
... indistinctement, devan...
... pour recevoir ...
... recevoir les prières ...
... aumône à déposer à se...
... aumône qu'après avoir obt...
... c'est bien saint Antoine qu...
... avoir donné du pain à se...
... se faire inscrire à l'Arc...
... séré est dans so...
... lors, avec son nom ...
... afin de particip...
... que tous les jour...
... de l'Archiconfré...

SAINT

ANTOINE DE PADOUE

ET

LE PAIN DES PAUVRES

SERMON PRÊCHÉ A BIARRITZ

Par le Père Exupère

Capucin

BAYONNE

IMPRIMERIE-LIBRAIRIE DE L. LASSERRE
rue Gambetta, 20

—

1894

MES FRÈRES,

Ce qui fait la beauté des saints, c'est leur ressemblance à Notre-Seigneur Jésus-Christ. Il doit être, a dit saint Paul, comme le premier-né, parmi la multitude des frères que Dieu a prédestinés à lui être semblables (1). Mais comment l'homme de la race d'Adam pourrait-il être semblable au Fils de Dieu, même aidé de la grâce qui guérit et qui élève l'âme? Aussi aucun ne lui ressemble pleinement et ne reproduit d'une manière complète sa perfection et sa beauté, excepté la Vierge Immaculée, Marie sa Mère. Tous les autres s'efforcent de le suivre dans les voies parfaites; tous les autres se renoncent et portent leur croix, et ils ne sont saints que parce que jusqu'à la fin de leur vie l'amour les pousse à porter leur croix à la suite de Jésus-Christ. Mais il semble que Dieu ait appelé chacun d'eux à reproduire avec plus de perfection, dans sa vie et dans ses vertus, quelques traits de sa beauté, quelques mystères de sa vie ou de sa Passion. Voilà pourquoi les étoiles du firmament de la sainteté diffèrent les unes des autres, quoique toutes reçoivent leur lumière du même soleil de justice. Jésus-Christ est toujours

(1) Rom. VIII. 29.

vivant dans son Église, et son Église est toujours sainte ; et peut-être à chaque instant de son histoire le regard de Dieu contemple en elle et dans les différents élus qu'elle renferme l'image parfaite de la beauté de Jésus-Christ.

I

Saint Antoine me semble avoir été appelé à reproduire, dans la suite de sa vie et au milieu de sa gloire du ciel, la compassion du Cœur de Jésus-Christ pour les pauvres. Ces paroles que nous lisons dans l'Évangile : « J'ai pitié de cette foule, car voici trois jours qu'elle attend, et si je les renvoie à jeûn, ils défailleront en route parce que plusieurs sont venus de loin » ; cet autre passage où l'historien sacré représente notre Divin Maître regardant avec pitié ce peuple qui était gisant comme un troupeau sans pasteur, me semblent contenir le récit même de la vie apostolique de saint Antoine de Padoue. Voilà la cause de ce renouveau de dévotion envers lui qui se produit en ce moment dans toute l'Église. C'est sa compassion pour les pauvres, pour les malheureux, pour les abandonnés, qui explique le caractère de sa vie apostolique et celui de ses miracles.

Certes, il ne songeait pas aux luttes, et encore moins aux gloires de l'Apostolat. Mais il eut pitié de ceux que l'hérésie ravissait au salut éternel ; il eut pitié de ceux à qui la tyrannie des hommes imposait un joug de fer et ravissait le pain ; il eut pitié de ses frères entraînés malgré eux par un supérieur indigne hors des voies séraphiques ; il eut pitié... et cette âme, qui n'avait rêvé que silence et solitude, que prière et piété, s'élança pleine d'ardeur au combat pour la défense des faibles et des petits. La compassion, qui l'avait obligé à commencer la lutte, soutint son courage, et enfin lui donna la victoire.

Les commencements de sa vie ne semblaient pas, en effet, annoncer ce caractère. Le sang de Godefroid de Bouillon, qui coulait dans ses veines, pouvait certainement faire d'Antoine un homme de courage ; mais il semblait que ce courage se tournât tout entier vers l'immolation de lui-même à la seule gloire de Dieu. Il chercha d'abord la vie religieuse dans le cloître des chanoines Augustins, et il y vécut dans la prière et dans l'étude, de manière à être le modèle des plus avancés dans la vertu. Tout à coup une voie nouvelle s'ouvre devant ses yeux; parce qu'elle est remplie de sacrifices et parce qu'il voit au bout la palme du martyre, il s'y élance avec une ardeur merveilleuse. Il a vu la beauté de la pauvreté, il a vu la bure des Frères Mineurs, et cette bure s'est montrée à lui empourprée du sang des martyrs du Maroc. Son grand cœur s'enflamme, rien ne peut le retenir; lui aussi sera l'enfant de la pauvreté, le témoin de Jésus-Christ au milieu des infidèles. Et il part pour arroser au milieu d'eux, avec son sang, la prédication chrétienne.

C'est une chose très remarquable que cette soif du martyre dans les saints. L'amour de Dieu envers les hommes ne s'est pas contenté de se donner, il s'est immolé. L'amour des hommes pour Dieu ne peut se contenter de se donner, il faut aussi qu'il s'immole. Ainsi avait pensé, senti et voulu François d'Assise; ainsi pensait, sentait et voulait également le plus parfait de ses enfants. Mais dans le secret de la sagesse de Dieu, il y a, pour réaliser ce désir des saints, des moyens que les saints mêmes ne soupçonnent pas. La tendre compassion de François pour Jésus crucifié l'immola plus longuement et plus cruellement que n'aurait pu faire le plus cruel des martyres ; la tendre compassion de saint Antoine de Padoue pour les membres souffrants de Jésus-Christ lui imposa des souffrances et des travaux plus accablants pour lui et plus glorieux pour Dieu que n'aurait pu le faire une prompte mort par la main du bourreau.

Jeté en Sicile par la tempête, il suivit ses frères appelés par saint François au Chapitre général d'Assise. Il y passa inconnu et compté pour rien : celui qui n'avait pas eu le martyre du sang voulait au moins le martyre de l'humiliation, de la pénitence et de la solitude ; la blancheur et le parfum de la pureté remplaceraient en son âme les roses de la charité. Le Chapitre fini, et aucun Supérieur ne réclamant pour sien cet inconnu à qui nul ne prenait garde, inconnu du Père, inconnu de ses frères, comme délaissé de Dieu et des hommes, Antoine dut avoir un moment de cruelles angoisses. Le Provincial de la Romagne eut pitié de cet humble religieux et l'emmena par compassion comme on emmènerait chez soi un pauvre inutile.

Antoine entra dans cette voie du silence où il faut aimer à être inconnu et compté pour rien. Le doigt de la Providence semblait le lui indiquer. Certes, il n'en serait jamais sorti de lui-même : aux yeux de son humilité, l'obscurité, le silence, la solitude, la charité pratiquée dans les conditions les plus humbles et les plus viles, et tout cela fait par l'ordre de la volonté divine, c'était la voie assurée du salut. Une circonstance imprévue l'en fit sortir.

Un Supérieur voulut qu'il parlât à son tour dans une assemblée de Frères Mineurs et de Frères Prêcheurs qui allaient à l'ordination. L'obéissance le força à dévoiler aux yeux surpris de ses frères les trésors de science et de charité qu'il avait cachés jusqu'alors avec tant de soin. Celui qu'on avait pris pour un faible esprit était un homme de génie; celui qu'on croyait ignorant était l'Arche du Testament; celui qui s'était tu jusqu'alors avait une parole de feu; celui qui avait obéi en silence était capable de dompter les foules et de les entrainer à sa suite, éclairées et convaincues.

L'action de saint François, qui avait ravivé la vie chrétienne dans l'Ombrie et la Toscane, commençait à se faire sentir par toute l'Église. Mais il y avait des contrées où le besoin de cette action était plus pressante : c'était principalement le midi de la France et l'Italie, livrés l'un et l'autre à l'hérésie, à la tyrannie et à tous les désordres qui suivent ces fléaux. Je ne m'arrêterai pas à détailler ces hérésies, ni à raconter après tant d'autres les troubles et la guerre qui en étaient la conséquence. Mais je ne puis en passer sous silence le caractère particulier, qui met tant de ressemblance entre cette période de l'histoire et celle que nous traversons nous-mêmes. Sous les noms divers de *Vaudois*, de *Patares*, de *Catarins* ou d'*Albigeois*, ces hérétiques cachaient, dans une vaste négation religieuse, la pensée de révolutions politiques et sociales. Il ne s'agissait pas pour eux de l'âme, de Jésus-Christ, de la vie éternelle. Il s'agissait de la vie présente du corps et d'une organisation différente

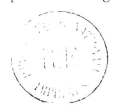

de la société. Alors comme aujourd'hui, c'était l'humanité pécheresse qui, loin d'accepter l'expiation du péché, écoutait à nouveau comme l'écho de l'antique enseignement satanique : Vous serez comme des dieux; comme des dieux par la délivrance de votre raison, comme des dieux par la sublimité de votre science, comme des dieux par l'abondance de vos plaisirs, par le triomphe de votre chair.

Au milieu de ces prédications fanatiques, comme il arrive toujours, le sang coulait avec plus d'abondance, les souffrances des pauvres étaient augmentées et les blasphèmes des hommes montaient jusqu'au ciel. Il est si facile de se faire écouter par les oreilles qu'on flatte, et de faire arriver jusqu'au cœur un enseignement qui favorise les passions! Voilà pourquoi, alors comme aujourd'hui, les foules, en se laissant aller aux inspirations de la terre, blasphémaient Celui qui les a délivrées, Jésus-Christ Notre-Seigneur. Alors comme aujourd'hui, au sein de l'Église, dans les ordres religieux nouvellement fondés, tels que celui des Frères Mineurs, il y avait des esprits pleins de tendresse, non pour les négations religieuses elles-mêmes, mais pour les progrès matériels, les réformes sociales et les espérances du bonheur universel qui étaient annoncés.

Ceux qui considèreraient ces temps avec les yeux de la sagesse humaine seulement, ne pourraient apercevoir aucune voie de salut. Mais Dieu se sert de la faiblesse pour confondre la force, et avec ce qui n'est pas il détruit ce qui est (1). Un saint, jusqu'à présent inconnu et qui vivra peu d'années, parcourra presque

(1) I. Cor. I 28.

avec la rapidité de la foudre tous ces pays livrés à l'esprit de mensonge. Partout il sèmera, ému de pitié, la parole de vie et le miracle qui la confirme. En même temps, par l'ordre de François, il instruira ses frères à parler de Dieu et du Sauveur Jésus-Christ avec des accents semblables aux siens, et dans peu de temps il pourra s'endormir comme un guerrier après la victoire.

Ce vaillant soldat du Christ, que la miséricorde poussait au combat, était une âme toute faite de pureté et d'amour, et ces deux vertus attiraient sur les saints les tendres caresses du doux enfant de Bethléem. Déjà on avait vu François, la nuit de Noël, recevoir ses faveurs. Antoine, à son tour, porte sur son cœur, entre ses bras, le doux petit Enfant de la crèche. On dirait un mystérieux attrait entre la simplicité et la pauvreté de Jésus naissant et la pauvreté et la simplicité de l'Ordre séraphique, qui aura bientôt à sa garde les Lieux Saints de l'enfance et de la Passion de Jésus-Christ, et les conservera à l'Église (on oublie trop, aujourd'hui que les dangers sont passés) au prix du sang d'un grand nombre de ses enfants.

Au contact de Jésus, la foi et la charité d'Antoine s'embrasent. Il ne craint pas de promettre de grands miracles pour prouver la présence réelle de Notre-Seigneur Jésus-Christ dans le Très-Saint Sacrement, et il force les animaux eux-mêmes à l'adorer. Si les hérétiques le repoussent, il prêche la parole de Dieu aux poissons de la mer, et il oblige ainsi ceux qui voulaient être sourds à entendre la parole de Dieu. C'est la pitié pour les âmes qui fait de lui le plus grand des thaumaturges que l'Église ait vus depuis les Apôtres.

Mais ce n'est pas assez de délivrer les hommes de la tyrannie de Satan, il faut encore les arracher au joug de ceux qui abusent du pouvoir pour devenir les suppôts de l'enfer. Les maux des peuples gémissant sous le joug de la tyrannie le touchent de compassion, et il ne craint pas d'engager la lutte, lui pauvre frère mineur, seul et désarmé, avec le tyran de Padoue et toutes les forces de ce monde. Là encore, le miracle le soutient. On croit à celui qui prouve ainsi sa mission divine, mais qui la prouve mieux encore s'il est possible par son courage et son dévouement. Oh! qui donnera à notre siècle de tels hommes qui ne craignent ni la vie ni la mort, mais seulement d'offenser Dieu et de trahir le peuple chrétien! Des hommes luttant sans relâche et sans trêve, avec assez de foi pour être sûrs de la victoire finale, même quand ils paraissent vaincus, avec assez de pureté et d'esprit de prière pour se reposer de leurs luttes de la terre dans la contemplation des choses du ciel, et de leurs combats avec les hommes dans les caresses de l'Enfant Jésus!

Mais l'Ordre religieux qui allait aux combats à la suite d'Antoine souffrait au dedans de lui-même les maux les plus cruels. Celui qui aurait dû continuer saint François et animer tout l'Ordre de l'esprit séraphique, celui-là, au nom de je ne sais quelle tradition et quelle science, détruisait l'œuvre de simplicité, de pauvreté, d'amour, que François avait élevée de ses mains stigmatisées. Que dis-je? Il persécutait avec une cruauté implacable ceux qui voulaient conserver en eux-mêmes les souvenirs des premiers jours de l'Ordre Séraphique, et reproduire dans leur vie sa première ferveur. Hélas! au lieu de marcher à

l'ennemi commun, terrible comme une armée rangée
en bataille, l'Ordre de saint François était lui-même
en pleine guerre civile, ou plutôt en pleine persécu-
tion. Les bons et les fervents étaient accablés par
l'autorité des supérieurs relâchés, et souvent on en
était arrivé aux mauvais traitements. Ah! comment
Antoine aurait-il assisté à ce spectacle de désolation,
sans qu'il éprouvât pour ses frères une compassion
semblable à celle qu'il avait éprouvée pour les étran-
gers? Il se fit le défenseur des opprimés Il résista au
nom de la perfection religieuse, au nom de saint
François, à son successeur indigne. Il éleva son cri
puissant et protecteur jusqu'au Vicaire de Jésus-
Christ. L'ami de saint François, Grégoire IX, entendit
la voix de celui qui était l'héritier des vertus séraphiques, et l'Ordre fut délivré du tyran qui l'avait
opprimé trop longtemps.

Quoi d'étonnant que tant de grandes choses faites
en si peu de temps, faites toutes par miséricorde, par
bonté de cœur, par pitié pour ceux qui souffraient de
quelque manière que ce fût, excitassent pour Antoine vivant et mort un enthousiasme immense, une
confiance sans borne, une certitude absolue de sa
sainteté? Six mois après sa mort, il était canonisé, et
le peuple chrétien, habitué à trouver en lui pendant
sa vie un protecteur et un défenseur, fut certain de le
trouver tel encore, mais plus puissant, après sa mort.
Les miracles autour de son tombeau n'ont pas cessé
depuis plus de six siècles, et le monde catholique
n'a pas discontinué d'entourer Antoine d'un culte
et d'une dévotion spéciale. La reconnaissance des
fidèles a été aussi persévérante que la miséricorde
du Saint à leur égard.

II

En France seulement cette dévotion paraissait singulièrement diminuée depuis la Révolution qui a diminué ou anéanti tant de saintes ou salutaires traditions. Cependant, plus que toutes les autres nations catholiques, la France qui avait reçu d'Antoine vivant les plus grands bienfaits, avait besoin de sa protection. Dans quelle nation catholique l'esprit du mensonge lève-t-il plus hardiment la tête? Dans quel peuple, hélas! est-il si aisément écouté? O peuple français, entre tous bon, entre tous prompt à t'égarer, comme tu es digne de pitié aux yeux de ceux qui te connaissent et qui ne peuvent te connaître sans t'aimer! Comment Antoine, ton apôtre et ton thaumaturge, du haut du ciel n'aurait-il pas eu pitié de toi!

Il y a peu d'années, dans une pauvre petite arrière-boutique de Toulon, saint Antoine commença à faire éclater de nouveau sa puissance miraculeuse. Ce furent des commencements si petits, si humbles, que nul n'aurait osé prévoir ce qui devait arriver dans peu de temps. L'esprit de Dieu soufflait de là, et bientôt ce souffle vivifiant eut passé sur la France entière. Bientôt il n'y aura plus une église qui n'ait sa statue de S. Antoine, et sous la statue son tronc pour le pain des pauvres. Les grâces, souvent miraculeuses, que saint Antoine a obtenues de Dieu pour ceux qui promettaient de donner un peu de pain à ses pauvres, ont été tellement abondantes que cette dévotion s'est étendue avec autant de rapidité qu'en avait eue la course apostolique d'Antoine pendant sa vie.

Le pain qu'il a ainsi donné à ses pauvres a été d'une abondance prodigieuse. A Bordeaux seulement, dans le seul mois de juillet, plus de 7,000 fr. ont été trouvés dans le tronc du pain des pauvres de saint Antoine. Ce ne sera pas une exagération bientôt de dire que saint Antoine donne à lui seul plus de pain aux pauvres que ne leur en ôtent ceux qui les trompent et qui les égarent, en leur donnant en pâture de mauvais journaux et de mauvais livres que les pauvres doivent payer; en les faisant assister aux réunions politiques où les pauvres payent encore, et en les entraînant à des grèves où les pauvres payent toujours. Peut-être un jour viendra-t-il où, entre celui qui leur donne sans leur rien demander que d'être bon et vertueux, d'aimer Dieu et d'espérer en lui, et ceux qui promettent beaucoup, qui ne donnent rien et qui trouvent, en égarant les pauvres, le moyen d'arriver aux honneurs et à la fortune, peut-être, dis-je, un jour viendra où le peuple comprendra quels sont ses véritables amis et saura choisir ses conseillers sincères. En attendant, le fait est éclatant que par la volonté de Dieu, saint Antoine a repris sa place dans la lutte contre les hérésies et dans la défense du peuple chrétien contre les tyrannies.

Cependant qu'on ne s'y trompe pas. Tout ne doit pas consister à demander des faveurs temporelles, en échange d'un peu de pain matériel donné aux pauvres. Comme autrefois Antoine ne faisait des miracles que pour rendre la foi aux âmes ou les affermir dans la charité, maintenant encore il intercède pour vous, surtout afin que vous ayez la vie éternelle. Dieu sait combien l'homme est matériel, et puisqu'il sait de quelle boue nous sommes pétris, il sait combien les choses de la vie présente nous sont sensibles, combien ce qui se rapporte à notre santé, à notre réputation, à notre fortune, nous touche. S'il daigne condescendre à notre faiblesse à cet égard, c'est afin de nous élever vers lui, au moins par la prière qui obtient le bienfait et l'action de grâce qui doit le suivre. A Lourdes, les miracles relatifs aux corps n'ont été si nombreux qu'afin de rendre incomparablement plus nombreux les miracles relatifs à l'âme. Aux pieds de saint Antoine, il doit en être de même. Il faut que les fidèles apprennent que ce qu'ils peuvent donner aux pauvres en vue d'obtenir une faveur temporelle, ils pourraient, s'ils le voulaient, le donner également pour l'amour de Notre-Seigneur Jésus-Christ et en vue de la vie éternelle. Ne le faisant pas, ils se convainquent eux-mêmes que leur charité, leur compassion pour les pauvres est bien loin de ressembler à celle dont saint Antoine leur donne l'exemple. Et cependant ils ne seront de vrais dévots de saint Antoine que lorsqu'à l'énergie et à la fermeté de sa foi, ils ajouteront la douce compassion et l'abondante miséricorde de sa charité.

Qu'il me soit permis de signaler aussi, dans ce fait, le développement d'un plan providentiel, merveilleux, qui se poursuit depuis le commencement de ce siècle. A mesure que ceux qui en étaient chargés ont abandonné la sollicitude du règne de Dieu sur la terre, Dieu a changé le chandelier de place et a conféré aux petits, aux humbles et aux faibles, les devoirs que les grands, les puissants, les riches, ne remplissaient plus. Lorsque les chefs des Etats ont cessé d'être les *évêques du dehors*, et que non-seulement ils n'ont plus pensé à étendre parmi les infidèles la foi de Notre-Seigneur Jésus-Christ, mais que, au nom de la politique ils y ont même fait obstacle, Dieu a suscité parmi les pauvres l'œuvre merveilleuse de la Propagation de la Foi : grâce à elle, l'apostolat catholique parmi les infidèles a été aussi prospère que jamais. Lorsqu'ils ont cessé de se soucier de la moralité de leurs peuples et de leur foi, oubliant qu'ils avaient reçu le glaive pour protéger le bien et empêcher le mal, selon la parole de saint Paul, Dieu a suscité les œuvres de saint François de Sales, de saint François Régis et autres semblables, aussi bien que la Société de Saint-Vincent-de-Paul, afin que le poste déserté par ceux qui avaient devoir de le garder fût rempli par la charité des hommes de bonne volonté.

Un grand devoir, qui était autrefois compris et qui paraît ne plus l'être au même degré, consistait à faire passer assez habituellement par les mains des prêtres les aumônes que les grands et les riches ont le devoir de faire aux pauvres. On comprenait alors que la charité matérielle est souvent le moyen d'arriver jusqu'aux âmes, et c'est à cette pensée qu'étaient dues la plupart des fondations charitables.

De son côté, l'Église le comprenait si bien que tous les bénéfices ecclésiastiques étaient considérés par elle comme bien des pauvres et devant intégralement revenir aux pauvres, après que le bénéficiaire en avait pris ce qui était nécessaire à l'entretien de sa vie. Aujourd'hui le clergé catholique est pauvre, et je ne crains point de dire que cette pauvreté est plus d'une fois la cause que les malades ne reçoivent pas tous les secours désirables, et que, faute de pouvoir donner assez, le prêtre n'est pas toujours reçu

au chevet des mourants. Eh bien ! c'est le moyen de
pouvoir faire largement l'aumône que saint Antoine
veut leur fournir en vous obligeant, à force de bienfaits, à donner vous-mêmes beaucoup pour le bien
de ses pauvres. Et le bénéfice ecclésiastique sera
désormais le patrimoine assuré des pauvres : ce sera
la reconnaissance du grand nombre des chrétiens
exaucés par saint Antoine de Padoue.

O grand Saint, ne vous arrêtez point dans vos
bienfaits miraculeux, ne vous contentez pas d'obtenir,
pour ceux qui vous les demandent, les grâces temporelles dont ils ont besoin. Donnez-leur votre foi,
donnez-leur votre amour pour Jésus-Christ, donnez-
leur votre énergique volonté de ne vivre que pour
lui. Et pour cela, suscitez des hommes qui soient,
comme vous, oublieux d'eux-mêmes et remplis d'une
compassion semblable à la vôtre envers tous ceux qui
pleurent, envers tous ceux qui souffrent, envers tous
ceux qui sont trompés. Hélas ! ces derniers sont les
plus nombreux, et, dans l'organisation actuelle de la
société, les plus à plaindre ! Faites revivre en leur
faveur, dans l'Ordre de saint François, l'esprit que
vous y avez trouvé et qui vous a animé vous-même.
Que cet Ordre produise des hommes dont la charité
soit inépuisable, dont le dévouement soit invincible,
et dont la parole ardente et lumineuse porte la conviction dans les âmes déjà touchées par leur charité.
Que votre œuvre moderne si rapide dans ses dévelop-
pements soit ainsi rendue durable dans les effets que
vous recherchez surtout, et qui sont l'accroissement
du règne de Jésus-Christ et le salut éternel des âmes.
Ainsi soit-il.

Bayonne. — Imp. Lasserre.

✝

NEUVAINE EN L'HONNEUR DE SAINT ANTOINE DE PADOUE

Répons miraculeux composé par saint Bonaventure (1)

Si quæris miracula,
Mors, error, calamitas,
Dæmon, lepra fugiunt ;
Ægri surgunt sani.
R. Cedunt mare, vincula ;
Membra resque perditas
Petunt et accipiunt
Juvenes et cani.

Perunt pericula ;
Cassat et necessitas.
Narrent hi qui sentiunt ;
Dicant Paduani.
R. Cedent mare....., etc
Gloria Patri et Filio et
Spiritui Sancto.
R. Cedunt mare ....etc.

V. Ora pro nobis, beate Antoni :
R. Ut digni efficiamur promissionibus Christi.

OREMUS. Ecclesiam tuam, Deus, Beati Antonii confessoris tui commemoratio votiva lætificet, qui spiritualibus semper muniatur auxiliis t gaudiis perfrui mereatur æternis. Per Christum Dominum nostrum.

Traduction du Répons :

Vous cherchez des miracles ? La mort, l'erreur, les calamités, les démons, la lèpre, les maladies, s'enfuient devant saint Antoine.

La mer obéit, les chaines se brisent, la santé revient, jeunes gens et vieillards l'invoquent et retrouvent les objets perdus

Les dangers s'évanouissent ; les besoins cessent. Racontez-le, vous qui l'avez éprouvé ; parlez, habitants de Padoue. Gloire au Père, au Fils et au Saint-Esprit, etc.

V. Priez pour nous, ô bienheureux Antoine ;
R. Afin que nous devenions dignes des promesses de Jésus-Christ.

ORAISON. Que votre Eglise, ô mon Dieu, soit réjouie et consolée par la fête du bienheureux Antoine, votre confesseur ; qu'elle soit continuellement aidée du secours de votre grâce, et qu'elle mérite de jouir de l'éternelle béatitude.

Litanies de saint Antoine de Padoue en usage dans l'Ordre de saint François

Seigneur, ayez pitié de nous.
Jésus-Christ, ayez pitié de nous.
Seigneur, ayez pitié de nous.
Jésus-Christ, écoutez-nous.
Jésus-Christ, exaucez-nous.

---

(1) 100 jours d'indulgence, chaque fois qu'on récite ce répons. — Indulgence plénière (aux conditions ordinaires) chaque mois, quand on l'a récité tous les jours du mois. (Pie IX, 23 janvier 1866).

nous.

                              ... priez pour nous.

... priez pour nous.

... de la grâce et de prophétie, priez pour ...

... priez pour nous.

... lumière de la sainte Église, priez pour ...

... prédicateur de la grâce, priez pour nous.

... propagateur de la foi évangélique, priez pour ...

... amour de la discipline régulière, priez pour ...

... prodige d'austérité, priez pour nous.

... d'une éclatante pureté, priez pour nous.

... modèle d'abstinence, priez pour nous.

... exemplaire d'obéissance, priez pour nous.

... ardent amateur de la pauvreté, priez pour nous.

... lys de chasteté, priez pour nous.

... ... de patience, priez pour nous.

... parfaite d'humilité, priez pour nous.

... perle étincelante de sainteté, priez pour nous.

... marteau des hérésies, priez pour nous.

... fervent zélateur du culte divin, priez pour nous.

... brûlant d'une soif ardente pour le salut des âmes, priez ...

... embrasé du désir du martyre, priez pour nous.

... saint et assidu imitateur de Jésus, priez pour nous.

... dévot serviteur de l'auguste Mère de Dieu, priez ...

... saint émule du séraphique François, priez pour ...

... illustre thaumaturge, priez pour nous.

... fidèle protecteur de ceux qui mettent en ...
... pour nous.

... procurez le pain aux pauvres, priez pour nous.

... qui effacez les péchés du monde, pardonnez-nous.

... qui effacez les péchés du monde, exaucez-nous, ...

... qui effacez les péchés du monde, ayez pitié de nous.

... ... ô bienheureux Antoine.

... devenus dignes des promesses de Jésus-Christ.

... votre Église, ô mon Dieu, soit réjouie et ...

... Antoine, Votre confesseur ; qu'elle soit ...

... ... et qu'elle mérite de jouir ...

                                    Cette première ...

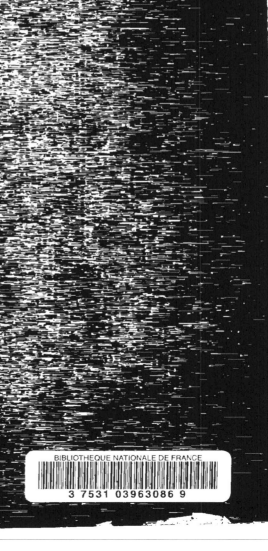

Imprimé en France
FROC031336020620
24149FR00015B/373